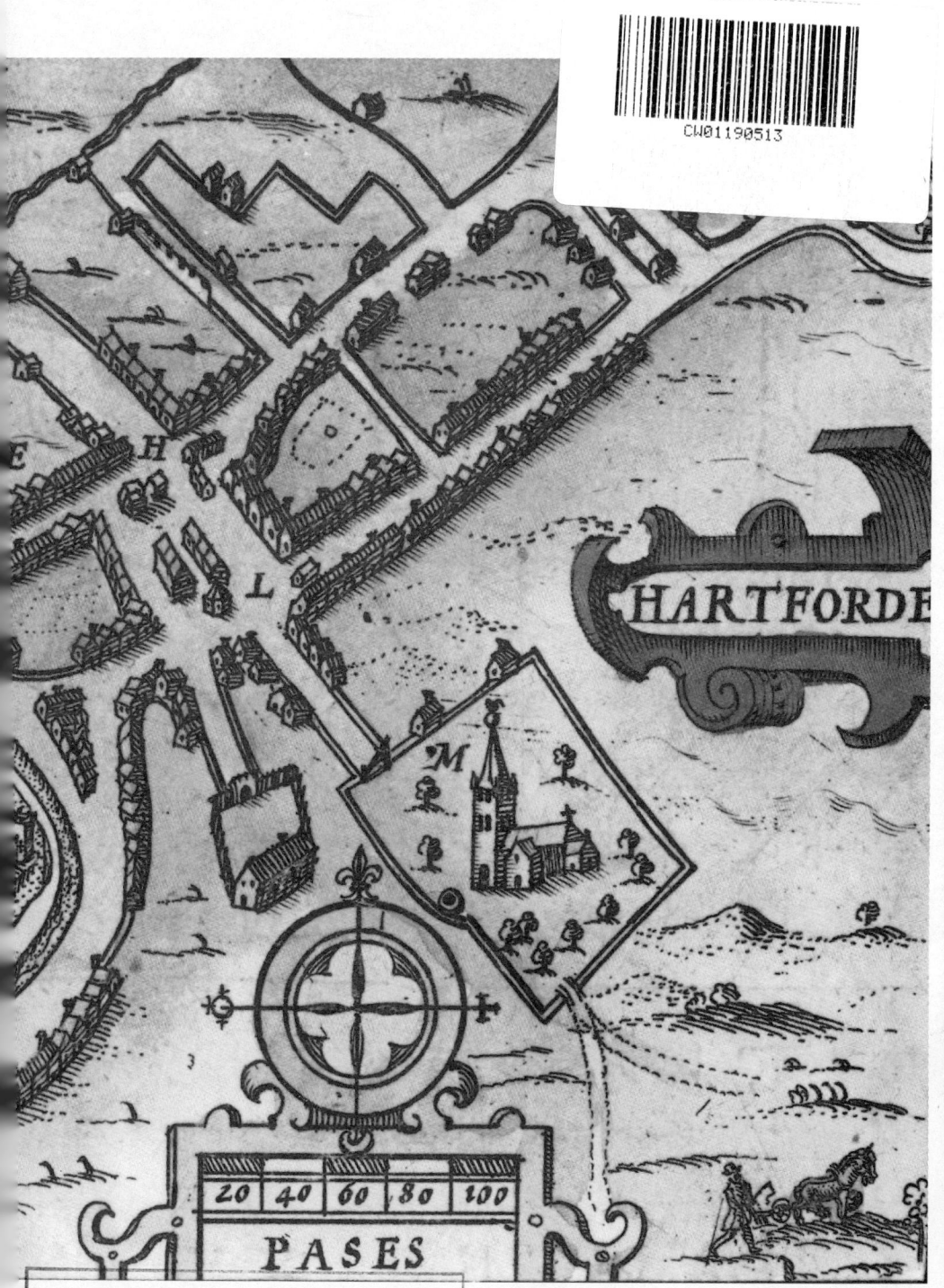

Inset from John Speed's map of Hertfordshire 1611, showing the town of Hertford, including the castle (centre) and All Saints (M) and St Andrew's (C) churches.

[Hertfordshire Archives &Local Studies]

Hertfordshire
COUNTY COUNCIL
Community Information

LOC
929.342

FOR REFERENCE ONLY

Please renew/return this item by the last date shown.

So that your telephone call is charged at local rate, please call the numbers as set out below:

	From Area codes 01923 or 020:	From the rest of Herts:
Renewals:	01923 471373	01438 737373
Enquiries:	01923 471333	01438 737333
Minicom:	01923 471599	01438 737599

L32 www.hertsdirect.org

An Inventory of the Goods and Chattells of John
Johnson late of the parish of Allsaints Hertford in the
County of Hertf. deceased taken & appraised by us Thomas
Herricke & James Goodman this twelveth day of
August in the yeare of our Lord 1673.

	£	s	d
Imprimis his wearing apparell & ready money	10	00	00
Item in his Parlour, One Bedsted & Matt curtaynes vallants, one feather bed & two Blanketts & a Coverlid, two feather bolsters & two pillowes	09	04	00
Item One Trundle bedsted & Matt one feather bed two Blanketts a bolster and one pillowe	03	16	00
Item One Table & formes, a livery Cubboard, a Glass Case, looking glasse, a small coffer, Box & basket	01	11	00
Item. In the hall, one long Table, six joint stooles, a presse Cubboard one formes foure Chaires, a Iron wheele & Reele, three Spitts, one paire of Ratts, two paires of Andirons, a fire shovell tongs & one Jacke	04	13	00
Item In the Little Parlour, one Settle, one hanging Cubboard a little Table & forme, & one Chaire	01	03	00
Item In the best Chamber One Bedsted with Curtaynes & Vallants, one feather bed, one straw bed & two feather bolsters two pillowes, a Rugg & Blankett	10	00	00
Item One Trundle bed & feather bed	03	00	00
Item One drawing Table two joynt stooles a Cubboard and two Chaires	03	08	00
Item a paire of Ratts fire Coales, a fire shovell, tongs, a painted Ironworke & bellowes, two Cushions, a smale table and bowle	04	00	00
Item. In the Chamber over the hall, One Bedsted, feather bed & bolster, two pillowes, one Coverled, Curtaynes & vallants, two Chests, one Chaire, one Box, one Table forme and one Carpett	10	04	00
Item. In two other Roomes above staires	02	10	00
Item. In the Kitchin, Brasse pewter & other things	08	00	00
Item. Nine paires of woolen sheetes	05	08	00
Item Cushions, Table linnen, pillowbeares & other linnen	06	04	04
Item A Gunn, and a pockring tongs	00	06	06
Item Chests & divers of Bottles	02	08	00
Item Cloaven Ladders & Stalls	04	00	00
Item fifteene Loads of Faggotts, Blocks & Round wood	11	05	00
Item two acres of Hey	06	00	00
Item A Horse	02	00	00
Item A Hovell whereon the hey lyes	06	00	00
Item three fowling pieces, a sword & Carbine	03	10	00
Item three drinke stalls	00	10	00
	130	10	10

Tho Herrick
James Goodman

Appraysers

Inventory of the 'Goods and Chattells' of John Johnson of All Saints parish Hertford; appraised by Thomas Herricke and James Goodman, 12th August 1673. (see pages 76-77 below).

[Hertfordshire Archives & Local Studies]

Hertfordshire Record Publications, Volume XIII

LIFESTYLE AND CULTURE IN HERTFORD

WILLS AND INVENTORIES FOR THE

PARISHES OF ALL SAINTS

AND ST ANDREW, 1660 - 1725

Edited with an Introduction by

Beverly Adams

Hertfordshire Record Society
1997

Hertfordshire Record Society

The Publication of this volume has been
assisted by a generous grant from

The Isobel Thornley Trust

© Beverly Adams

ISBN 0 9523779 2 6

Typeset and Printed by: The Broadwater Press, Luton

Contents

                                page

List of Illustrations	iv
Acknowledgements	v
Preface and Editorial Conventions	vi

Introduction

Part I   Lifestyle and Culture in Hertford

1. The study in context	viii
2. The significance of Hertford's location	x
3. Hertford's religious climate	xi
4. The probate process	xiii
5. Problems of interpretation	xiii

Part II   Hertford's Material World

1. Wills, inventories and occupations	xv
2. The value of goods and chattels	xvii
3. Status and wealth	xviii
4. Borrowing and lending	xviii
5. Household goods	xviii
6. Change over time	xxii
7. A feminine touch?	xxii
8. The use of space	xxiv
9. The domestic interior	xxiv

Part III   Hertford's Cultural Environment

1. Making the will	xxv
2. A question of literacy	xxvii
3. Religious beliefs	xxvii
4. Beneficiaries and bequests	xxviii
5. Family, friends and neighbours	xxxi
5.1 Appraisers	xxxi
5.2 Overseers and executors	xxxii

Part IV   Conclusion   xxxiii

References	xxxv
Appendix A - Coding scheme for occupational titles	xliii
Appendix B - Statistical method	xlvi
Bibliography	xlviii
Archdeaconry Court of Huntingdon: Wills and Inventories for the Parishes of All Saints and St Andrews, 1660-1725	1
Glossary	143
Index of Names	151
Index of Places	156
Index of Subjects	158

List of Illustrations

Inventory of the 'Goods and Chattells' of John Johnson, 1673	Frontispiece
All Saints church, Hertford, drawn by R.M. Batty, c. 1800	f.p.3
St Andrew's church Hertford c.1820, from a watercolour by George Shepherd	f.p.124
The will of Hertford yeoman and maltster Nathaniel Hale, 1671	f.p.125
The town of Hertford 1611; inset from John Speed's map of Hertfordshire	Endpapers

Acknowledgements

This publication has been made possible with the generous assistance of the Isobel Thornley Fund.

The introduction to this volume is an abridged version of a dissertation submitted for the MA degree at the Institute of Historical Research, London in September 1995. I wish to thank my tutors at the University, especially Professors John Miller of Queen Mary and Westfield College and John Turner of Royal Holloway College who prompted me whenever ideas were running short, and Dr. Peter Denley, who provided valuable guidance through the rigours of computer analysis. I also wish to thank Dr. Kate Thompson, Hertfordshire County Archivist, for permission to publish the manuscripts in her keeping.

In addition, I am indebted to Susan Flood, Senior Archivist at the Hertfordshire Archives and Local Studies, for her kindness and provision of research facilities throughout the process of transcription; to Robin Harcourt Williams, Librarian and Archivist to the Marquess of Salisbury, who shared his considerable knowledge with generosity and good humour; to Lionel and Diana Munby for their comments on the text and kind hospitality; to Dr. Alan Thomson of the University of Hertfordshire, which provided research funding, for his encouragement and direction; to Richard Busby for compiling the Indexes and to Susan Flood for typing them on to a computer disk. Errors of transcription or fact, together with any opinions expressed in the text, are of my own making.

Finally, this volume is dedicated to my family and friends.

Queen Mary and Westfield College, London
June 1997

Preface

This volume combines an edition of previously unpublished probate records for the Borough of Hertford in the period from 1660 to 1725 with an analysis of their content in the light of current historical interest in material culture. All surviving seventy-six probate inventories exhibited in the Archdeaconry Court of Huntingdon for the parishes of St Andrew and All Saints for the period[1], together with forty-four wills and details of any administration bonds, have been transcribed from manuscript and analysed by computer using *Kleio* database software[2]. The original manuscripts, together with contemporary copies, are held at the County Record Office in Hertford. In any study of this type, both the historical context and the limitations of the source need to be taken into account. The Restoration period in English history has been the subject of considerable scholarship in the past twenty years, much of it challenging the concept of a sterile period set between the upheaval of the civil war and the 'constitutional' gains of the Glorious Revolution. Economic historians have also reviewed their position on the period and on the changes both in industrial production and consumer spending.

Wills and inventories have been used extensively to reconstruct communities and their attitudes to property and kinship. But this source cannot be used uncritically; we need to take account both of the process which generated the documents and any limitations which constrain their use. Whilst acknowledging these constraints, this introduction aims to outline traditional views of the period and ask a number of questions of Hertford's community culture at a time of considerable change and upheaval.

Editorial conventions
To make these probate documents accessible to as wide an audience as possible, certain amendments have been made to the original. Whereas spelling and capitalisation have not been altered, some punctuation has been added and modernised for ease of reading. The widespread habit of abbreviating words and proper names has been countered by extending shortened forms with square brackets. Missing letters or words are replaced by question marks where the original was illegible. The thorn has, throughout, been replaced with 'th', but other early modern usages, including the interchangeable 'i' and 'j', 'u' and 'v', have been left unaltered. Unfamiliar terms may be found in the Glossary at the end of this volume.

For ease of publishing, the inventories have been set out according to a standard format. Whereas many of the originals did list the contents of each room across the page and separated by commas, many others wrote individual items on separate lines, resulting in lengthy documents. Valuations have been standardised to pounds, shillings and pence with double numbers. The arithmetic of the appraisers is sometimes erratic: no attempt has been made to correct their calculations, but indications have been given where a figure appears to be a subtotal or an amount carried forward.

The heavily abbreviated Latin clauses of probate and exhibition have been omitted, although the date of legal process has been extracted and noted with the transcription.

Coding and Statistical Sampling
Details of coding schemes employed in the analysis are provided in Appendix A; statistical method is described in Appendix B.

Introduction
Part I
Lifestyle and Culture in Hertford, 1660-1725

1. The study in context

When John Dryden described the Restoration period as 'time's whiter series'[3] with the Restoration, he was, of course, indulging in partisan polemic. Yet his optimistic public verse could be taken to reflect a society moving steadily towards enlightened modernity. The evidence for progress and development seems compelling; the late seventeenth century witnessed the 'scientific' achievements of Isaac Newton, read the temperate deliberations of John Locke and experienced a cultural climate in which utility and reason joined hands to promote improvement. Aesthetics also enjoyed an injection of 'reason': Gothic 'crinkle crankle'[4] was dismissed as vulgar, to be replaced by a classical uniformity of style, reflecting a harmonious universe in which disorder or enthusiasms were outlawed. Within this rhetoric, the urban triumphed at the expense of the rural.

Changing intellectual style was mirrored in altered patterns of consumer behaviour. Whereas existing explanations for such changes are legion, the received picture nevertheless focuses on the transition from 'traditional' to 'modern'. One aspect of this picture is an increased demand for consumer goods, the latter underwritten by a general re-assessment of attitudes to material luxury and enjoyment. From such a perspective, a diffusion of wealth down the social scale allowed unprecedented participation in a wave of consumerism in the relentless pursuit of status, while snobbery masqueraded as good taste and virtue[5]. Combined with population growth, such an environment appeared the perfect breeding ground for larger-scale development in the later eighteenth century, when industrialisation would provide an abundance of affordable commodities[6]. Tapping into new markets, entrepreneurs expanded demand through advertising and new marketing techniques to which an aspiring 'middling sort' was considered especially susceptible[7].

This persuasive argument is endorsed by contemporary critiques of social mimicry. Most notorious of these was Bernard Mandeville's biting commentary on social climbing, *The Grumbling Hive,* originally published in 1705. The poem provoked outcry and official sanction, not merely for exposing fashion victims with such cynicism but, more insidiously, for suggesting that economic growth might actually benefit from the whims of fashion and an expansion of 'getting and spending'[8]. Even though Mandeville outraged contemporary moralists, the debate reflected a changing intellectual environment in which the idea of luxury lost its pejorative meaning[9]. Thus throughout the eighteenth century, increased consumption and the dictates of fashion came to be regarded not as corrupting and emasculating, but economically beneficial[10]. The possible benefit to be gained from vice was a much-disputed and long-running moral question also addressed by eighteenth-century philosopher David Hume, who clarified the fine distinction between socially-beneficial 'refinement' and 'vicious luxury' which might impinge on human duty and generosity[11]. By the later eighteenth century, trade, consumption and luxury had thus been sufficiently 'de-moralised' for the changed economic thinking to come to maturity and acceptance in Adam Smith's model of the economy, a model which, in broad terms, held sway until challenged by John Maynard Keynes in the 1930s[12]. But to see this climate as that which prevailed in the later seventeenth century is, perhaps, to anticipate later developments. Restoration England was a period more concerned with its recent past, when the re-establishment of order and stability was highest on the political and intellectual agenda.

While society was being re-ordered and competing ideas weighed in the balance, change was becoming evident in the fabric of English towns. A focal point for the surrounding countryside, towns provided a concentration of skilled craftsmen and amenities which underwrote the burgeoning world of commodities[13]. Towns were also qualitatively different; Peter Borsay defines them as distinct social, intellectual and cultural spaces[14], echoing the classical distinction between town and country[15]. Yet if some provincial towns witnessed an urban renaissance in this period[16], benefits were far from universal, for urban development created a heightened awareness of social distinction[17]. Nor is the rigid divide between town and country necessarily similar in all regions of England. As Lionel Munby points out, Hertfordshire's rural and urban spaces are of a piece, neither being entirely 'natural' and both constantly changing and inter-relating[18].

Developing communications and the subsequent increase in internal trade certainly provided consumers with a far wider choice of goods and services, and probate evidence confirms that a range of household possessions became increasingly commonplace throughout the eighteenth century. Lorna Weatherill stresses the strategic importance of the middling sort to this new consumerism since, if involved in positions of local prominence, they may have been concerned to mark their status materially through the display of possessions[19]. Both she and Colin Campbell, however, challenge the idea that increased consumption was necessarily the result of competing with neighbours, defending the middle ranks from the charge that they were easy prey for advertising and marketing strategies, despite those commentaries which suggested otherwise[20].

Such challenges to the traditional historical picture warn historians of the danger in accepting the one-dimensional caricature of an expansive and increasingly 'modern' post-Restoration society. For this period was marked by tension and upheaval. The reactionary pull of custom and precedent often held out against forces for innovation, revealing in the process the energies and divisions of a society attempting to come to terms with political, religious and social change. As such, the spectre of disorder was never far away in a century which had witnessed civil war and regicide, the institution of a republic and subsequent restoration of the monarchy in the absence of viable alternatives and an ongoing struggle for an elusive political and religious settlement. If this was a century of revolutionary ideas and radical action, it was also one of great uncertainty. We need, perhaps, to ask whether such an scenario would stimulate change, risk-taking or more flippant behaviour.

2. The significance of Hertford's location

If such abstract considerations sound a cautionary note, other questions arise from an examination of Hertford's physical environment. As Hertfordshire's geography demonstrates, physical location affects settlement, the local economy and communications with the world beyond parish boundaries. The county town has served as the administrative centre of a shire in close proximity to London, and itself prevented from developing a discrete county identity by virtue of physical characteristics, not least the lack of a major east-west route. It is therefore possible that the capital's relative accessibility by road and the navigable River Lea increased Hertford's susceptibility to changing cultural influences spreading out from London. Certainly, by 1719, the parish church of All Saints, not unlike its style-conscious metropolitan counterparts, was promoting its role as fashion venue on the basis of musical excellence and innovation[21].

As a market and regional centre[22] and ancient incorporated borough, Hertford was nevertheless a small town of some 1500 adults at the time of the Compton Census in 1676, its economy heavily reliant on malting barley for London brewers[23]. In the county's urban hierarchy, Hertford had already lost its standing by the early eighteenth century, for Daniel Defoe, always seeking evidence of commercial success, described St Albans as the capital town of the shire[24], its corn market vital to the economy of the south-east. In terms of communication, however, there was a threat closer to home, since Ware enjoyed the competitive edge by virtue of its location further down the River Lea and had staged rival, illegal markets from the medieval period onwards. Lionel Munby describes the bitter conflict over control of river traffic from as far back as 1191, when Hertford inhabitants took the drastic protectionist measure of vandalising the Ware bridge![25]. Yet despite ongoing sibling rivalry and Ware's undoubted commercial advantages, Hertford's growth compared to other regional centres in the Restoration period suggests that it was enjoying moderate success in terms of urban development[26].

Any growth, however, paled into insignificance when compared to the capital. Swelling from 200,000 to 900,000 people between 1600 and 1800, London's prodigious expansion was unique in Europe, ensuring a disproportionate dominance over the rest of England, both socially and economically. Since mobility ensured that a sixth of the population would have visited London at some stage in their lives, the transmission of ideas and tastes was almost guaranteed[27]. This rapid development, however, was not achieved without cost and if London, described by Thomas Dekker as the 'Queene of Cities', was a luxury to be met by other regions[28], Hertfordshire's proximity ensured that she would have to foot at least part of the bill.

As the focus for political, legal and commercial activity, not to mention the home of a politically volatile populace, the distended capital needed to ensure ready supplies of food, water and raw materials. Protecting these vital supplies required investment and this in turn encouraged product specialisation in neighbouring counties. London financiers had already committed considerable resources to Hertfordshire by the sixteenth century, and one of Hertford's primary tasks was to grind Bedfordshire grain for the capital's insatiable appetite[29]. Communication routes by road and river were thus already well-established in response to the capital's needs, and the relationship deepened with the ongoing development of the Lea Navigation after the sixteenth century. Although not the ambitious canalisation scheme originally envisaged by the City of London's sponsors in 1571, the flash-lock technology employed in the improvement of the navigation nevertheless stood witness to engineering prowess long before the age of Brunel[30].

3. Hertford's religious climate

If the town was subject to external economic demands, it asserted its spiritual independence in the strength of nonconformist dissent which far exceeded the regional average. Despite the lingering presence of a small group of Roman Catholics in the area, the Compton Census registered as protestant dissenters a third of all adults over the age of sixteen, a level unrivalled in the county[31]. Nonconformity took the form of a strong Independent (Congregationalist) and Quaker presence[32], but was not evenly distributed across the town, for dissenters and conformists were much more evenly balanced in St Andrews, a factor which may have created substantial cultural differences between neighbourhoods.

Fig. 1 Religious Affiliation in Hertford St Andrew and All Saints - 1676

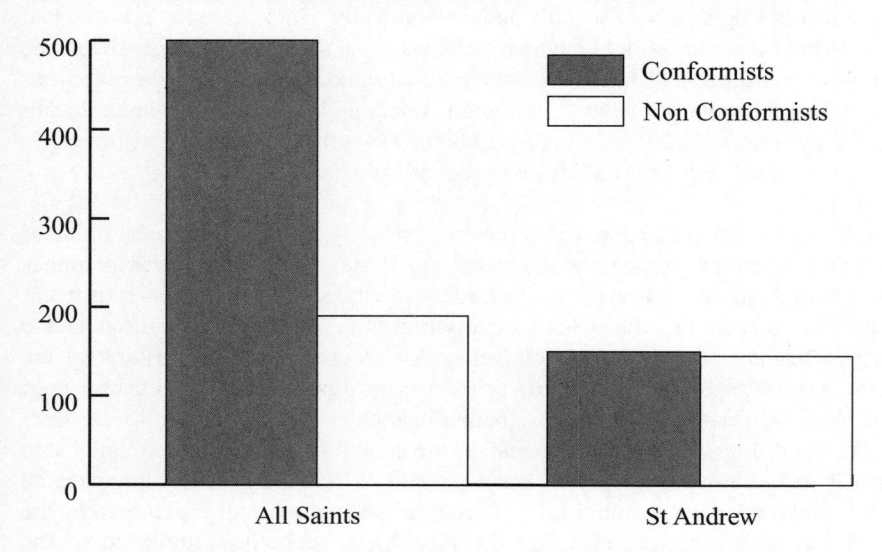

Source: Whiteman A., *The Compton Census of 1676: a critical edition* (OUP for the British Academy, 1986)

Fig. 2 Religious Affiliation in Hertford (parishes combined)

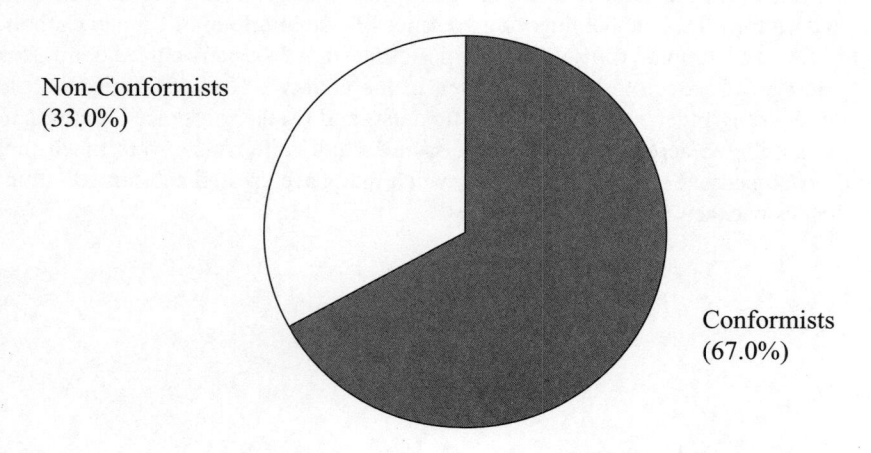

Source: Whiteman A., *The Compton Census of 1676: a critical edition* (OUP for the British Academy, 1986)

4. The probate process
Historically, the county was divided between the bishoprics of London, in the east, and Lincoln, in the west. The latter was divided between the Archdeaconries of St Albans and Huntingdon, Hertford Deanery falling within Huntingdon's jurisdiction. When we examine the probate process itself, it is apparent that will-making only became an established, if atypical, activity after the fourteenth century, filtering down the social hierarchy with the gradual extension of written culture and bureaucracy[33]. Originally two separate documents, the *voluntatum* was concerned with realty, the *testamentum* with personal goods and debts. As a result of the medieval system of land tenure, realty could only be devised through the mediation of manorial courts, whereas personalty could be bequeathed, and it was only in the sixteenth century that the Statutes of Wills made provision for land to be willed to a chosen heir[34]. Formalised inventory-taking was also established by statute in 1529[35], requiring the appraisal of possessions in excess of £5 by at least two 'honest and skilful' men within three months of death[36].

The whole process carried a spiritual dimension, reflected in instructions to clergy in the 1662 Book of Common Prayer: their involvement was encouraged to enable the smooth transition of property and avoid family and community conflict. Nevertheless, intestacy was widespread. Mechanisms for dealing with such cases were established by statute under Edward I, and revised in the later seventeenth century, whereby letters of administration were granted upon security before any property could be distributed[37]. Until 1858, probate came within the jurisdiction of the various ecclesiastical courts: the local archdeaconry court for testators with property in one archdeaconry and for those people of 'small means'[38]; the bishop's consistory court for testators with holdings in more than one parish, and for wills which were a cause of local dispute; and the Prerogative Courts of York and Canterbury for those testators holding property in more than one diocese or seeking the status of a higher jurisdiction[39].

5. Problems of interpretation
Such a process raises a number of difficulties for the historian, since a study based only on documents proved in the local Archdeaconry Court is automatically biased in terms of property ownership and, quite probably, in social structure. Certainly, locally-proved probate material is absent for the Rector of All Saints, Ralph Battell; William Mynors, who served as alderman in 1687 and Mayor in 1689, and Adlord Bowde, all of whom ranked as wealthy in Hearth Tax terms, although William Edmonds, who was Mayor in 1665, and John Bach, alderman, are included in the sample[40].

Using probate evidence to reconstruct material and cultural environments also raises a number of problems, not least the attribution of personal meaning and value to everyday things: those items of furniture, utensils, tools and 'household stuff' recorded in wills and inventories. Inferring lifestyle from such evidence is fraught with danger, since a household may have spent any surplus income in ways which are lost to us, perhaps on a change of diet, or shorter working hours[41]. Prudence, thrift and restraint are other aspects of behaviour which might be difficult to detect without corroborating evidence from diaries or household accounts. For a lack of possessions does not necessarily signify relative poverty, but may reflect a moral objection to living in a more material world. Indeed, 'luxury' and 'necessity' are other challenging concepts, since their definition is constantly changing, underpinned by a range of circumstances and attitudes. Nor, as Christopher Berry points out, is it easy to understand the fine distinction between the two, since one's luxury may well prove to be another's necessity[42].

Trying to date changes in household consumption from inventories is also hampered by their 'snapshot' effect. Without the benefit of household accounts and bills, it is difficult to assess how much appraised property represented recent purchases. Nor is probate material reliable for estimating individual wealth; wills are notoriously vague about financial liabilities, land values, or the means by which money bequests are to be financed. Moreover, Margaret Spufford demonstrated that even where such information is available, there is no clear connection between the value of household goods and total wealth[43]. The Hertford 1663 Hearth Tax returns are of little more help in this respect, since the two sources have only thirteen names in common and, as might be expected with such a small sample, there is no obvious pattern to link the number of hearths with the recorded value of household goods.

The concept of status or occupation poses further difficulties, since status tends to evolve throughout a person's lifetime. Daniel Defoe's 'mechanick' may well have climbed a skills ladder from apprentice to journeyman before achieving middling status as a master craftsman. It is thus quite possible that the information provided in a will or inventory overestimates the strength of some social groups[44]. Nor are the occupational or status titles themselves without bias, since they could change with the owner's *claim* to status; there were undoubtedly some for whom titles such as 'gentleman' were little more than social pretence.

A recital of pitfalls does not end there - wills and inventories should not be seen as a reliable source for linking particular occupations with material wealth. Before death overtook the testator, the perfectly legitimate transfer of property to other family members could be well under way, so that an occupational title and the appraised value of personal property might not suggest an accurate picture, even if they were associated at the outset. Another problem is the 'disappearance' of goods; in some cases they were removed in haste before the appraisers could make their inventory, or even deliberately excluded from appraisal. Appraisers' skills, too, were often greater in reputation than reality; property valuations and arithmetic were sometimes highly suspect[45]. A neatly-rounded valuation of seven guineas for a motley assortment of goods, for example, suggests a rather pragmatic approach on the part of the appraiser![46].

Having assessed the pitfalls of this particular source, however, it is fair to say that problems of interpretation are a fact of life and are hardly restricted to probate material. Wills and inventories do, after all, provide complementary, but quite distinct views of disparate social groups, many of whom were not part of a written culture and for whom we have little other evidence.

Part II
Hertford's Material World

1. Wills, inventories and occupations[47]
When examining Hertford occupations, we find that specialist trades such as peruke-maker, watchmaker and tobacconist were located in the town during this period[48], confirming the picture of a thriving urban centre with well-developed services. Thirty separate occupations or ranks are represented in the inventory sample and, whilst acknowledging that titles or labels change their meaning over time, the majority - gentleman, bachelor and yeoman excepted - are relatively unambiguous. A fifth of testators were widows and spinsters, whilst tradesmen in 'low and intermediate' status occupations accounted for a further two-fifths. Even those defined as gentlemen are, by virtue of the sample, probably 'lesser' gentry, lending this group a strongly middling character. Grouping testators by economic activity only reinforces this picture for, despite an unwieldy category of those without any recorded occupation, dealing and manufacturing emerge as the most common means of earning a living[49].

Fig. 3 Social Status of Testators Leaving Inventories

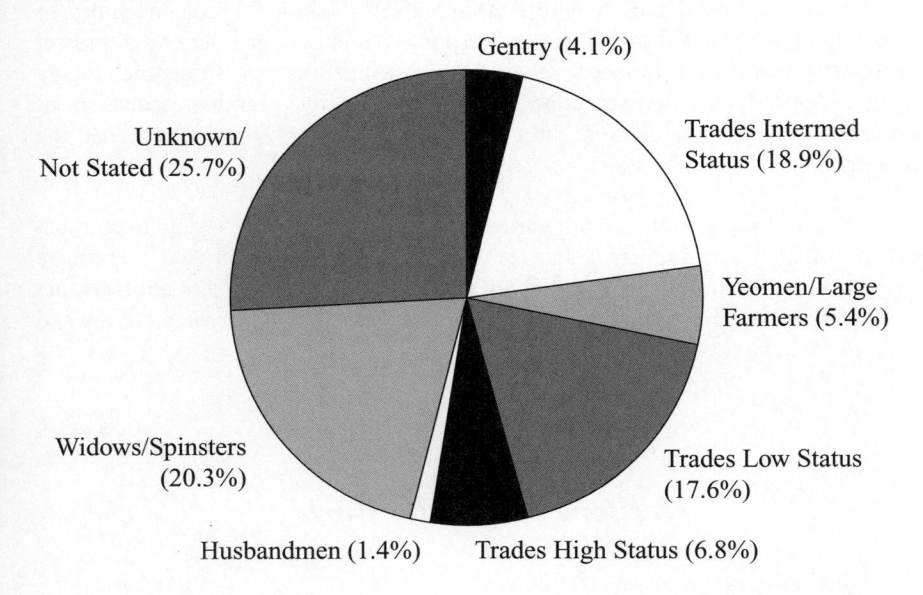

- Gentry (4.1%)
- Trades Intermed Status (18.9%)
- Yeomen/Large Farmers (5.4%)
- Trades Low Status (17.6%)
- Trades High Status (6.8%)
- Husbandmen (1.4%)
- Widows/Spinsters (20.3%)
- Unknown/Not Stated (25.7%)

Fig. 4 Testators grouped by economic sector

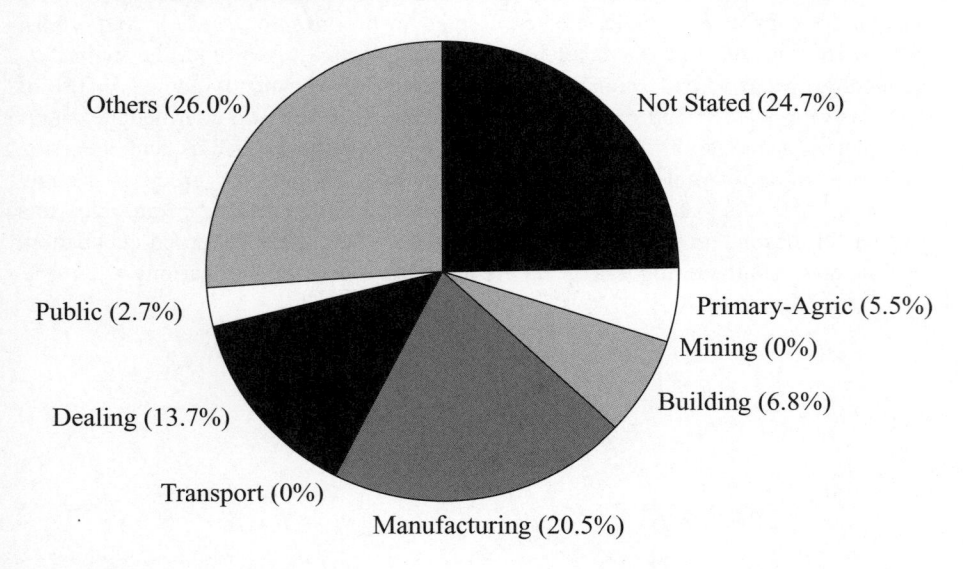

- Not Stated (24.7%)
- Primary-Agric (5.5%)
- Mining (0%)
- Building (6.8%)
- Manufacturing (20.5%)
- Transport (0%)
- Dealing (13.7%)
- Public (2.7%)
- Others (26.0%)

2. The value of goods and chattels

Economic disparity is the key to this group of testators. Whereas only a handful held property in excess of £500, over one fifth had property (including outstanding debts) valued from £101-£250. Comparing the pattern both to Lorna Weatherill's broad study and Michael Reed's work on Ipswich, Hertford is peculiar in the relative strength of this particular group, although this may reflect the social bias of the sample and its poor representation of husbandmen and labourers[50].

Fig. 5 Hertford Inventory Totals in £ sterling, 1660-1714 Grouped Frequency Distribution

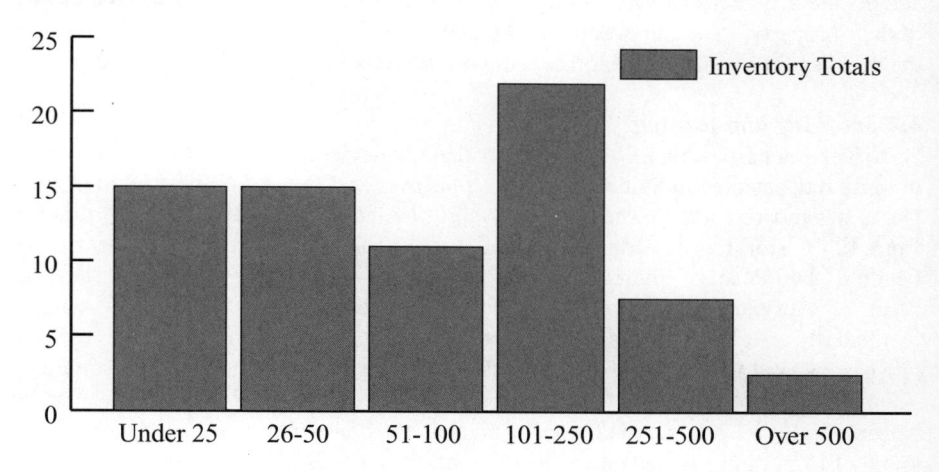

Fig. 6 Hertford Inventory Totals, 1660-1714: Percentage Distribution

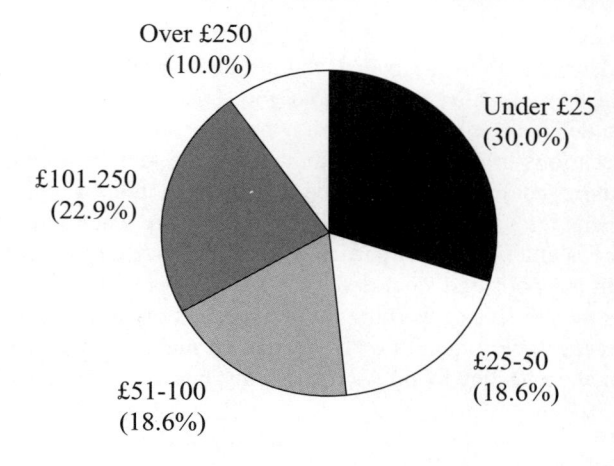

3. Status and wealth
If levels of inventoried wealth were, indeed, linked to status, we might expect certain trades to fall within the same band of inventory values. Yet status groups occur haphazardly across the full range; yeomen held property valued from £28.6s.9d to £577.8s.5d, gentlemen from £26.10s.5d to £454.18s.5d., confirming Lorna Weatherill's observation that the gentry were an ill-defined group of individuals[51]. Certainly, tradesmen do occur more frequently in the lower bands; cordwainers, carpenters, tailors, a locksmith, tanner and glazier all had total goods of less than £100, but the inventories of another tanner, a bricklayer, a currier and two bakers were valued at between £101 and £250. Dealers, too, occur with similar frequency in both bands, and if solidarity really existed amongst occupational groups, it is not manifested clearly in their property. Nor can differences be explained by inflation over the period, since the decades following the Restoration did not witness rapidly-increasing prices[52].

4. Borrowing and lending
Historian Rachel Garrard has suggested that moneylending in a community could indicate that selected individuals had a surplus over and above their desired lifestyle[53]. Debts in Hertford were owed to twenty-eight of the seventy-six testators[54], ranging from £1.10 shillings to Robert Stothard to £180.16s.2d owed to the older James Pendred, the maltster. Whereas some of these debts would represent the outstanding debts of everyday commerce, it is clear that other testators, all of them widows incidentally, were local sources of loan capital[55]. Mary Pomfrett, sister of the prosperous Will Catlin, had seven separate amounts out on loan, ranging from £5 to Thomas Hutchin to £100 to Will Hawkings, and spread geographically as far as Nazeing in Essex. Her personal goods and chattels, however, were modest, amounting to only £13.5s. and deemed unworthy of mention at appraisal[56]. Joane Baker was owed £100 and Joan Treherne £115 when their goods were appraised, both appearing to show little concern for new material possessions[57].

5. Household goods
When debts are deducted from the overall value of inventoried property, a clearer picture emerges of the real value of household goods and stock, for over two thirds left possessions valued at less than £100. Again, this does not provide evidence to link the values of possessions to social rank. Although bakers, tanners and maltsters did appear to have more comfortably furnished homes than their woodworking and building sector peers, the evidence is far too fragile to make wholesale assumptions about the possessions and lifestyle of particular groups of tradesmen. Yet those with the greatest wealth in goods and stock did include three yeomen and two maltsters, perhaps reflecting the rewards of working in these sectors of the economy[58]. Indeed, since Defoe noted the superb quality of Hertfordshire malt, its producers may well have expected to make a healthy living[59]. Frustratingly, however, their inventories only

include the values of working equipment and stock, not their furnishings. To the appraisers concerned, the trappings of domesticity were evidently far less significant than the means of getting a livelihood.

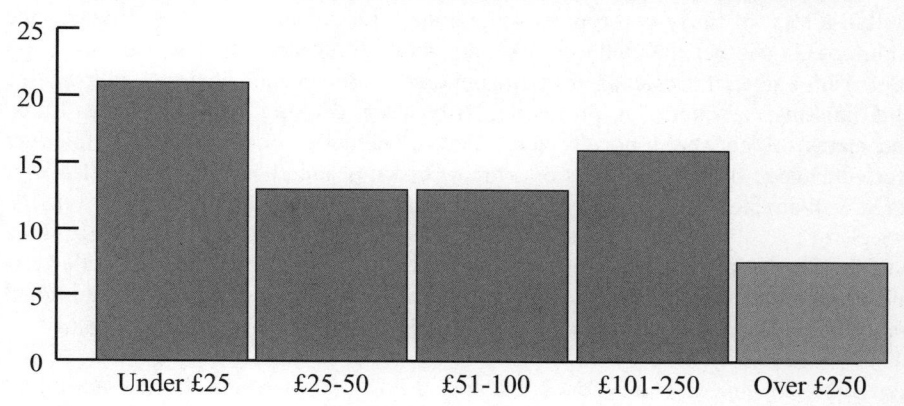

Fig. 7 Moveable Goods excluding Debts - Grouped Frequency Distribution

Joseph Saward's appraisers took a more comprehensive approach, detailing books, arms to the value of £5, grain amounting to over £260, horses, cows and hogs, a clock in the hall and a parlour cluttered with two tables, a looking glass and no fewer than seventeen chairs. Although we are given no status title for Saward, his will and inventory portray him as a prosperous landowner and farmer, probably one for whom the title of yeoman had real substance. Another for whom it was relevant was Nathaniel Hale. His material world fits well with Mildred Campbell's perception of the traditional yeoman enjoying an unpretentious but comfortable lifestyle[61]. His household inventory, taken in 1671 and valued at £355.10s. shows that he had no money out on loan, perhaps since he was in the habit of reinvesting surpluses into the home and his well-stocked farm. He composed and wrote his own will, owned one of the few clocks in the neighbourhood, had a separate parlour furnished with carpeted tables and leather chairs, and five upstairs chambers all equipped with bedsteads and feather bedding. In addition to livestock, grain and farming equipment, he had a healthy sum of liquid equity, for he willed a total of £205 in money bequests to his five sons and three daughters, one of whom had married into the Saward family. His inventory also provides a clearer picture of his domestic interior than many, for the chambers pair exactly with ground floor rooms and reveal a clearly-defined use of space within the house. The parlour was quite possibly used for visiting, its leather upholstery and absence of settles or stools suggesting a touch of formal 'frontstage' display and earnest respectability.

If many inventories provide only the barest information, John Bach's appraisers recorded a positive embarrassment of detail. We have a sense in which the process of making the inventory itself marked the status and success of the deceased. For the material lifestyle of this gentleman, alderman and former mayor could serve as a benchmark for the middle ranks. In addition to his domestic living space, he occupied rooms in no fewer than five inns: the Magpie; Dolphin; Ship; Groom and Anchor. Within a total of thirty-two rooms, some hung with coloured paper or drugget, one wainscoted, another painted, he had amassed thirty-three tables, two of them 'Spanish', eighteen bedsteads, over one hundred chairs, dozens of sheets, pillowcases and napkins, crockery in profusion, fifty-three cooking pots and even three saucepans, which were a novelty and reflected changing cooking methods. Interiors were enhanced by thirteen pairs of window curtains and five mirrors. He also kept three well-stocked cellars, partly for his occupation but also, no doubt, for oiling the wheels of the administrative machine. The wine cellar housed eight hogsheads, three half-hogsheads, quantities of sack and red and white port, while the little cellar was reserved for cider, and the beer cellar held fifteen and a half hogsheads, an additional ten of 'stale beere' and a further four of mild. He also owned two pairs of pistols[62].

Yet although his inventory does include 'key goods', which Lorna Weatherill considered an important factor in assessing new attitudes to consumption[63], we have no way of knowing from this source alone whether he, or members of his household, were directly responsible for the lavish expenditure necessary to acquire so many possessions. If nothing was specifically described as 'new', neither was it 'old', a qualification used far more frequently in the sample[64]. What is clear, however, is that the opulence of Bach's home and sheer quantity of possessions marked his status in the community. Whether all this material wealth represented a desire to show off to his neighbours, however, or merely reflected the expectations of rank and office, must remain a mystery.

At the other end of the material spectrum, spinster Mary Humberston's inventory detailed a meagre £5.12s.4d. of household goods, although these did include a feather mattress, a possession that Neil McKendrick described as a mark of wealth[65]. She owned a single cooking pot and four little pewter dishes, and was evidently not caught up in the spending habit, many of her possessions carrying the marks of age. Quite possibly they had been willed to her, as she was to will them to her sister Anne[66]. Barber-surgeon Edward Tuffnell, whose goods were appraised in 1665, was also without many possessions, although he too enjoyed the comforts of feather bedding. Like Mary Humberston, he possessed a single skillet, owned five shillings worth of pewter, and slept in the little parlour. Fashionable changes in the use of rooms had not impinged on his lifestyle, yet to assume from his sparse belongings that he was relatively poor would be misguided. For Tuffnell owned the rights to the Swan Inn at Hatfield, held free - and copyhold property in Bengeo, and the Maydenhead Inn in Hertford itself. Evidently, his approach to material possessions was highly functional, untouched by the impulses of fashion. His inventory also reinforces Lorna Weatherill's observations that the 'new consumerism' is far less appropriately applied to the later seventeenth century than the eighteenth[67].

Yet if these two extremes are unrepresentative, those with goods valued between £101 and £250 might convey more accurately Hertford's middle rank lifestyle. Certainly, in terms of 'key goods', twelve of the sixteen owned tables, five owned cooking pots, eleven some form of pewter. Only one, however, owned a saucepan, and none of this group had a clock, although whether such a novel and desirable item would have survived to the point of appraisal is another question! Three in this group had looking glasses, four had table linen and three some silver. Only the baker, John Radford, curtained his windows; this concession to interior decor seems not to have been a high priority[68]. Books, on the other hand, do not appear to have been necessities, only one being recorded. Yet it seems possible that appraisers included books under the general heading of 'other household lumber', for in a town riven by partisan and religious strife, it would have been surprising if the less expensive pamphlets and broadsheets had not found their way into some of these homes.

Eating habits in Hertford show little innovation at this time, for there are no recorded sets of knives and forks, but ample table napkins. We know from Braudel's research that the use of individual forks was spreading across Europe from Italy, but there was still an immense cultural gulf between Renaissance Venice and seventeenth century Hertford. Braudel found no evidence of table forks in England before the Restoration[69], and Hertford inventories mention them only twice, once, predictably, in John Bach's inventory, which records thirty-six forks and forty-eight knives, the other in the inventory of yeoman, John Richardson, whose goods were appraised at the turn of the century. Innholder Robert Stothard had a shredding knife and meat fork, but all other knives and forks were household implements, not table cutlery. As for food storage, fifteen owned a livery cupboard, whilst nine owned more substantial court cupboards behind whose doors all types of 'household lumber' might be concealed. Others had cupboards or trunks of indeterminate size and construction, most failing to motivate the appraisers to description unless used for a specific purpose. Perhaps Benjamin Bradney's 'cubbard' was little more than a small wooden box for it housed only his tobacco[70].

If storage was highly functional, these testators were convinced of the benefits of comfortable bedding which attracted far greater attention on appraisal. Their descriptions convey a vivid impression of high and standing bedsteads, trundle and half-headed beds, all layered with mats, mattresses, bolsters and pillows, 'pillowbeers' and sheets, blankets, coverlets and rugs. Bedsteads, too, were incomplete without their curtains and valance and, on occasion, a tester canopy. Straw mattresses were the least common, whilst flockbeds were far less popular than feather. Nor did these distinctions appear to be related either to status or to the total value of household goods. If, as Francis Steer observed in a contemporary Essex sample, sheets were a luxury, they were one enjoyed explicitly by over thirty-five per cent of Hertford testators. When, in addition, 'all the linen' is taken into account, even more sheets and pillowcases would probably come to light.

6. Change over time

Bedding notwithstanding, the overwhelming impression remains of modest consumption, and only sporadic innovation. If Hertford consumers were heading for a lifestyle punctuated by frequent bouts of spending, this ought to be revealed by the appraisal of novel consumer goods, especially amongst those with surplus money to hand or in similar social or occupational groups across time. Yet the data once again proved inconclusive. The inventories of three bakers, appraised between 1663 and 1712, certainly show an increase in total value, and whereas the earliest includes only tables and pewter, the second, appraised some seven years later, does mention a looking glass and window curtains. Unfortunately, the compilers of the most recent inventory suffered from appraisal-fatigue and recorded only malt, oats, debts and clothing[71]. Three maltsters' inventories for the period between 1664 and 1712 are even less enlightening. Richard Goodman had no 'key' items and the Pendreds' domestic goods were not recorded.

Ranking key goods over time is unreliable, since appraisal became rather less detailed as time passed. Nevertheless, taking 1684 as the mid-point of the sample[72], several items do seem to occur with increasing frequency. The first clock was recorded in 1669, not again until 1683 and then five times between 1688 and 1725. Saucepans appear only once before 1688, but then three times before 1704, and books, looking glasses, decorative turkey work goods and window curtains also appear more often after the mid-1680s. Perhaps then these patterns do suggest a glimmer of change in lifestyle and the quality of the domestic interior.

7. A feminine touch?

Whether consumption decisions by women were responsible for such change over time is unclear. Alice Clark believed that an expanding world of consumer goods was related to the changing role of women and their place in the domestic economy[73], a concept further elaborated by Amanda Vickery[74]. Yet how, from inventory evidence, do we decide who was responsible for household purchases? By linking the ownership of household goods to individual testators, we are suggesting that lifestyle was decided by the material tastes of the deceased, rather than the whole family. This in turn carries assumptions about decision-making within the family which may be wholly misguided! Only if we are lucky enough to have supplementary evidence is it possible to judge with any accuracy which goods were purchased solely by women, and possible reasons for that choice.

Whilst acknowledging these difficulties, there is nevertheless a suggestion that ownership amongst women was biased towards items which contributed to personal comfort, privacy and interior decoration. Whereas there is little difference between men and women in the possession of functional items such as tables, dishes and plates, appraisers recorded more turkey work goods, feather bedding, table linen and window curtains in households headed by women; perhaps this in itself reveals something of decision-making in those households with a man at the helm.

Fig. 8 Ownership of selected key goods by gender

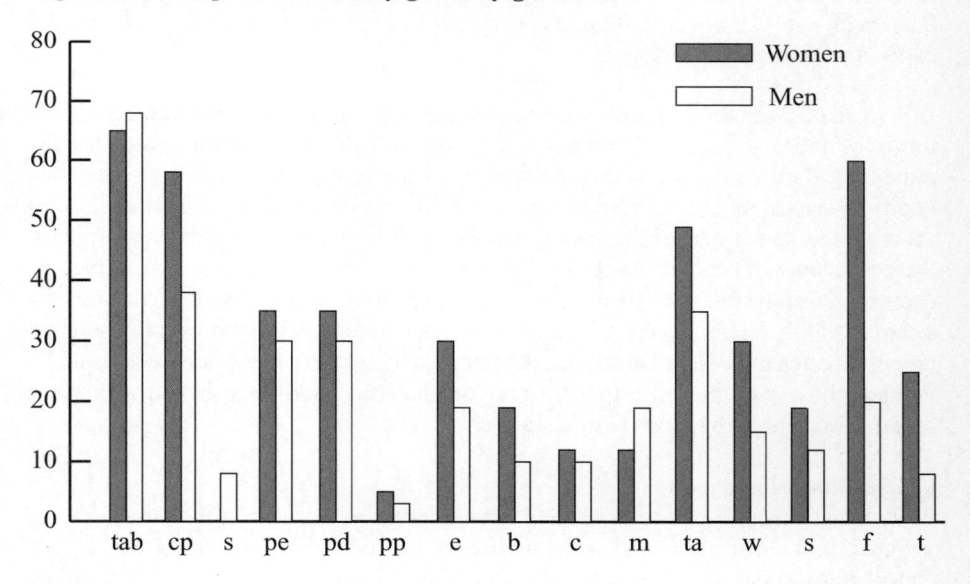

Key:

tab	tables	c	clocks
cp	cooking pots	m	looking glasses
s	saucepans	ta	table linen
pe	pewter	w	window curtains
pd	pewter dishes	s	silver
pp	pewter plates	f	featherbedding
e	earthenware	t	turkey work
b	books		

8. The use of space
If the possession of material goods underwent subtle changes over time, so did the use of rooms, reflecting changing aspects of lifestyle[75]. Although the pretension and formality of the middle-class parlour would provoke acid criticism from Cobbett in the early nineteenth century, the arrival of the parlour as a separate room was a much earlier innovation, occurring with the partitioning of the main hall and the provision of a separate area for display and activity[76]. Appraisers tended to name rooms at random, if they recorded them at all which, in nearly a third of inventories, they failed to do. Yet they do provide some indication of the number of rooms available to the household - amongst this group, an average of eight and nine rooms or separate storage areas. If we try to link the number of rooms with the overall value of goods, it does seem that no testator with goods valued at under £50 occupied more than four separate rooms. Thereafter, the pattern becomes confused, although it is clear that those with over £250 worth of goods occupied a minimum of six rooms, and in some cases considerably more.

If the use of a separate parlour marked changing attitudes to the use of rooms, two-thirds of those with named rooms had given into the new fashion, whereas the remaining third continued to use the hall as central living space. None of these had goods in excess of £250, whereas the wealthiest six all had a parlour, as did all yeomen and gentlemen, regardless of the value of their goods. In this area, at least, there is an aura of genteel sensibility. Yet it would be wrong to assume that all parlour users reserved the room for display, for over one quarter of these still used the area for sleeping. This, again, appears to have some association with the overall value of property, since only John Goodman, the tanner, had goods valued in excess of £70[77]. Perhaps those who placed a higher value on material goods also hoped to make a social statement by having a formal parlour.

9. The domestic interior
Any changes from function to fashion should, perhaps, be seen in the possession of pictures, soft furnishings and decorative china, teapots and coffeepots, but all are conspicuously absent[78]. The voluminous bedding, sporadic cushions and few turkey work chairs make little impression on a generally workmanlike approach to possessions and interior decoration, an image endorsed by a lack of descriptive language in the inventories. If this group of early modern consumers included fashion victims, someone must have removed the evidence before the appraisers started work.

For furniture, if described, was jointed, rather than carved or turned, almost certainly of oak. The more fashionable walnut is never mentioned, elm and pine only recorded twice, cedar and deal once. Brass was the most popular metal, followed by pewter, some iron, a little tin-ware and copper[79]. Even the more precious little silver items are scattered about the neighbourhood, showing no preference for the status of their owner; the seven who possessed silver ware included three widows, two gentlemen, a mealman and a maltster, their inventory values showing the usual wide range[80]. Nor can we paint these interiors with any precision, since the colour of fabrics and furnishings is rarely mentioned. Where it is, however, green is predominant, with an occasional item in red or a dark, 'sad' colour. Above all, the interior might have been strangely silent to the desensitised twentieth century ear, for despite tools and hand-turned implements, cooking, eating and conversation, there is no suggestion of games or music, except, in Mary Cornell's house, for the sound of a pair of virginals[81].

Part III
Hertford's Cultural Environment

1. Making the will

If the material world of the inventory only really comes alive once seen in its cultural setting[82], that is provided, in part, by the will and testament. For once the formal legal formulae have been penetrated, wills convey a wealth of human detail: James Pendred's frank confession that he has difficulty with the names of his many nieces and nephews[83]; ill-concealed family tensions; personal insecurities and anxieties. Even the long-suffering scribe, possibly driven to distraction by a client's inability to make firm decisions about the disposal of goods, helps to paint a picture of contemporary lifestyle. Margaret Webb's will consisted of eight sheets, detailing the intricacies of twenty-seven separate bequests, but even before signing and sealing the document, she experienced a change of heart, subtracting £45 from eight of the bequests, and redistributing her household linen[84]. One only hopes that her scribe was well paid for his services! Few wills were made well in advance of death despite everyday reminders of mortality. Only when illness or old age sounded a warning, perhaps when, like Will Catlin, people had become 'ancient and crazie in body'[85], did the need to make a will become pressing.

Yet wills need not have been written in advance for us to glean something of prevailing attitudes; for those unable to settle matters before their last illness might be pressed to declare their intentions. Not that witnesses were to be blamed for their insistence, since Christian observance did demand preparation for death, including the settling of affairs in this life before embarking upon eternity. Without the clutter of legal phrases, the two nuncupative wills allow us to glimpse the sombre deathbed scene, whilst throwing into relief the potential for double-dealing by others. Those who insisted that Joane Baker declare her will were obviously creating an unwelcome intrusion and she responded with justifiable irritation. When asked by Mary Rooding to confirm whether she willed all her property to her sister Mary Clarke, Joane assented, adding with some bite, 'to whome shou'd she give it else'[86].

The cynical might suspect that husbandman Thomas White's deathbed declaration in 1660 was reported less faithfully, since it suggests that the dying man was almost too aware of his social obligations. Reported with a certain dramatic licence, the words were designed to move their judicial audience: 'applying himself to his then master...(White) said, master my estate is but small not above twelve pounds. And I have layen suche a great while at yor Charges....my will and desire [is] that you will pay the Debts that I owe and see mee buried. And if there bee any surplusage of my estate I give it to you in consideracon of yor great love towards me in my sicknesse'[87]. It is, of course, quite possible that Thomas Bratt's motives in caring for his employee were truly altruistic; financially, he had little to gain. But with a nuncupative will, the suspicion of avarice and self-interest always hovered around the witnesses.

Conditions attached to bequests also reveal family tensions or individual anxiety. Daniel Smith feared discord in the wake of his death, for he felt the need to 'charge, desire and entreate all and every of my said Sisters not to act or doe any thing with intent to defeat or destroy this my devise'[88]. Edward Tuffnell also alluded to ill-feeling between his sons, for he included a clause of forfeiture if Conor should 'anywaies disturbe or trouble' his brother[89]. Such was the legal power of testators to act from beyond the grave, and it could be used to chilling effect in the case of a widow's re-marriage. Goody stresses that the whole question of remarriage was fraught in early modern European society, and was obviously a cause for concern amongst children whose widowed mother was still of child-bearing age.

It might appear that carpenter, John Helder, was motivated by personal jealousy when he insisted that his wife, in the event of any remarriage, would forfeit her property to her sons 'as if shee were as truly dead'[90]. In reality, however, he was acting as the guardian of his children's heritage by ensuring that family property remained intact. Helder's character emerges between the lines of his will, revealing open tensions with his son-in-law, who had fallen behind with the rent, and its austere tone sits well with a man of rigid and uncompromising principle: presented at the Quarter Sessions in 1662 for failure to attend church, Helder committed himself, in the face of legally-sanctioned hostility, to building work on the Quaker Meeting House[91]. John Radford, too, was concerned at the prospect of his wife's remarriage, including a clause in his will to insure his property against future alienation. Thus any prospective suitor for his widow Frances would have to provide security of £300[92]. Having seven children, he was almost certainly concerned with their future solvency.

2. A question of literacy

Of the forty-two written wills, most would have been drafted by a scribe. In some cases, however, and with sufficient pride for the fact to be mentioned, testators committed their own intentions to paper[93]. The whole concept of literacy is, however, laden with the judgements of our own twentieth-century values. Surely, the inability to sign one's name at this time should not automatically signify 'illiteracy', a term which suggests that those excluded from written culture were somehow impoverished. As David Cressy points out, the ability to write at this time was neither as valuable nor as enlightening as some might claim[94]. Certainly, amongst the Hertford wills, many who made their mark took the trouble to draw unique pictograms which, in a small community, would have been as recognisable as any formal signature. Nor does the use of a mark rather than a signature indicate lack of reading ability, since reading was always taught before handwriting[95].

Unsurprisingly, however, men were far more commonly able to write their names. Of thirteen female testators for whom there are wills, only one, Mary Pettit, in 1690, gave a signature, whereas nearly half of the men signed their names. Mary Pettit was not a wealthy woman in terms of household goods, her inventory being valued at £75.7s.10d. In 1663, however, she inhabited a house with seven hearths, placing her firmly amongst the more prosperous middling sort. Her circle of friends included Henry Marson, probably the Quaker of the same name[96], and Will Guyse, who was a prominent Congregationalist[97]. Since the Quakers kept a school in Hertford from the 1660s, it is likely that a desire for book-learning permeated her social circle.

3. Religious beliefs

Whereas religious belief is undoubtedly relevant to social values, the extent to which it can be inferred from will preambles is far from clear. The influences of traditional rubrics, local custom and the preferences of scribes must all have played their part. What is clear is that Hertford's solidly protestant culture had excised any lingering vestiges of traditional religion from its formal modes of expression. Whereas Caroline Litzenberger's analysis of sixteenth century wills identified three types of religious expression - traditional, protestant and neutral[98], those for Hertford in this later period show few such distinctions, their local context being one in which the divide was not between the Church in England and Catholicism, but parish protestantism and dissent. Unsurprisingly, therefore, the Virgin Mary, the holy company of heaven and the saints are all absent, as are allusions to the more 'neutral' Holy Trinity. Yet at the other end of the doctrinal spectrum, expressions of orthodox Calvinism also fail to appear; explicit references to predestined election are missing, although self-confident assurances of salvation are recorded in a fifth of preambles; Jesus Christ's role as a *personal* saviour or redeemer and the merits to be gained from his human experience are recorded in more than half, while a tenth showed an acceptance of God as providential provider through the 'loan' of worldly goods. Nor are changes evident across time; the formulae remain consistent, the concepts unchanged. The overall outlook comes across as stable, conservative, even austere, for only five testators mention joyful or happy prospects in eternity; perhaps the whole process of will-making precludes too much levity.

An avowedly protestant world-view is also evident in bequests for charitable purposes, for there are no gifts to the altar, for lights, or prayers for the souls of the dead. Although many historians have observed a general transition to secular charitable giving after the English Reformation, the level of charitable bequests suggests that a doctrine of salvation earned through good works carried little appeal. Forty-five Hertford testators bequeathed an approximate £3,200 in cash bequests, and of this total amount, only £30.10s. were bequeathed to the poor, although Thomas Noble did bequeath an annuity of £15 to relieve poverty in the parish of All Saints. By far the most generous legacies for the poor were made by Quakers; the tanner John Moores left £5 to 'poore Friends' at the Hertford meeting, with another £5 to any others working in the 'service of truth'[99]. James Pendred, too, willed £10 to his fellow Friends[100]. Compared with the usual bequests of ten or twenty shillings, these amounts demonstrate unequivocal mutual support amongst dissenters. Yet if bequests to the poor lacked vigour, those for public works were non-existent. It appears that keeping personal property within the family was most important, one which fits well with the picture of a group determined to retain financial independence in the face of an unpredictable and relatively pressing existence.

4. Beneficiaries and bequests

Also of interest is the manner in which property was bequeathed, and the relationships created or perpetuated in the process. Even where inheritance patterns reflect family connections and rifts, they are nevertheless dominated by links of kinship and marriage[101]. Common law favoured primogeniture, a system which for some underpinned the existing privileges of an unequal social hierarchy, but for others enriched English culture by preserving inheritances in one piece[102]. Certainly, one only has to examine the French system of partible inheritance to see the differences in landholding, agriculture and national economies. Yet the philosopher John Locke was starting to lay stress on the natural law concept of property which suggested that human justice should be based on equal rights to subsistence. The notion that all children had equal rights of inheritance formed part of an increasingly vocal challenge to primogeniture throughout Europe. Those who framed the 1670 Statute of Distribution evidently took notice, for the act included provision for personalty to be divided equally between all children in cases of intestacy. Evidence does confirm that primogeniture was observed far less rigorously in the early modern period, a pattern which Joan Thirsk believes helped to spread wealth down the social order[103].

Yet Hertford's inheritance patterns are obscured. The wills cannot be used in isolation to determine whether partible inheritance, primogeniture or 'borough English' was the preferred system, since sibling position was rarely noted. Nor do they detail property transferred in advanced during the testator's lifetime. Indeed, it was common practice for older children to receive their 'portion', possibly newly-acquired land or an apprenticeship premium, well in advance, while younger siblings might have to wait for a parent's death to inherit[104]. What does emerge from wills, however, is the importance attached to landholding and attempts to retain control over those types of property rights.

Those men who inherited land included thirteen sons, four grandsons and five brothers. Thomas Gray bequeathed land to each of his three sons[105], John Helder to two sons, his wife (with conditions attached) and two of his brothers[106], and Edward Tuffnell to his sons, Conor and Thomas, despite the former's reputation for trouble-making[107]. It appears that testators aimed to spread equity amongst a variety of family members. Nor were children automatically favoured in the process. Although relationship labels were vague, particularly the use of 'cousin' and 'kinsman', grouping beneficiaries by generation reveals that more than a third were contemporaries, whilst those in the same generation as grandchildren and parents accounted for a further fifth.

Fig. 9 Beneficiaries Grouped by Generation

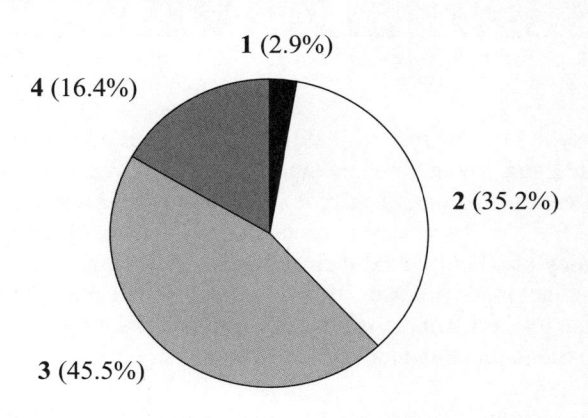

1 (2.9%)
4 (16.4%)
2 (35.2%)
3 (45.5%)

Key: 1 - same generation as testator's parents
       2 - same generation as testator
       3 - testator's children and other beneficiaries of that generation
       4 - testator's grandchildren

Siblings formed the single largest group of contemporaries (two-fifths), followed by 'kin' (roughly one quarter), some of whom could be identified as members of the extended family, but others who were evidently trusted friends and neighbours.

Fig. 10 Relationship of Beneficiaries in Testators' Own Generation

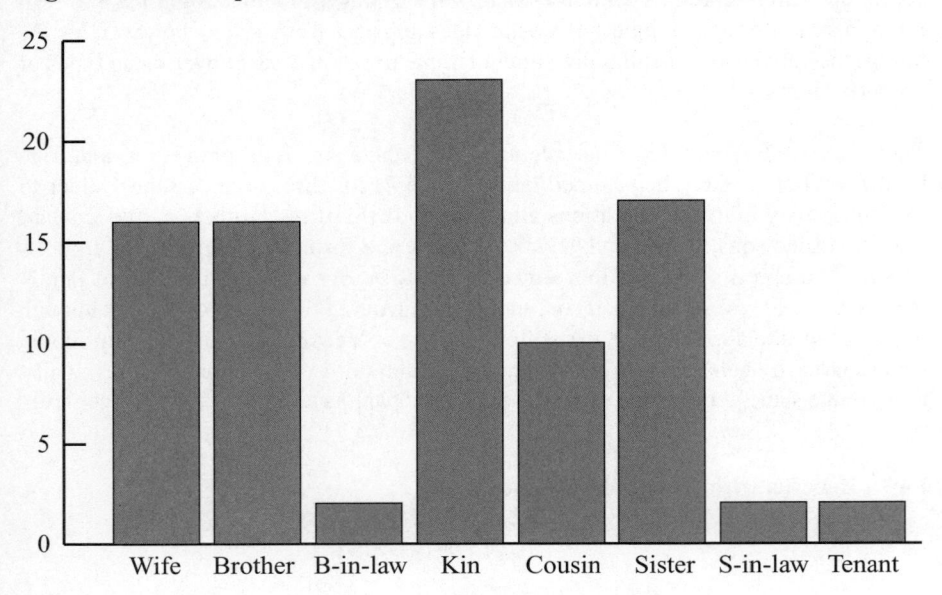

Relationship	Count
Wife	16
Brother	16
B-in-law	2
Kin	23
Cousin	10
Sister	17
S-in-law	2
Tenant	2

It is also interesting that there is little difference in the gender of beneficiaries. Even if this balance came about through the accident of birth and death, there is also evidence of a certain egalitarian attitude in bequests of personal goods, a fact which concurs with E.P.Thompson's own research on the behaviour of freeholders and tradesmen, many of whom willed their property on an equal basis[108]. Mealman John Babb, for example, made no distinction between his male and female grandchildren, willing 'the same Goods Chattells reale and personal Estate.... to be equally divided between them Share and Share alike'[109].

Daniel Smith, too, was concerned to emphasise the sharing principle, although with five sisters, he probably had little choice if he hoped for a quiet life and peaceful end. They were not in the habit of behaving in sisterly harmony, if the baker's pleas for compliance were any indication[110] and, although his 'honoured' mother and older sister were to act as joint executrices, an uncle, Benjamin Turner, was given the unenviable position of overseer!

If there were no obvious gender preferences in the number of bequests, the goods bequeathed did show differing attitudes to men and women. For if men were more likely to be willed land, and almost certain to receive working tools, women were compensated with far more linen (78% compared to 22%), and household goods (61.3% compared to 38.7%), revealing a particular view of propriety in the ownership and management of material property.

5. Family, friends and neighbours

If the inheritance process was centred on a limited number of individuals, the machinery of probate involved a much wider circle of contacts and shows something of this small town's collective life. The perpetual quest for local stability was manifested both formally - through the organisation of poor relief for example - and informally, through people's own networks of friendship and support[111]. Since many historians have shown that families lived as 'nuclear' units in this period, kinship and neighbourliness were important factors in the local community and one way of maintaining daily activities and lifestyle[112].

5.1 Appraisers

A singularly male activity, not least because of the need to write, appraisal was a rather more detached task than witnessing or administering a will, and was rarely performed by those with a direct material interest. Only three of the eighty-six appraisers were also beneficiaries, whilst eleven acted as witnesses to the relevant will and six were appointed overseer. John Burton and Archibald Palmer, both described as loving friends of the relevant testator, performed all three tasks, perhaps involved more intimately with the family's welfare. A reputation for skill and honesty in appraisal obviously carried weight, since over a quarter of all appraisers acted on more than one occasion and nearly a third of these in four or more cases. Of these, Adlord Bowde and William Guyse each appraised eight sets of goods and John Hill seven, while John Barfoot passed his skills to his son, Barfoot men appraising no fewer than eleven households between 1663 and 1714. This select band whose services were in repeated demand must have formed working relationships, for John Barfoot worked with Bowde on the inventories of John Helder, Grace Smart and Robert Stothard, whilst Guyse teamed up with Bowde for the demanding appraisal of John Bach's goods.

Adlord Bowde's liability for nine hearths in the 1663 tax returns places him, in theory at least, amongst Hertford's more prosperous inhabitants. His thirty-five years of appraisal experience involved him with a variety of individuals across the social spectrum, from alderman John Bach, to carpenter John Helder, cordwainer Richard Kerbye with only £7.6s.2d worth of household goods, Grace Smart, one of the least prosperous widows, and both innholders, Richard Churchman and Robert Stothard.

Bowde comes across as a stalwart community man, his many connections and solid social status permitting him ease of commerce amongst Hertford people.

5.2 Overseers and Executors

Overseeing a will, like appraisal, was again delegated solely to men, two-thirds of overseers being described as trusted or loving friends, the remainder male relatives. In contrast, the task of executing the will fell, in seven out of ten cases, to family members, wives forming the largest single category and accounting for over a fifth of the whole group[113].

Fig. 11 Relationship of Executors to Testators

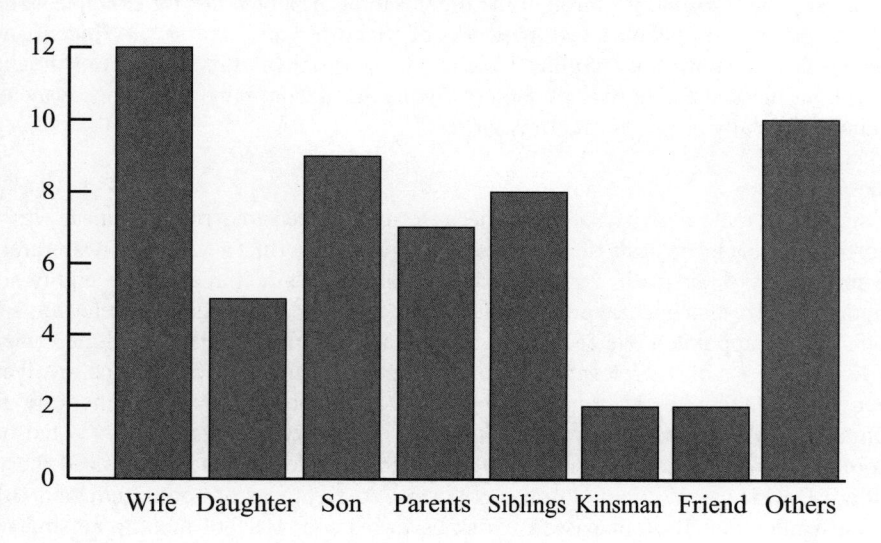

Examining the social world as a piece suggests a pattern of close family ties and functional business relationships, all woven into a community fabric by kinship and connecting figures such as Adlord Bowde and Will Guyse. Despite the undoubted priority given to family relationships, it was a world in which friendship and neighbourliness were fundamental.

Part IV
Conclusion

Although those bequeathing probate records may not be entirely typical, it seems fair to say that they exhibited little evidence of fevered expenditure. If the new consumerism really did extend down the social scale to include the lower middling sort and beyond, its effects were well-concealed, and confirm Lorna Weatherill's belief that a consumerist approach is not really appropriate at this time[114]. In contrast, there is ample evidence of modest comfort and genteel respectability of the type described by Cobbett as 'plain manners and plentiful living'[115]. Even where novel consumer items did make an appearance over time this, in itself, does not have to imply a hidden agenda of social climbing or competitiveness with one's neighbours. The colourful display in the alderman's many rooms is not necessarily proof of conspicuous consumption, but might have reflected the demands of hospitality and expectations of rank, rather than a concern to adopt the latest London fashions. At a practical level, patterns of inheritance also suggest a determination to maintain family independence by spreading resources as widely as possible, a strategy which might have stopped expenditure on non-essential fripperies. In a predominantly agrarian economy, investment in land was probably a more secure option than obeying the dictates of fashion in order to purchase a clock or china teapot.

Explanations for an apparent lack of 'getting and spending' fall into two main categories; firstly, the possibility that goods were not available to this group at the right price or, alternatively, that goods were available but not coveted. The work of David Eversley and Joan Thirsk challenges the former suggestion, for both observed a healthy supply of consumer items to all sections of the community, regardless of status, much earlier in the seventeenth century. It is also unlikely that Hertford suffered any shortage of appropriately-priced goods, being well-served by commerce with the capital. Reasons for a lack of spending can only, therefore, be conjectured. Perhaps, as Christopher Berry points out, spending on 'luxury' goods continued to be frowned upon until the eighteenth century, and spending on non-essentials might well have earned some sort of moral censure. When combined with the town's strength in dissent, a certain disregard for a more material lifestyle seems plausible. There is clear evidence that dissenters were rounding on those who displayed extravagant and worldly tastes. Writing to her fellow Quaker women in 1678, Maria Penington suggested that money given to them by their husbands 'to lay out in superfluous things, either in the house or upon our bodys' should be given up to the Lord's service[116]. Given the strength of Quakerism in Hertford and the efficient networks of communication built up by the movement, this message against unnecessary consumption may well have found willing listeners in the neighbourhood.

If a lifestyle based on consumer spending is not in evidence, one based on sociability and mutual support between family, friends and neighbours fits the picture well; there is ample evidence that those of varying wealth and religious affiliation were bound together in some sort of community framework. Certainly, in this atmosphere of mutual support and material restraint there were few, if any, 'slaves to prodigality'[117] who set themselves apart from a broad general mentality. Perhaps Hertford consumers favoured the 'middle way' as a response to a turbulent time of religious and political partisanship - parish protestants set against dissenters, Whigs lined up against Tories - a relatively plain and modest lifestyle which sat happily with a need to keep the community in one piece. Ultimately moderation may have reflected this desire for stability, and it was this need, articulated so forcefully by Dryden, that won the day.

References

[1] Historically, the county was divided between the bishoprics of London, in the east, and Lincoln, in the west. The latter was divided between the Archdeaconries of St Albans and Huntingdon, Hertford Deanery falling within Huntingdon's jurisdiction. The probate records are held in the County Record Office, Hertford.*

[2] Designed specifically for historians by Manfred Thaller at the Max Planck Institut in Göttingen.*

[3] J.Dryden 'Astraea Redux' in Sir H.Grierson and G. Bullough, *The Oxford Book of Seventeenth Century Verse* (Oxford, Clarendon Press,1934), 832.

[4] A phrase used by the son of Christopher Wren. B.Ford, ed., *Eighteenth Century Britain* (Cambridge University Press, 1992), 5.

[5] Peter Borsay maintains that an 'urban renaissance' was grounded in surplus wealth, which promoted an increase in conspicuous consumption. P.Borsay, *The English Urban renaissance: Culture and Society in the Provincial Town 1660-1770* (Oxford University Press, 1989).

[6] N. McKendrick, J. Brewer and J.Plumb, eds., *The Birth of a Consumer Society: the Commercialisation of Eighteenth Century England* (Europa Publications, 1982).

[7] Matthew Boulton, a contemporary manufacturer, based his marketing philosophy on the assumption that emulation travelled down the social hierarchy: 'The variety of the great will ever be affecting new modes, in order to increase that notice to which it thinks itself exclusively entitled. The lower ranks will imitate them as soon as they have discovered the innovation' Cited in M. Berg, *The Age of Manufactures 1700-1820* (Routledge, 1994), 130. The argument that England was about to embark on a wave of consumerism is demonstrated in McKendrick, Brewer and Plumb, *Birth of a Consumer Society*.

[8] Bernard Mandeville, *The Fable of the Bees*, Edited with an Introduction by Phillip Harth (Penguin Books, 1989).

[9] In the 1690s, the import of cheap, colourful fabrics by the East India Company tapped into latent home demand, challenging the received wisdom that demand was 'inelastic' and creating sufficient alarm that Tory landowners and their allies demanded new sumptuary laws for the suppression of this 'bare-fac'd Luxury, the spreading Contagion of which is the greatest Corrupter of Publick Manners'. To defend the trade of the East India company and the consumption of imports required that such moralising be deflected. McKendrick, Brewer and Plumb, *Birth of a Consumer Society,* 14-19.

[10] B. Mandeville, *Fable of the Bees* 1714 (Penguin, 1989). Berry detects a watershed with Nicholas Barbon's pamphlet *Discourse of Trade* (1690). Barbon's radical

*References 1 and 2 are in the Preface, the remainder are found in the Introduction.

pamphlet was a critique of traditional moralistic thinking, since he maintained that prodigality may be prejudicial to the individual but not to national trade. C.J. Berry, *The Idea of Luxury: a conceptual and historical investigation* (Cambridge University Press, 1994), 112.

[11] D.Hume *Of the Standard of Taste and other essays,* edited by J.W.Lenz. (US, Bobbs-Merrill, 1965), 56-59.

[12] There was a distinct change from 'bullionist', moralistic accounts, which maintained that any deficit in the trade balance caused by the consumption of overseas imports was detrimental to the defence and integrity of the state, to concepts of trade which favoured consumption, since it provided employment. The new thinking was encapsulated by Adam Smith in *The Wealth of Nations,* 1776.

[13] Although Daunton challenges the notion that towns were central to eighteenth century change, he agrees with this point. L. Weatherill, *Consumer Behaviour and Material Culture in Britain 1660-1760* (Routledge, 1988), 70.

[14] P.Borsay 'The development of provincial urban culture', in P.Borsay, ed., *The Eighteenth Century Town* (Longman, 1990), 181 Certainly, Lorna Weatherill found that urban inventories listed certain types of good more frequently than rural inventories, although regional differences also played their part .Weatherill, *Consumer Behaviour,* 75.

[15] The essential difference between the two may be traced back to classical concepts. R. Williams, *The Country and the City* (Hogarth Press, 1993), 1.

[16] Peter Borsay identifies a period of urban renaissance based on metropolitan cultural values, when the service sector in many provincial towns blossomed to serve the interests of both visiting and resident gentry, and middlemen benefited in the process. P.Borsay, *The English Urban Renaissance*. This concept is discussed in P.Clark's 'Introduction' in P.Clark, ed., *Country towns in pre-industrial England* (Leicester University Press, 1981), 22. The view of urban renaissance is not without its critics, however, for J. Barry maintains that urban middling groups were not necessarily subordinated to the cultural values of a landed elite. He also suggests that the purchase of land may have been a rational investment decision rather than a commitment to the social values of the landed gentry. Revisionist accounts have nevertheless reinforced Hexter's challenge to the importance of the middling sort by emphasising the dominance of ruling elites. J. Barry, 'Introduction', in J. Barry and C.Brooks, eds., *The Middling Sort of People: Culture, Society and Politics in England,* 1550-1800 (Macmillan, 1994), 6-9.

[17] In the course of the eighteenth century, the middle of the urban hierarchy - towns of between 2,500 and 100,000 - 'filled out', their population increasing from 7.5% to 20% of the whole. P.Borsay 'Introduction' in P.Borsay, ed., *The Eighteenth Century Town 1688-1820* (Longman, 1990), 5. Not all towns experienced similar fortunes,

however, and those disadvantaged by poor communications suffered at the expense of their better-placed rivals. Berkhamsted in Hertfordshire, for example, had diminished from a thriving market town to an 'overgrown village' by the 1770s. *Clark, Country Towns,* 30.

[18]Munby L., *The Hertfordshire Landscape* (Hodder and Stoughton, 1977), 254.

[19]Weatherill, *Consumer Behaviour,* 14.

[20]Weatherill L., 'The Meaning of Consumer Behaviour', in J.Brewer and R.Porter, eds., *Consumption and the World of Goods* (Routledge, 1993), 208 and C.Campbell, 'Understanding traditional and modern patterns of consumption in eighteenth-century England: a character-action approach', in Brewer and Porter, *Consumption,* 40.

[21]G.Sheldrick, ed., *The Accounts of Thomas Green 1742-1790* (Hertfordshire Record Society, 1992), xii.

[22]C.W.Chalkin described Hertford as a regional centre because of its marketing and servicing functions. Cited in P.Borsay, 'Urban Improvement and the English Economy' in *The Eighteenth-Century Town 1688-1820* (Longman, 1990), 148.

[23]Population estimates for periods before 1801, when the decennial census was introduced, are based either on parish registers, which record life events, or various surveys, such as the Compton Census of 1676, an enquiry into religious conformity in the Province of Canterbury. Both Lionel Munby and the Leicester Small Towns Project, headed by Professor Peter Clark, have produced estimates for Hertford in 1676 based on the number of communicants, ostensibly of both genders, over the ages of 16. Lionel Munby, however, used the standard multiplier of 1.5 to produce a figure of 1499 for that year. Professor Clark's team, in contrast, used a multiplier of 3.0 in all jurisdictions where the census takers counted only male communicants and estimate the population as 2997. Since the Leicester team's own estimate for 1662 was only 1314, a population of 1500 for the year of the Compton Census seems more realistic. It would also fit with Professor Clark's estimate for Hitchin, the larger town, of 2400 in 1670. See L.M. Munby, *Hertfordshire Population Statistics, 1563-1801* (Hertfordshire Local History Council, 1964); P. Clark, K. Gaskin and A.Wilson, *Population Estimates of English Small Towns* 1550-1851 (Centre for Urban History, University of Leicester, [Working Paper No.3], 1989); P.Clark and P.Slack, *English Towns in Transition 1500-1700* (Open University Press, 1976), 83.

[24]D.Defoe, *A Tour Through the Whole Island of Great Britain* (originally published 1724; Dent, Everyman edition, 1962), 171.

[25]Lionel Munby, *The Hertfordshire Landscape* (Hodder and Stoughton, 1977), 103.

[26]Hertford grew by 28.4% between 1676 and 1753, York by 5.3% between 1670 and c.1730 and Northampton by 14.1% from 1676-1746. P.Borsay, 'Urban Improvement and the English Economy' in *The Eighteenth-Century Town 1688-1820* (Longman, 1990), 148.

[27]McKendrick, Brewer and Plumb *Birth of a Consumer Society,* 21-22.

[28]F.Braudel, 'Pre-modern Towns', in P.Clark, ed., *The Early Modern Town* (Open University Press, 1976), 83-87.

[29]VCH Vol IV, 216.

[30]Several laws were passed since 1425 to preserve the navigation: 9 Henry VI.c.9 (1431); 13 Elizabeth.c.18 (1571) - 'For bringing of the River of Lee to the North side of the City of London', at a cost of £80,000 to the City; 12 George II - to improve the navigation from Hertford to Ware. L.Turnor, *History of Hertford* (Hertford, Stephen Austin and Sons, 1830) 388-89. See also Keith Fairclough's doctoral thesis: K.R. Fairclough, *The River Lea: the development of a river navigation, 1571-1767* (London, unpublished PhD thesis, 1984).

[31]A. Whiteman, *The Compton Census of 1676: a critical edition* (OUP for the British Academy, 1986). Recorded protestant dissenters for the Province of Canterbury: 4.4%.

[32]Congregationalist and Quaker records are held in the County Record Office, Hertford.

[33]Nesta Evans found that of 42 adult male burials in Flixton between 1560 and 1600, wills only survive for ten men. N.Evans 'Inheritance, Women, Religion and Education in Early Modern Society as revealed by wills' in P.Riden, ed., *Probate Records and the Local Community* (Gloucester, Alan Sutton, 1985), 55.

[34]32 Henry VIII c1; 34 and 35 Henry VIII c5.

[35]21 Henry VIII, c5.

[36]F.Steer, ed., *Farm and Cottage Inventories of Mid Essex 1635-1749* (Colchester, Wiles and Son, 1950), 5.

[37]13 Edward I c19, 31 Edward III c11 and 22 and 23 Charles II c10, 1 James II c17.

[38]PRO Information Leaflet 31.

[39]K.Tiller, *English Local History* (Gloucester, Alan Sutton, 1992), 158.

[40]William Edmonds is probably the same man listed in the Hearth Tax returns as having eleven hearths. Since the Edmonds in the sample is by no means the wealthiest in terms of household goods, his inventory total being £223.5s, this supports the idea that the number of hearths and wealth in household goods are not automatically correlated. Yet there is no will for Edmonds, and it is impossible to discover his holdings in real estate, but the inventory reveals his property on the ground as covering no fewer than 66 acres. This could well place him amongst Hertford's wealthiest men. CRO H22/372. Other probate documents for Hertford are held in the Public Record Office, having come within the jurisdiction of the Prerogative Court of Canterbury.

[41]It is, perhaps, also important to recognise that purchasing decisions may not have been the sole responsibility of the head of household.

[42] C.J.Berry, *The Idea of Luxury: a conceptual and historical investigation* (Cambridge University Press, 1994) Various approaches to the concept of need are covered in Chapter 7. Whereas Collingwood maintained that needs are universal and have no history, Marx stressed that new needs were identified over time, effecting qualitative change in humans in the process.

[43] J.S.Moore, 'Probate inventories - problems and prospects', in P.Riden, ed., *Probate Records,* 12.

[44] P.Earle, 'The Middling Sort in London' in Barry and Brooks, eds, *The Middling Sort,* 150-51.

[45] J.West, *Village Records 2nd edn* (Chichester, Phillimore, 1982), 95.

[46] CRO H22/171.

[47] See Appendix A for social structure of all Hertford testators and for listings of the occupational and status titles in the source.

[48] This figure is based on all Hertford testators for the period, not just the inventory sample.

[49] Refer to Appendix A for coding conventions.

[50] Refer to Appendix C for details of sampling

[51] Weatherill, *Consumer Behaviour,* 169.

[52] The Schumpeter-Gilboy price index, cited in P. Matthias, *The First Industrial Nation: the Economic History of Britain 1700-1914, 421* reveals a period of fluctuating, rather than increasing prices.

[53] R.Garrard, 'English Probate Inventories and their use in studying the significance of the domestic interior, 1570-1700' in *AAG Bijdragen 23 -Probate Inventories,* 1980, 57.

[54] Debts included good and bad, 'sperate' and 'desperate'. Eight were for £10 or less, nine between £11-30, eight from £31-100, and two for over £100.

[55] Lionel Munby has observed that the case of widows is unique: often they were left part of a house which had been bequeathed to a son or daughter. Little personal property might be recorded on appraisal since the widow would be in the habit of sharing household amenities with other family members. This would then allow for any surplus capital to be placed out on loan in the community.

[56] CRO 104HW23.

[57] Joane Baker's household goods amounted to £15.12s.10d, Joan Treyherne's to £18.15s.0d.

[58] The eight highest values were £267.12s.7d, £350.2s.7d, £355.10s, £363, £374.5s.2d., £454.18s.7d, £577.8s.7d, and £640.12s.

[59] Defoe, *A Tour Through the Whole Island,* 34.

[60] CRO 10HR27 and 122HW11.

[61] Garrard, 'English Probate Inventories', 56.

[62] CRO 14HW38 and 8HR73.

[63] L.Weatherill identified a number of 'key' goods which were recorded consistently, particularly if novel, and conducted her analysis of ownership and change from within this framework. Her key goods are: tables, cooking pots, saucepans, pewter, pewter dishes and plates, earthenware, knives and forks, china, utensils for hot drinks, window curtains, table linen, looking glasses, pictures, books, clocks, and silver. *Consumer Behaviour,* 204-207. These categories, where present, have formed the basis for an examination of household goods in this study, but have been combined with observations of feather bedding and decorative turkeywork items, as possible indicators of domestic comfort. There remain the perennial problems that certain items, books for example, might have been subsumed under the title of 'other lumber'.

[64] Goods were described as 'old' on 118 occasions, and as new on only three.

[65] McKendrick, Brewer and Plumb, *Birth of a Consumer Society,* 27.

[66] CRO 57HW66.

[67] Weatherill. *Consumer Behaviour,* 16.

[68] CRO 111HW37.

[69] F.Braudel, *The Structures of Everyday Life* (Collins, 1981), 206.

[70] CRO H22/141.

[71] CRO 122HW32.

[72] 1660-1683 and 1684-1725.

[73] A. Vickery, 'Women and the world of goods: a Lancashire consumer and her possessions', in J.Brewer and R.Porter, (eds), *Consumption and the World of Goods* (Routledge, 1993), 294.

[74] Vickery, 'Women and the world of goods', 294.

[75] Garrard, 'English Probate Inventories', 58.

[76] N.Pounds, *The Culture of the English People* (Cambridge University Press, 1994), 141.

[77] Goodman's inventory was appraised in 1664, and his use of space may reflect the earlier tradition.

[78] Weatherill had noted that 13% of her sample owned pictures, 4% decorative china and 4% sets of knives and forks. *Consumer Behaviour,* 8.

[79] Brass is recorded 77 times, pewter 51, iron 34, tin 13 and copper 8.

[80] The inventory totals of owners of silver ware ranged from £35.15s to £454.18s.7d

[81] CRO H23/499; Appraised in 1714.

[82] T.H.Breen, 'The meaning of things' in Brewer and Porter (eds), *Consumption and the World of Goods,* 250.

[83] CRO 8HR38.

[84] CRO 3HR20.

[85] CRO 8HR136.

[86] CRO 14HW14 Joane Baker.

[87] CRO 3HR106 Thomas White.

[88] CRO 10HR149.

[89] CRO 4HR172.

[90] CRO 59HW1.

[91] V.A. Rowe, *The First Hertford Quakers* (Hertford, Religious Society of Friends, [1970]), 50.

[92] CRO 111HW37.

[93] The exact number of individually written wills cannot be measured, since many only survive as contemporary copies made by the probate court and recorded in a register of wills. The greater number of wills in this sample were transcribed from the original court registers, but the few original documents include John Hill's will, which, in 1703, included in the preamble the words 'with my owne handwriteing'. CRO 59HW98.

[94] D. Cressy 'Literacy in context: meaning and measurement in early modern England' in Brewer and Porter, eds., *Consumption and the World of Goods,* 306.

[95] Cressy, 'Literacy in context', 312.

[96] Henry Marson was also a 'loving friend' of alderman John Bach, which extends her social circle to include even more prestigious characters.

[97] W. Urwick, *Nonconformity in Hertfordshire* (1884), 542.

[98] C.Litzenberger 'The Analysis of Sixteenth Century Wills as it pertains to the Religion of the Laity in Gloucestershire (1541-1580)' in S. Bocchi and P.Denley, eds., *Storia & Multimedia: Proceedings of the 7th International Congress Association of History and Computing* (Bologna, Grafis Edizioni, 1994).

[99] CRO 8HR159.

[100] CRO 8HR38.

[101] J.Goody, Introduction, 3 and 'Inheritance, property and women' 14, both in J.Goody, J.Thirsk and E.P.Thompson, *Family and Inheritance. Rural Society in Western Europe 1200-1800* (Cambridge University Press, 1976).

[102] S.Staves, in J.Brewer and S.Staves, eds., *Early Modern Conceptions of Property* (Routledge, 1995), 199.

[103]22 and 23 Car. II, c10. Joan Thirsk also compares the intellectual debates about primogeniture in England and the European mainland in J. Thirsk 'The European debate on customs of inheritance, 1500-1700' in Goody, Thirsk and Thompson, *Family and Inheritance,* 171-191.

[104]Borough English was a form of land tenure under which all land descended to the youngest son. This form was found in parts of Hertfordshire. L. M.Munby, ed., *Life and Death in Kings Langley 1498-1659* (Kings Langley Local History and Museum Society, 1981), xvii.

[105]CRO 3HR29.

[106]CRO 59HW1.

[107]CRO 132HW8.

[108]E.P.Thompson 'The grid of inheritance: a comment' in Goody, Thirsk and Thompson *Family and Inheritance,* 357.

[109]CRO 15HW78.

[110]CRO 119HW26.

[111]K.Wrightson, *English Society 1580-1680,* (Unwin Hyman, 1982), 40.

[112]Wrightson, *English Society,* 45.

[113]Wives were the largest category (21.8%), followed by sons (16.4%), daughters and brothers (9.1% each). The remainder included parents (12.7% combined), friends and kin (3.6%each).

[114]Weatherill, *Consumer Behaviour,* 16.

[115]McKendrick, Brewer and Plumb, *Birth of a Consumer Society,* 28.

[116]Friends House Library. Penington MS, Vol. 4, f.159. David Scott's research into the York Quaker community revealed an earnest middling sort respectability, its morality 'a more acutely realised version' of protestant bourgeois values. D. Scott, *Quakerism in York, 1650-1720* (University of York, Borthwick Paper No. 80).

[117]B.Mandeville, 'Grumbling Hive' in *The Fable of the Bees* (Penguin Books, 1989), 68.

Appendix A: Occupational and Status Coding of all Hertford Testators, 1660-1760

The coding schemes employed in this study are those used by Lorna Weatherill in her general study: Weatherill, L., *Consumer Behaviour and Material Culture in Britain 1660-1760* (Routledge, London and New York, 1988). Whereas the economic groupings derived from the Booth-Armstrong schema relate more properly to a nineteenth-century industrial base than a seventeenth-century economy, it was felt that both her schema for 'key' goods and coding schemes should be retained for the sake of consistency and comparison.

1. Gregory King 1688 social status ranking
Fig. A1 Status of Hertford Testators

- Husbandmen (1.7%)
- Gentry/Prof/Clergy (5.9%)
- Widows/Spinsters (21.0%)
- Unknown/Not Stated (20.0%)
- Trades: Dealers (23.5%)
- Yeoman/Large Farmers (3.5%)
- Labourers (1.2%)
- Trades: Crafts (23.2%)

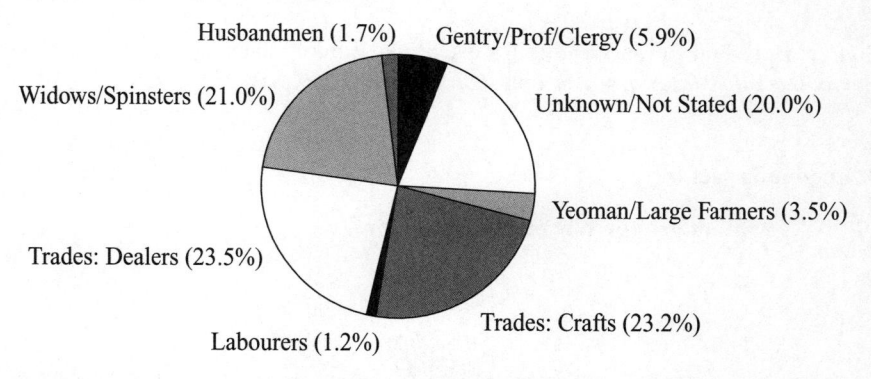

Source: Based on Lorna Weatherill's adaptation of Gregory King's hierarchy, *Consumer Behaviour and Material Culture in Britain 1660-1760* p.213

2. Dr. Vivien Brodsky Elliott's social status groupings
Fig. A2 Social Status of Hertford Testators

- Husbandmen (1.7%)
- High Status Trades (6.9%)
- Widows/Spinsters (21.0%)
- Intermed Status Trades (21.0%)
- Labourers (1.2%)
- Yeoman/Large Farmers (3.5%)
- Unknown/Not Stated (20.0%)
- Low Status Trades (21.2%)
- Gentry (3.5%)

xliii

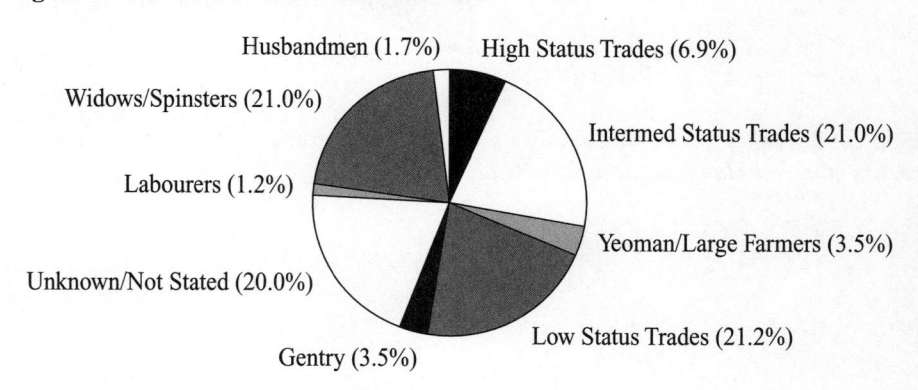

Fig. A3 Status of Hertford testators excluding widows and spinsters

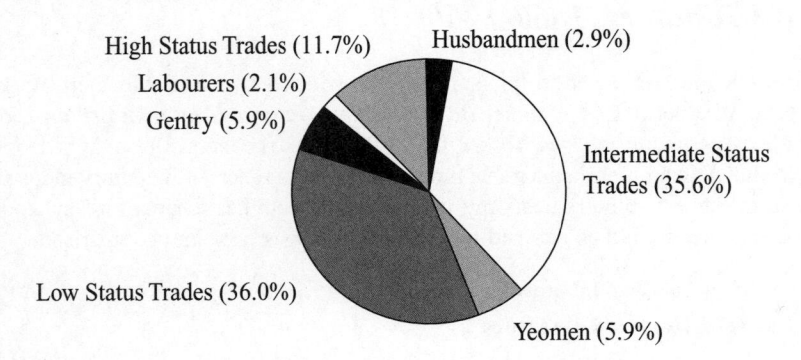

- High Status Trades (11.7%)
- Husbandmen (2.9%)
- Labourers (2.1%)
- Gentry (5.9%)
- Intermediate Status Trades (35.6%)
- Low Status Trades (36.0%)
- Yeomen (5.9%)

Source: Based on Lorna Weatherill's use of Dr. Elliott's schema, *Consumer Behaviour and Material Culture in Britain 1660-1760,* p.212

3. Economic sectors

Fig. A4 Testators grouped by economic sector

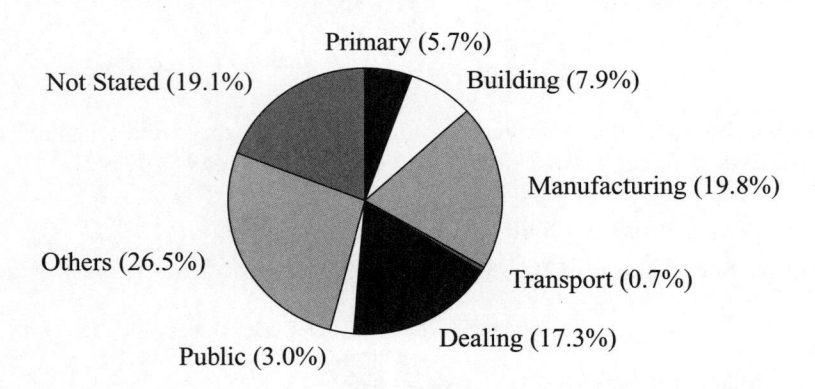

- Primary (5.7%)
- Building (7.9%)
- Not Stated (19.1%)
- Manufacturing (19.8%)
- Others (26.5%)
- Transport (0.7%)
- Public (3.0%)
- Dealing (17.3%)

Source: Based on Lorna Weatherill's use of W.A. Armstrong's schema, *Consumer Behaviour and Material Culture in Britain 1660-1760,* p.214

Key to Coding Systems

1. General Criteria (based on Gregory King's social hierarchy)

Category	Code
Gentry/professional/clergy	1
Yeomen/large farmers	2
Husbandmen/small farmers	3
Tradesmen:crafts	4
Tradesmen:dealers	5
Labourers	6
Widows/spinsters	7
Unknown	8

2. Social Status (Dr. Ellliott Brodsky's schema)

Category	Code
Gentry	1
High status trades	2
Intermediate status trades	3
Yeomen/large farmers	4
Low status trades	5
Husbandmen	6
Labourers	7
Widows/spinsters	8
Tradesmen-unknown	9
Unknown	10

3. Economic Sector (Booth-Armstrong)

Category	Code
Primary-agriculture	1
Primary-mining	2
Building	3
Manufacturing	4
Transport	5
Dealing	6
Public/professional	7
Others	8

Appendix B: Statistical analysis and sampling

The quantitative methods employed are those of description and interrogation and rely heavily on the techniques of exploratory data analysis advocated by Catherine Marsh in *Exploring Data* (Polity Press, Oxford UK and Cambridge, Mass, 1988). The Hertford inventory sample, which represents some 20% of all Hertford testators for the century from 1660, is still small and susceptible to distortion both through uneven recording by appraisers and social bias. Exploratory data analysis employs resistant measures, frequency distributions, grouped where appropriate, and graphics output such as boxplots to examine the spread and central tendency of a series of values. Minitab Release 8 computer software in conjunction with Microsoft Works Spreadsheet package provided the statistical descriptions and diagrams.

Sampling and inference

Any statistical analysis demands that measures be reliable and valid; they should represent accurately the underlying population. For a sample to be representative, however, it must be random or subsequent results will be biased and any generalisations invalid.

The Hertford inventory sample and underlying population

It is therefore necessary to check that the inventory sample is broadly representative of Hertford testators whose wills were proved in the Archdeaconry court. All three observations are based on the occupational coding systems employed by Lorna Weatherill in her study of consumption behaviour.

Fig. B1 Representativeness of sample – Economic Sector

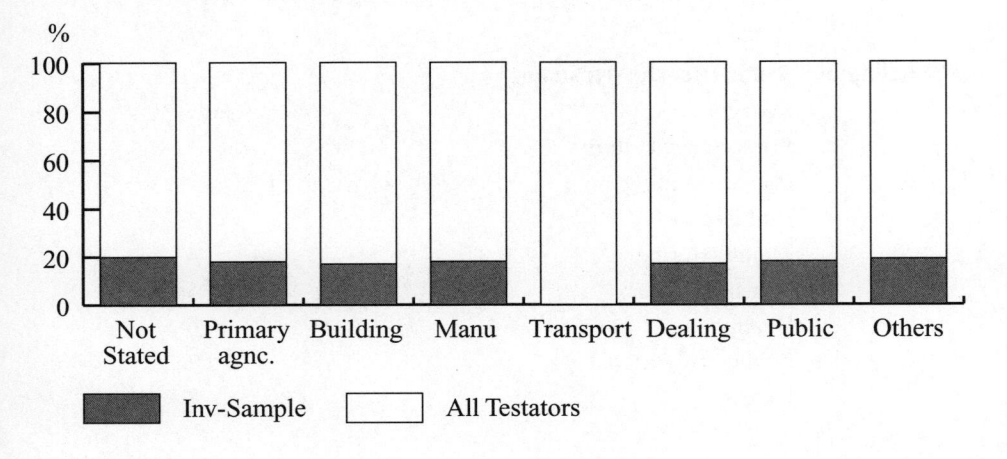

In this categorisation, those in transport are not represented, but since the whole population only included three wills for that category, sampling would not have been realistic. The marginally higher proportion in the sample with no occupational or status title accounts, in part, for the three per cent under-representation of those in the dealing category.

Fig. B2 Representativeness of sample – Gregory King's social groupings

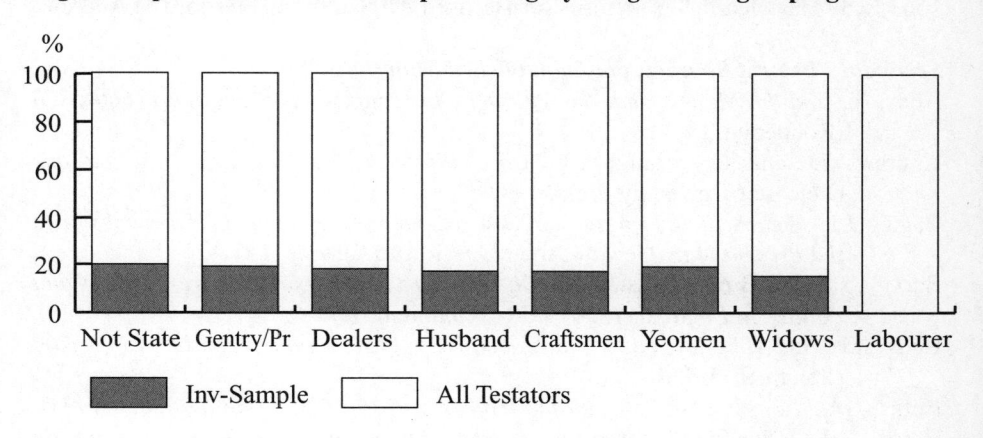

[Bar chart showing percentages for Not State, Gentry/Pr, Dealers, Husband, Craftsmen, Yeomen, Widows, Labourer — with Inv-Sample and All Testators]

Fig. B2 Representativeness of sample – Elliott's status groupings

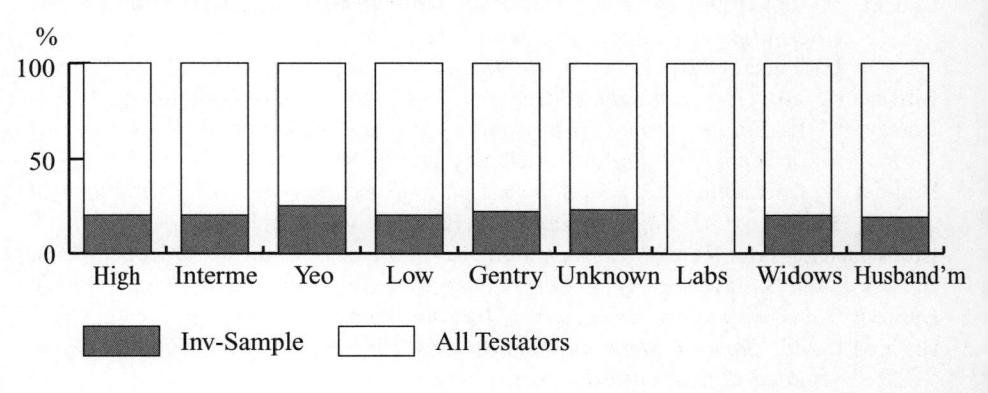

[Bar chart showing percentages for High, Interme, Yeo, Low, Gentry, Unknown, Labs, Widows, Husband'm — with Inv-Sample and All Testators]

In both social status groupings, labourers are not represented in the sample, whereas gentry, professionals and those without titles are marginally over-represented. Thus although the inventory selection cannot be described as an wholly accurate stratified sample of the overall population, it is sufficiently similar in profile to suggest, with extreme caution, that observations about property ownership might apply to the broader population of Hertford testators whose wills were proved locally.

Bibliography

Primary Sources
Wills and Inventories for the town of Hertford, proved in the Archdeaconry Court of Huntingdon, 1660-1725.
1663 Lady Day Hearth Tax Returns for Hertford All Saints and Hertford St Andrew

Secondary Printed Sources and Unpublished Material
Addy, J., *Death, Money and the Vultures: inheritance and avarice, 1660-1750* (Routledge, 1992).
Andrews D. and Greenhalgh M., *Computing for Non-Scientific Applications* (Leicester University Press, 1987).
Bagley J.J., *Historical Interpretations Vol. II: Sources of English History 1540 to the Present Day* (Newton Abbot, David and Charles, 1972).
Barry C. and C.Brooks, eds., *The Middling Sort of People: Culture, Society and Politics in England, 1550-1800* (Macmillan, 1994).
Beier A.L. and R.Finlay, eds., *The Making of the Metropolis: London 1500-1700* (Longman, 1986).
Berg, M., *The Age of Manufactures 1700-1820* (Routledge, 1994).
Berry, C.J., *The Idea of Luxury: a conceptual and historical investigation* (Cambridge University Press, 1994).
Bocchi, S. and P.Denley, eds., *Storia & Multimedia: Proceedings of the 7th International Congress Association of History and Computing* (Bologna, Grafis Edizioni, 1994).
Borsay P., ed., *The Eighteenth Century Town 1688-1820* (Longman, 1990).
Borsay P., *The English Urban Renaissance: Culture and Society in the Provincial Town 1660-1770* (Oxford University Press, 1989).
Braudel F., *Civilisation and Capitalism 15th-18th Century Vol.I The Structures of Everyday Life English Translation* (Collins, 1981).
Brewer J. and Porter R., eds., *Consumption and the World of Goods* (Routledge, 1993).
Brewer J. and S.Staves, *Early Modern Conceptions of Property* (Routledge, 1995).
Burke P., *New Perspectives on Historical Writing* (Polity Press, 1991).
Bush M.L., ed., *Social Orders and Social Classes in Europe since 1500: studies in social stratification* (Longman, 1992).
Carr E.H., *What is History?* (Penguin Books, 1990).
Chauncy Sir H., *The Historical Antiquities of Hertfordshire* (originally published 1700, reprinted 1826).
Clark J.C.D., *English Society 1688-1832* (Cambridge University Press, 1985).
Clark J.C.D., *Revolution and Rebellion: State and Society in England in the 17th and 18th Centuries* (Cambridge University Press, 1986).

BIBLIOGRAPHY

Clark P., ed., *The Early Modern Town* (Open University Press, 1976).
Clark P., ed., *Country Towns in Pre-Industrial England* (Leicester University Press, 1981).
Clay C.G.A., *Economic Expansion and Social Change: England 1500-1700* (Cambridge University Press, 1984).
Crone P., *Pre-industrial Societies* (Oxford, Blackwell, 1989).
Davis N.Z., *Society and Culture in Early Modern France* (Duckworth 4th Ed., 1975).
Davison L., T.Hitchcock, T.Keirn, R.B.Shoemaker, eds., *Stilling the Grumbling Hive: The Response to Social and Economic Problems in England, 1689-1750* (Gloucester, Alan Sutton, 1992).
Defoe D., *A Tour through the whole island of Great Britain* (originally published 1724, Dent, Everyman edition, 1962).
Denley P. and Hopkin D., eds., *History and Computing* (Manchester University Press, 1987).
Denley P., Fogelvik S. and Harvey C., eds., *History and Computing II* (Manchester University Press, 1989).
Fisher F.J., ed., *Essays in the Economic and Social History of Tudor and Stuart England* (Cambridge University Press, 1961).
Flood S., ed., *St Albans Wills 1471-1500* (Hertfordshire Record Society, 1993).
Ford B., ed., *Eighteenth Century Britain* (Cambridge University Press, 1992).
Goody J., Thirsk J. and Thompson E.P., eds., *Family and Inheritance. Rural Society in Western Europe 1200-1800* (Cambridge University Press, 1976).
Greenstein D., *A Historian's Guide to Computing* (Oxford University Press, 1994).
Grierson, Sir H. and G.Bullough, *The Oxford Book of 17th Century Verse* (Oxford, Clarendon Press, 1934).
Heard N., *Stuart Economy and Society* (Hodder and Stoughton, 1995).
Heath C., *The Book of Hertford* (Chesham, Barracuda Books, 1975).
Hill C., *Reformation to Industrial Revolution* (Penguin Books, 1967).
Hill C., *Change and Continuity in 17th Century England* (Yale University Press, 1991).
Holmes G.S., *The Making of a Great Power: Late Stuart and early Georgian Britain* (Longman, 1993).
Hoskins W.G., *Local History in England* (Longman, 3rd Edition, 1984).
Howe D.R., *Data Analysis for Database Design* (Edward Arnold 2nd Ed., 1989).
Hume D., *Of the Standard of Taste and Other Essays* (US, Bobbs-Merrill, 1965).
Hunt L., ed., *The New Cultural History* (University of California Press, 1989).
Jones-Baker D., ed., *Hertfordshire in History* (Hertfordshire Local History Council, 1991).
Lucie-Smith E., *Furniture: A Concise History* (Thames and Hudson, 1979).
Macfarlane A,. *A guide to English historical records* (Cambridge University Press, 1983).
Mandeville B., *The Fable of the Bees* (originally published 1714), Edited with an Introduction by Phillip Harth (Penguin Classics, 1989).
Marsh C., *Exploring Data* (Polity Press, 1988).
Matthias P., *The First Industrial Nation: the Economic History of Britain 1700-1914* (Routledge, 2nd Ed, 1983).

BIBLIOGRAPHY

Mawdesley E., Morgan N., Richmond L. Trainor R., eds. *History and Computing III* (Manchester University Press, 1990).
Mawdesley E. and Munck T., *Computing for Historians* (Manchester University Press, 1993).
Munby L.M., *The Hertfordshire Landscape* (Hodder and Stoughton, 1977).
Munby L.M., *All My Worldly Goods* (Bricket Wood Society, 1991).
Munby L.M., ed., *Short Guides to Records* (Historical Association Pamphlet- undated)
Munby L.M., ed., *Early Stuart Household Accounts* (Hertfordshire Record Society, 1986).
Munby L.M., ed., *Life and Death in Kings Langley. Wills and Inventories 1498-1659* (Kings Langley Local History and Museum Society, 1981).
Norden J., *Speculi Britaniae. The Description of Hertfordshire* (originally published 1598, reprint 1971).
Phythian-Adams C., *Rethinking English Local History* (Leicester University Press, 1987).
Plumb J.H., *The Commercialisation of Leisure in Eighteenth Century England* (University of Reading Press, 1973).
Porter R., *English Society in the Eighteenth Century (*Penguin Revised Edition, 1990).
Pounds N.J.G., *The Culture of the English People* (Cambridge University Press, 1994).
Prior M., ed., *Women in English Society 1500-1800.* (Methuen, 1985).
Riden P., ed. *Probate Records and the Local Community* (Gloucester, Alan Sutton, 1985)
Rule J. *The Vital Century 1714-1815* (Longman, 1992).
Sheldrick G., ed., *The Accounts of Thomas Green 1742-1790* (Hertfordshire Record Society, 1992).
Slack P., *Poverty and Policy in Tudor and Stuart England* (Longman, 1988).
Steer F., ed., *Farm and Cottage Inventories of Mid Essex 1635-1749* (Colchester, Wiles and Son, 1950).
Stephens W.B., *Sources for English Local History* (Manchester University Press, 1973).
Thirsk J., *Economic Policy and Projects: The development of a consumer society in early modern England* (Oxford, 1978).
Thomas K., *Religion and the Decline of Magic* (Penguin, 1971).
Tiller K., *English Local History* (Gloucester, Alan Sutton, 1992).
Victoria County History - Hertfordshire (1906-14).
Weatherill, L., *Consumer Behaviour and Material Culture in Britain 1660-1760* (Routledge, 1988).
Willey B., *The Seventeenth Century Background* (Ark, 1934).
Williams R., *The Country and the City* (Hogarth Press, 1973).

BIBLIOGRAPHY

Williams R., *Keywords: a Vocabulary of Culture and Society* (Fontana, 1988).
Wilson A., ed., *Rethinking Social History* (Manchester University Press, 1993).
Wrightson K., *English Society 1580-1680* (Unwin Hyman, 1982).
Wrightson K. and Devine D., *Poverty and Piety in an English Village: Terling 1525-1700* (Academic Press, 1979).

Journal Articles

Barry, J., 'The Making of the Middle Class?' [Review Article], *Past and Present,* 145, (1994), 194-208.
Beckett J.V., 'The computer and the historian', *Archives,* Vol. 19, No.84 (1990), 192-198.
Borsay P., 'The English Urban Renaissance: the development of provincial culture c. 1680-1760', *Social History,* 5 (1977), 581-603.
Borsay P., 'Culture, status and the English urban landscape', *History,* 67 (1982), 1-12.
Carr L. and Walsh L., 'Inventories and the analysis of wealth and consumption patterns in St. Mary's County, Maryland 1658-1777', *Historical Methods,* 13 No. 2 (1980), 81-104.
Chartres J.A., 'City and towns, farmers and economic change in the eighteenth century', *Historical Research,* 64, No. 154 (June 1991), 138-55.
Clay C., 'Marriage, inheritance and the rise of large estates in England, 1660-1815' *Economic History Review,* 2nd Series XXI (1968), 503-18.
Cowan A., 'Urban elites in early modern Europe: an endangered species?', *Historical Research,* 64, No.154 (June 1991), 121-37.
Denley P., 'Models, sources and users: historical database design' in the 1990s', *History and Computing,* 6 (1994), 33-43.
Dils J., 'Deposition books and the urban historian', *The Local Historian* Vol. 17 No. 5 (February 1987), 269-80.
Everitt A., 'Social mobility in Early Modern England', *Past and Present,* 33, (1966), 56-73.
Gittings C., 'Probate accounts: a neglected source', *The Local Historian,* (May 1991), 51-59.
Hanson Jones A., 'Estimating the wealth of the living from a probate sample', *Journal of Interdisciplinary History,* 13, 2 (1982), 273-300.
Harvey C. and Press J., 'The business elite of Bristol: a case study in database design', *History and Computing,* 3 (1991), 1-11.
Hollen Lees L., 'The challenge of political change: urban history in the 1990s', *Urban History* Vol. 21 pt. 1 (April 1994), 7-19.
Overton M., 'English probate inventories and the measurement of agricultural change', *AAG Bijdragen,* 23 (1980), 205-15.

BIBLIOGRAPHY

Overton M., 'Computer analysis of an inconsistent data source: the case of probate inventories', *Journal of Historical Geography*, 3, 4 (1977), 317-26.

Page S.J., 'Research methods and techniques - researching local history: methodological issues and computer-assisted analysis', *The Local Historian*, (February 1993), 20-30.

Schurer K., 'The future for local history: boom or recession?', *The Local Historian*, (August 1991), 99-108.

Speck W.A., 'Social status in late Stuart England', *Past and Present*, 34 (1966), 127-29.

Stave B., 'A conversation with Thomas Bender: Urban History as Intellectual and Cultural History', *Journal of Urban History*, Vol.14, No.4 (August 1988), 455-91.

Stone L., 'Social mobility in England 1500-1700', *Past and Present*, 33 (1965), 16-55.

Thaller M., 'Historical information science: is there such a thing? New comments on an old idea', *Accademie Nazionale dei Lincei Conference Proceedings*, Rome (1993), 51-86.

Thaller M., 'The Historical Workstation Project', *Computers and the Humanities*, 25, (1991), 149-62.

Winchester I., 'What every historian needs to know about record linkage for the microcomputer era', *Historical Methods*, Vol. 25, No.4 (1992), 149-65.

Wrigley E.A., 'City and country in the past: a sharp divide or a continuum?', *Historical Research*, Vol. 64, No.154 (June 1991), 107-120.

ARCHDEACONRY COURT

OF HUNTINGDON:

WILLS AND INVENTORIES
FOR THE PARISHES OF
ALL SAINTS AND ST ANDREWS
HERTFORD, 1660 - 1725

Reproduced by kind permission of
Hertfordshire County Record Office

HERTFORD CHURCH

The old church of All Saints, Hertford, drawn by R.M. Batty, c. 1800. The building was destroyed by fire on 21 December 1891 and rebuilt in red Runcorn stone shortly afterwards (from the Knowsley extra-illustrated edition of Clutterbuck's History of Hertfordshire, vol V, p 168A).

[*Hertfordshire Archives & Local Studies*]

WILLS AND INVENTORIES FOR HERTFORD, 1660-1725

Hertford Wills
1660 – 1725

1	Thomas Gray	Grant of Probate: 26 March 1661	Will Ref: 3HR29
	Yeoman	Estate valued at: £12.9.6	

In the name of god Amen, the Seaventh day of September in the year of our Lord God 1658 I Thomas Gray late of Tewing and now of Hertford, in the countie of Hertford, yeoman, being at this time in good and perfect health in bodie and mind allthough lame in my limbs, doe ordaine and make this my testam[en]t, and last will in maner and forme following, first I do will my Soule in to the hands of Allmightie God my Father by whose Blessing I received those worldly goods that I enioy, and my Body to bee buried where my Executor hereafter named shall thinke moot in assured hope of my resurrection to Eternall life through Jesus Christ my saviour. Item I give and bequeath Forty shillings to bee distributed by my said Executor amongst the poore people of Tewing aforesaid within one month after my decease. Item I give and bequeath unto Joseph Gray my youngest sonne all that my messuage or tenem[en]t, called by the name of Cromers lyeing and being at Chaymer and in the p[ar]ish of Bengeo and Sacombe in the countie aforesaid with all Appurtenances thereunto belonging both freehold and customary and to his heires for ever, And as for my land at great Munden holden of that Manor by foure severall coppies: Thomas Gray. wittnesse Tho[mas] Bevis, John Rogers, [Ri]Ch[a]rd Dighton and Mary Stronge, of Court Roll the Lands mentioned in three of them, I have surrendred into the hand of the lord of the said Manor by two customary tennants thereof, namely Henry Marston and James Paswater, in which three coppies are mentioned Fifty Acres and one Rood, more or lesse of coppiehold land called or knowne by the name of Floodgates also [known as] Floodgaty Parke, or p[ar]cell thereof, as by the said three coppies remaining in the hands of my said sonne Joseph Gray more at large it doth and May appeare, All which lande I doe hereby give and bequeath unto my said sonne Joseph Gray and to his heires for ever upon condition that hee or his heires shall pay unto my said sonne John Gray the sume of threescore pounds within one yeare after my decease, in regard I have herein given the best part of my land unto my said sonne Joseph, And it is my mind and will that my said sonne Joseph shall have the said lande tythe Free as my said sonne John Gray is to have the land specified in the said fourth coppie tythe Free, It being allsoe p[ar]cell of Floodgates als[o known as] Floodgaty parke: as by the said coppie remaining in the hands of my said sonne John Gray more at large it doth and may appeare which land I have surrendred to the use of my said sonne Thomas Gray, wittnesse Tho[mas] Bevis, John Rogers, [Ri]Ch[a]rd Dighton and Mary Stronge, John Gray but doe intend it shall discend to him as heire at law,. Item it is my mind and will that my said sonne Joseph Gray shall pay to my said sonne

WILLS AND INVENTORIES FOR HERTFORD, 1660-1725

John Gray Fifteene pound a yeare for two yeares next after my decease out of the lands last mentioned in regard hee is to bee at the charges of my Funerall and allsoe to pay the Legacies herein menconed. Item I give and bequeath unto the three children of Richard Penyfather my sonne in law, tenn pounds of good and lawfull money of England to bee equally divided amongst them, when they come severally to the age of one and twenty yeares, and in case any of them dye before they receive their proportions it shall bee equally divided amongst the survivors of them. Item I give and bequeath unto William Pryor the Elder of Hartingfordbury twenty shillings of good and lawfull money of England. Item I give and bequeath unto my Cozen Samuell Fordham of great Munden the like sume of twenty shillings of lawfull money of England. Item I give and bequeath unto my maid Joane which was my late servant the like sume of twenty shillings of lawfull money of England which three sums last menconed are to bee paid by my fore? Thomas Gray, wittnesse John Rogers, [Ri]Ch[a]rd Dighton and Mary Stronge, said Executor, within one yeare after my decease, and it is my mind and will, that the great table in the hall at my house at Tewing with the Frame and the side Bench under the window and the wainscote shall not bee removed, but shall remaine for my eldest sonne, and for the cupboard in the hall with the stoole table my will is that my youngest sonne shall have them. Item I give to my said sonne John the cupboard in the chamb[e]r over the said hall, and as for the two chests in the same chamber and the two other chests in the next chamber to it, my mind and will is that my said sonne John shall first chuse one out of them and then my said son Joseph shall chuse two and the fourth chest I give with two paire of sheets to the sonne of my sonne in law: Richard Penyfather. It is allsoe my mind and will that the furniture in the kitchin shall not bee removed from the place where now it standeth, neither shall the great trough in the Bowling house bee removed but that both shall remaine for my said sonne John and his heires. Item I give and bequeath unto my sonne Penyfathers eldest daughter the Bedd whereon I now lye in Hartford, Thomas Gray, wittnesse, Tho[mas] Bevis, John Rogers, [Ri]Ch[a]rd Dighton and Mary Stronge, aforesaid with the curtaines thereunto belonging with the Bedding, excepting one of the best blanketts, with three paire of sheets which I have now in use in Hartf[ord]: aforesaid it being my mind and will that my sonne Penyfathers youngest daughter shall have them, and as for the bedsted that is none of mine. Item all the rest of my goods chattells and debts, not before bequeathed, my debts legacies and funerall charges being first paid and satisfied, I give and bequeath to my Executor, hereafter named. Item I ordaine and Make my sonne John Gray of London, full and whole Executor of this my last will and testam[en]t, revoaking all other wills formerly by mee made, and my good friende John Stronge of Hertf[ord] aforesaid and Robert Nash of Digswell: overseers, and desire them to see this my will performed and for theire paines I give to each of them tenn shillings to bee paid unto them by my said Executor soe soone as they have seene it performed, lastly I have caused this my will to bee, I Thomas Gray, wittnesse Tho[mas] Bevis, John Rogers,

WILLS AND INVENTORIES FOR HERTFORD, 1660-1725

[Ri]Ch[a]rd Dighton and Mary Stronge, written and it hath bin read unto mee, and I have sealed this six sheets or leafes of the same together at the topp and have subscribed my name with my owne hand and sett my seale to every one of them, and have published and declared it to bee my testam[en]t, and last will in the presence of those whose names are hereunto subscribed Thomas Gray, Signed, Sealed and published in the presence of us Thomas Bevis, John Rogers, [Ri]Ch[a]rd Dighton, and Mary Stronge. For my wearing apparrell when the lord shall bee pleased to call mee away it is my mind and will, to bestow it if they shall except of it on these first my cozen Strong where I now soiourne to have my cloake, the next my mind and will is to my friend Robert Nash of Digswell to have my best great coate, I allsoe give and bequeath to my cozen Edward Gray of Haddon my best short coate, next I give and bequeath to Thomas Larken of Bengo my best dublett, next I give and bequeath to my cozen Samuell Foordham of much Munden my best breeches, for my other sute I bequeath to my sonne Joseph Gray, my Jerken coate and two of my breeches, next I bequeath to Will[ia]m Pryor of Hartingfordbury my dublitt, next I give and bequeath to my cozen Edmund Larken of Stapleford my best hat, next I give and bequeath to my cozen Oddall of wardsmill my old coate. Item I allsoe give unto my sonne John Gray his eldest daughter one of my best handchercheifs. Item I allsoe give to Matthew Gray, Josephs daughter the other of my best handchercheifs: these things I desire may bee performed within two months after my decease

Thomas Gray: September, the 30th 1658

2   John Smith   Grant of Probate: 24 April 1662   Will Ref: 3HR111
     Locksmith

In the name of God Amen, the seventh day of october Anno D[omi]ni 1642 in the yeare of the Reigne of our Sovereigne Lord Charles Stuart by the grace of God of England Scotland France and Ireland King Defender of the faith etc I John Smith of Burrough of Hartf[ord] in the County of Hertford, for I Smith being sicke in body but of good and perfect memory, thankes bee given to God and Creator with confidence that for the merritts of Jesus Christ his only sonne my Redeemer hee will except and receive mee into everlasting happines being sanctified by the holy ghost. My body which was made of earth I willingly comitt to the earth to bee buried decently in the Church yard and as concerning all my worlds estate I will that it bee disposed in manner and forme following, that is to say, my will is that my Executor hereafter to bee herein named shall deliver to the overseers of the poore of the parrish of All Saints in Hertford abovesaid to the use of the poore of the said parrish the sume of twentie shillings to bee distributed within one month after my decease to the poorest of them as soone as they can. Item my will and meaning is and I doe give and bequeath unto my loveing wife Mary all my Landes Ten[emen]ts and hereditaries as well free hold as coppie hold with their and every of their app[ur]tenancies to have and to hold to her the said Mary and her assignes for and during the whole terme of her naturall life, to that end and trust shee will maintaine our children and bring them up with a motherly care. Item my will is that the said Mary my wife shall pay yearely unto William Smith my eldest sonne the sume of foure poundes the said paym[en]t to beginne after hee shall have acomplished the age of three and twentie yeares. Item I give and bequeath unto my said sonne William the house wherein I now live in the markett place in Hertford called or knowne by the corner house with all and singular its app[ur]tenancies To have and to hold unto him and his heires for ever after the decease of my said wife, upon condition that hee the said William shall paye or cause to be paid the sume of thirtie pounds unto Jane Smith my daughter and to George Smith my sonne the sume of tenn poundes within one yeare after that he the said William shall come to possesse the said house, soe that it decends to his brother. Then my will is that hee or they to whom the said house shall soe decend shall pay the said sumes of thirtie pounds and tenn pounds to the said Jane and George. Item my will and meaning is that my said wife shall have my stall in the shambles at her disposing for ever. Item I give and bequeath unto John Smith my sonne my house with the app[ur]tenances coppie hold of the mannor of Brickendon situate in Castle Street To have and to hold to the said John Smith his heires and assignes forever from and immediately after the decease of the said Mary, my wife upon condition that the said John his heires and assignes shall pay unto Ann Smith his sister twenty pounds and unto George Smith his brother tenn pounds within one year after hee shall possesse the said house. Item I give and bequeath unto my daughter Elizabeth Smyth the sume of fiftie pounds of lawfull money of England to bee payd unto her by my Executrix on the day of her marriage or within one year after my decease which[ever] first shall happen. Item I give unto Mary Smyth my daughter the sume of fifty pounds to bee paid unto her by me Executrix when shee shall accomplish the age of one and twenty years or on the day of her marriage which of these shall first happen. Item I give and bequeath unto my Daughter Jane Smyth tenn pounds and to my daughter Ann Smith twenty pounds to bee paid unto them respectively when they or either of them respectively shall accomplish the ages of one and twenty yeares or on the dayes of their severall marriages which shall first happen. Item I will and bequeath unto George Smith my youngest sonne all those my two peeces of meadow customary of the mannor of Brickendon containing two acres more or lesse lyeing in Loc-meads in Hertford aforesaid To have and to hold to him and his heires forever after the decease of my said wife. Item my will and meaning is that if my said children to whom I have willed a portion of money shall happen to dye before their said portion shall be payable then the money to bee given and disposed shall bee equally divided amongst the other of my children as shall bee liveing. Item as concerning all the rest of my moveables goods and chattles debts and creditts whatsoever, I give and bequeath unto my loveing wife whome allso I make and constitute my whole and sole Executrix of this my last will and testam[en]t trusting to her faithfullnes that shee will pay my debts and legacies and my funerall charges discharge as it behoveth, and revokeing all other will or wills I ratifie this my present Testament to stand firme and effectuall onely whereof allsoe I make my loveing freind John Pegge and my loveing brother William Smith and my brother in lawe Edward Reason overseers and for their paines I give them six shillings eight pence a peece to buy them gloves, and in witnesse hereof I have hereto sett my hand and seale the day and yeare first abovewritten John Smith in presence of John Pegg and Edward Reason.

Inventory Reference: 119HW26
Date of Appraisal: 23 April 1662

An Inventory of the goods and Chattells of John Smyth of Hertford Locksmyth deceased, taken and appraised by us whose names are here underwritten the three and twentieth day of Aprill Anno D[omi]ni 1662

Imprimis in the hall	one pres, one table	01.00.00
In the Kitchin	three bottles, six pewter platters, three spits, two drippinge pans, two skillits, three flagons, one great flagon, fower chamber pots, paire of Andirons	01.10.00
In the parlor	one drawinge table, one bedstead, fether beds	03.00.00
In the hall chamber	one bedstead, one fether bede, rugg, curtaines vallainces, one chest, six stooles, two chaires	08.00.00
	One table	00.10.00
In the Kitchin chamber	one table, one chest, one box, one bedstead, one fether bedd	02.00.00
In the new chamber	one fether bedd, rugg, blankets, curtaines and vallainces, beddstead, Andirons, a Liverie Cubbard, fower stooles	10.00.00

WILLS AND INVENTORIES FOR HERTFORD, 1660-1725

In the shopp chamber	one forme	00.07.00
	Linnen, twelve paire of sheets, three dozin of napkins, six table cloths	08.00.00
	cloaths, purse	05.00.00
[Total]		**39.01.00**

[Appraisers]
John Downes, John Burton

Exhibited: 28 June 1662

3	Margaret Webb	Grant of Probate: 2 January 1661	Will Ref: 3HR20
	Widow	Estate valued at: £135.18.8	

In the name of god Amen. I Margrett Webb of Hertford in the countie of Hertf[ord] widd[ow] being of perfect mind and memory praised bee god doe ordaine and make this my last will and testam[en]t, in maner and forme following, First it is my mind and will that my Bodie bee decently Buried by mine Executor with the Advice and comfort of mine overseeres, all hereafter named. And as for those Lands Goods and possessions which it hath pleased God to endow mee withall, I will dispose of in such maner as I shall herein expresse, And touching all and singular the houses, landes, meadowes, and pastures, and all other my Estate in any houses or Lands whatsoever which I have or ought to have in the p[ar]ish of Great Munden in the countie aforesaid, with their and every of their Appurtenances I doe hereby will and ordaine by my said Executor with the Advice and Approbation of my said overseers to the best Advantage for paym[en]t of my legacies here after mentioned, And allsoe upon trust and confidence that my said Executor, his heires Executors, or, [The Marke of Margarett Webb] wittnesse William Carter and [Ri]Chard Dighton Administrators, shall well and truely pay or cause to bee paid the aforesaid legacies in currant money of England unto such person or persons or to the severall Executors, Admi[ni]strators, or Assignes of them or any of them whose names are hereafter mentioned vizt: I give and bequeath unto my Sister Damport the sume of thirty pounds of lawfull money of England and to her sonne Will[ia]m Damport the sume of five pounds of like lawfull money of England. Item I give and bequeath unto my Cozen Joane Haynes wife of Thomas Haynes of Hertf[ord] aforesaid the sume of tenn pounds and to her six children the sevrall sumes of five pounds a peece of Lawfull English money and if any of them do part this life before theire legacies become due unto them, then such legacies to bee

WILLS AND INVENTORIES FOR HERTFORD, 1660-1725

equally divided amongst such of them as shall survive. Item I give and bequeath unto Margarett, now wife of Will[ia]m Browne of great Amwell, the sume of Fifty pounds. Item I give and Bequeath unto my cozen Margarett daughter of John Gaze, the sume of tenn pounds. Item I give and bequeath unto Elizabeth Skingle, Sister of Daniell Skingle the sume of twenty pounds. Item I give and Bequeath unto Joane Stoakes daughter of my Brother [The marke of Margarett Webb] with wittnesse Will[ia]m Carter and [Ri]Chard Dighton, Thomas Reynolds, the sume of threescore pounds. Item I give and Bequeath unto my cozen Will[ia]m Smart of London the sume of Twenty pounds. Item I give and bequeath unto Mary the wife of Thomas Arnold the sume of Fifty pounds and to her daughter Mary the sume of Five pounds and to her sonne John the like sume of five pounds. Item I give and Bequeath unto Margarett Browne, daughter of the aforesaid Will[ia]m Browne the sume of five pounds, and to her Brother Will[ia]m the like sume of five pounds, And I allsoe give and Bequeath to her Brother Edward Browne and to his sister Jane Browne, the like sume of five pounds apeece, to goe to the longest liver of them. Item I give and Bequeath to my cozen Frances daughter of Will[ia]m Harvey deceased, the sume of one hundred pounds, and to Will[ia]m Harvey her Brother, the sume of one hundred pounds, and to Jane Harvey his sister the sume of one hundred pounds, and to Mary Harvey their sister the sume of threescore pounds. Item I give and Bequeath unto Robert Lea of Hertf[ord] the sume of twenty pounds, and to his Brother Thomas Lea of Hodsdon the sume of tenn pounds. Item I give and Bequeath, unto my cozen Dorothy now wife of John Read of (The Marke of) Margaret Webb widd[ow], wittnesse [Ri]Chard and Will[ia]m Carter) [for] her l[i]f[etime] and to her sonne John after her decease, the sume of forty pounds to bee paid by mine Executor, into the hands of my cozen Will[ia]m Stoakes within a yeare and three quarters after my decease, who shall with the Advice and approbacon of my overseers improve the same, soe as to pay Forty shillings by the yeare halfe yearely to the said Dorothy during her naturall life, And incase shee depart this life before her sonne John attaine the the Age of one and twenty yeares, then the said Forty shillings by the yeare, to bee paid halfe yearely towards the bringing up of the said John her sonne till hee bee of the said Age of one and twenty yeares, and then it is my mind and will, that my said cozen Will[ia]m Stoakes shall pay the said Forty pounds into the hands of the said John Read, sonne of the said Dorothy. Item I give and Bequeath unto the poore people of great Munden the sume of twenty shillings, And I allsoe give and Bequeath unto the poore people of the p[ar]ish of St Andrewes in Hertf[ord] the sume of twenty shillings which sums to the poore of both p[ar]ishes are to bee distributed unto them by mine Executor with the Approbacon of my overseers within one month after my decease. Item I give and Bequeath unto John sonne of Thomas Gifford my kinsman the sume, (The Marke of Margarett Webb widd[ow], wittnesse Will[ia]m Carter and [Ri]Chard Dighton) of five pounds. Item I give and Bequeath unto the forenamed Joane Haynes my kinswoman, and to the heires of her Body lawfully begotten for ever, all that my tenem[en]t with all and every the Appurtenances to the same now belonging except my shopp which Thomas Haynes her husband now hath in his occupacon, which are situate lyeing and being in the p[ar]ish of St Andrewes in Hertf[or]d aforesaid now in the occupacon of the said Thomas Haynes her husband, But it is my mind and will that the said Thomas Haynes my kinsman shall enjoy the same (excepting the said shopp) during his naturall life. Item I give and bequeath unto my said kinswoman Jane Harvey all that my messuage or tenem[en]t, wherein I now live with my said shopp which is now in the occupacon of the said Thomas Haynes, and all and every the Appurtenances to the same messuage or tenem[en]t and shopp belonging, and to the heires of her Body lawfully begotten for ever, which said messuage or tenem[en]t, and shopp are all standing and being in the said p[ar]ish of St Andrewes in Hertf[ord] aforesaid, And as concerning the Legacies of the children not of Age herein menconed and willed to bee paid unto them, It is my mind and will that they shall bee severally paid unto them within one yeare and three quarters. (The marke of Margarett Webb wid[ow] wittnesse Will[ia]m Carter and [Ri]Chard Dighton) after my decease. And it is my mind and will, that all those children to whome I have herein given legacies shall have their legacies when they are payable, provided that they bee in the meantime putt into safe hands by mine Executor with the Advice and Approbaton of my overseers then liveing and improved for them, till they Attaine to their severall Ages of one and twenty yeares, and they, and all others, herein named shall have their legacies duely paid unto them by mine Executor, hereafter named vizt, all that are of Age within one yeare and three quarters, after my decease. Item I doe hereby ordaine and make my kinsman, Daniell Skingle of Stondon my full and sole Executor of this my last will and testam[en]t, revoaking all other wills formerly by mee made. Lastly I ordaine and make my loving friends Will[ia]m Turner and Thomas Bevis of Hertf[ord] aforesaid Gent[lem]en overseers of this my last will and testam[en]t, desiring them to see the same performed, and if any sentence or clause herein shall seeme darke, I desire it may bee by them and my Executors interpreted according to the best sense and meaning, and for my said overseers cares and paines, I give and Bequeath unto them the severall sums of twenty shillings a peece to buy each of them a Ring, to bee paid unto them by [The marke of] Margarett Webb wid[ow], wittnesse Will[ia]m Carter and [Ri]Chard Dighton, my said Executors, within one month after my decease, And all my Goods and Chattells, whatsoever unbequeathed, my debts which I justly owe, and legacies being first paid and satisfied, and my funerall expences with the Advice and approbaton of my said overseers discharged, I give and Bequeath unto my said Executors, In wittnesse whereof I the said Margarett Webb to this my last will and testam[en]t containing Eight Leaves or sheets of paper have to Every sheet or leafe of the same, sett my hand or marke, and seale, this eight day of January in the twelfe yeare of the Raigne of King Charles the second over England, etc And in the yeare of our Lord God one thousand six hundred and sixtie, The marke of Margaret Webb wid[ow], Read subscribed Acknowledged declared and published to bee the last will and testam[en]t, of the said Margarett Webb in the presence of us Will[ia]m Carter and [Ri]Chard Dighton.

Memorandum that before the sealing hereof by the within menconed Margarett Webb shee tooke of Forty five pounds which was herein menconed, vizt, five pounds from Will[ia]m Damport, Tenn pounds from Margarett daughter of John Gaze, five pounds from Mary Arnold, Five pounds from John Arnold, Five pounds from Margrett daughter of Will[ia]m Browne, Five pounds from her Brother Will[ia]m Browne, and Five pounds a yeere from her Brother Edward Browne and her Sister Jane Browne in the presence of us Will[ia]m Carter and [Ri]Ch[a]rd Dighton. It is my further will that my sister Damport shall have one paire of towen sheets and some of my wearing Apparrell, and my Executor Daniell Skingle of Stondon to pay her halfe a crowne a weeke weekly during her life, I further give to Mary Arnold tenn pounds more than is expressed in the other part of my will and one paire of towen sheets, to bee both presently delivered to her by my said Executor, I give further to Margarett Heyward tenn pounds more then is in the other part of my will, to bee presently paid her by my said Executor, and one paire of towen sheets to bee presently delivered unto her by him, I further give to Jane Harvey and her sister Frances my plate to bee equally divided, and to each of them 2 paire of flaxen sheets, and to each of them a tablecloth and to each of them a paire of pillowbeers vizt 3 holland ones and one flaxen, I further give Dorothy Read five pound more than is expressed in the other part of my will, to bee by my executor paid presently into the hands of Mr Turner of Hertf[ord] to bee by him payd unto her at his discrecon wittnesse my hand and seale the day and yeare above menconed. the marke of Margarett Webb wid[ow] Signed, Sealed and published to bee a part of the last will and testam[en]t, of Margarett Webb of Hertf[ord] wid[ow] in the presence of us: Elizabeth Finch and Elizabeth Loyd.

4 Thomas White — Husbandman
Will Ref: 3HR106 [nuncupative will]

The xviii th day of September 1660 I Thomas White of Hertford in the County of Hertford husbandman made and declared his last will by word of mouth as followeth: The said White applying himselfe to his then master Thomas Bratt said 'master my estate is but small not above twelve pounds And I have layen suche a great while at yor Charges, And I owe sevrall moneyes to diverse persons, therefore my will and desire that you will pay the Debts that I owe and see mee buried and if there bee any surplusage of my estate I give it to you in consideracon of yor great love towards me in my sicknesse'. This was made in the presence of three or fower credible witnesses.

Witnesses to this Will: Jonathan Squire, John Bratt.

WILLS AND INVENTORIES FOR HERTFORD, 1660-1725

5   Richard Goodman   Grant of Probate: 27 October 1664   Will Ref: 4HR146
Maltster

In the name of God Amen the twelveth day of February Anno D[omi]ni 1663 I Richard Goodman of the parrish of All Sts als[o known as] Allhallowes in Hertford in the County of Hertford, maulster being aged and weake in body but of perfect minde and memory, doe make and ordaine this to be my last Will and testament in writeing in manner and forme following, vizt, First I give will and bequeath my soule into the hands of Almighty God my Creator and my body to the earth of which it was made in full assurance of a glorious resureccon to everlasting life throug the onely merritts and mediacon of Jesus Christ my only Saviour and blessed Redeemer. And for my temporall estate of which it hath pleased God to make me his unworthy steward I will and bequeath the same in manner following. First I give and bequeath unto my kinsman James Goodman of Hertford aforesayd and Sarah his wife All those two tenements in Castle Streete the one called Gilliaports and is now in the occupacon of Robert Faireman Schoolm[aste]r, the other in the occupacon of Jane Harvey wid[ow] and Robert Faireman aforesayd which I lately purchased of Finch, both which are customary or coppy hold lands and holden of the Mannor of Brickendon-berry, To have and to hold to the said James Goodman for ever Provided neverthelesse and upon the condicon notwithstanding that if the sayd James Goodman shall not agen or otherwise dispose of the sayd tenements or tenement or all or any of them but shall thereof dye seized, that then the sayd tenements with their and every of their appurtenances I will shall be and remaine unto Samuell Nash and Elizabeth Nash the sonne and daughter of Samuell Nash of Munden Parva in the sayd County of Hertford to be equally devided betweene them and their heires and assignes forever. Item I give and bequeath unto Sibbell Goodman my wifes sister for and dureing the terms of her naturall life the full sume of eight pounds by the yeare to be payd unto her by James Goodman his Executors Adminnistrators or assignes as aforesayd at the foure most usuall Feasts in the yeare by even and equall portons that is to say at the Feast of the Annuntiation, the Feast of St John Baptist, the Feast of St Michaell the Archangell and the birth of our Lord and Saviour comonly called Christmas, the first payment to be payd and done by the sayd James Goodman his Executors Adminnistrators or assignes to the sayd Sibbell Goodman or her assignes the next of the Feasts aforesayd which first and next happen after my decease. All the rest of my goods Chattles and debts unbequeathed I give and bequeath unto the abovenamed James Goodman whome I make name and appoint ordaine and Authorize to be my full and sole Executor of this my last Will and testament and revokeing all former and other wills doe make this to be my last Will and testament. In Witnesse whereof I have put my hand and seale the day and yeare first abovewritten, Richard Goodman signed sealed published and declared to be the last Will and testament of the said Richard Goodman in the presence of John Pegg [and] Jo. Best

WILLS AND INVENTORIES FOR HERTFORD, 1660-1725

Inventory Reference: 48HW45
Date of Appraisal: 12 January 1664

An Inventorye of the Goods and Chattells of Richard Goodman late of Brickendon in the parish of All Sts In Hertford in the Countye of Hertford deceased taken and appraised by Tho[mas] Kirbye and Adlord Bowde of Hertford, the 12th day of Jan[ua]ry 1664

Bonds	20.00.00
a Bedstead, feathir bed, bolster, Rugge, 2 blanketts, a chaire, a chest, a Cupbord	05.00.00
his wareinge cloathes, money in his pockett	05.00.00
[Total]	**30.00.00**

[Appraisers]
Thomas Kirby, Ad[lord] Bowde

Exhibited: 27 Oct 1664

6   Thomas Noble   Grant of Probate:1 October 1662   Will Ref: 4HR18
    Gentleman

In the name of God Amen the fourteenth yeare of our Reigne of our Soveraigne Lord Charles the Second over England Scotland France and Ireland King defender of the Faith etc I Thomas Noble of Hertford in the County of Hertford, Gentleman being of perfect health of body and of sound minde and memorie thankes be given to God for the same yett well knoweing the incertaintie of this life and being willing to settle my affaires in this world and to reserve the Remainder of my daies in provideing for eternitie, doe make this my last Will and testament in manner and forme following That is to say: First I resigne into the hands of my creator the spirit which he gave me and my body I First comitt to the Earth from whence it came to be decently buried in the parrish church chancell of All Saints as neere to my family there already buryed as conveniently as can bee according to the discretion of my Executor, hereafter to be named, assuredly believeing that through the merritts of my blessed Saviour they shall againe meete and unite in a Joyfull resurrecton to life everlasting. And for my temporall Estate wherewith it hath pleased God to entrust me here I doe devise and dispose thereof as followeth: First to the end that all my debts may bee iustly and truely payd I give and bequeath to my trusty freinds John Downes my sonne in lawe of Hertford aforesayd gentleman and William Mills of Hadham in the County of Hertford yeoman my brother in lawe to Robert Lawson of Hertford aforesayd Gent and Joseph

WILLS AND INVENTORIES FOR HERTFORD, 1660-1725

Browne of Hertford Gentleman and their heires forever All that my messuage app[ur]tenances called or knowne by the name of the thre crosses scituate standing and being in the parrish of Bennington in the County aforesayd togeather with all lands meadowes pastures wood and wood Grounds whatsoever to the same messuage and Farme belonging or appertaineing or therewith usually occupyed or enjoyed as part parcell or member thereof as the same late was in the Tenure and occupacon of Richard Fairman or his Assignes. And allso all other the messuages Lands Tenements and hereditaments whatsoever of me the sayd Thomas Noble scituate lyeing and being in the parrishes of Bennington Aston Watton att Stone and Walkerne in the sayd County of Hertford and every of them To have And to Hold the aforesayd messuages farme and premisses with all and singular the appertenances unto the sayd John Downes, William Mills, Robert Lawson and Joseph Browne their heires and Assignes forever, neverthelesse upon the especiall trust and confidence and to the uses intents and purposes hereafter menconed and declared That is to say upon the trust and to the intent that the sayd John Downes, William Mills, Robert Lawson and Joseph Browne and theire heires or the Survivor or Survivors of them shall soe soone as conveniently they can after my death make sale of all and singular the premisses of them devised as aforesayd to the best advantage and out of the monies thereby ariseing shall in the first place make speedy paym[en]t of all and singular my iust debts which I shall stand indebted in unto any p[er]son whatsoever at the tyme of my decease; and upon this further trust that after sale thereof to be made as aforesayd and my debts as aforesayd and discharged my sayd trustees their heires or Assignes shall out of the surplusage or Remainder of the money ariseing by sale of the aforesayd premisses secure raise and pay all and singular the legacies and bequests hereby given and limited to be payd as hereafter is payd as aforesayd that my sayd trustees their heires and assignes shall pay unto my Executor hereafter named the remainder and surplusage of the sayd purchase money. Item to my neece Susan Dellawood of Hoddesdon in the County of Hertford wid[ow]ow I give the anuity or yeerly sume of fifteene pounds of lawfull English money to be payd her yearly and evry yeare for and during the terme of her naturall llife. And doe give and devise unto my sayd sonne in lawe John Downes the annuity or yearly sume of fifteene pounds of lawfull English money to comence and to be payd unto him imediately from and after the death of the sayd Susan Dellawood yeerly and evry yeare for and during the Terme of his naturall life if hee shall happen to survive the sayd Susan and after the deceases of them the sayd Susan Dellawood and John Downes, I give and bequeath unto my sayd foure Trustees theire heires and assignes forever the anuity or yearly sume of fifteene pounds of lawfull English money in Trust and upon speciall confidence that they shall dispose thereof yearly and evry yeare for the use and benefitt of the poore of the parrish of All Saints in Hertford aforesayd for the time being forevermore. Item to the children of my sayd brother Mills I give the sume of twenty pounds to be equally divided amongst them. Item to my two neeces Elizabeth Waterman and Ann Waterman I give the sume of five pounds a peece. Item to my servant Christopher Grimes I give the sume of tenn pounds. Item to my nurse

WILLS AND INVENTORIES FOR HERTFORD, 1660-1725

Gable I give the sume of forty shillings. Item to the poore of the parrish of Saint Andrews in Hertford I give forty shillings. Item to the poore of the parrish of All Saints aforesayd I give tenn pounds. Item to my sayd foure freinds and Trustees I give the sume of forty shillings a peece and desire theire care in performance of this my Will All which sayd Annuities and Legacyes by me devised as aforesayd my will and meaneing is shall be secured raised and paid out of the surplusage money which shall arise upon sale of the aforesayd premisses and which shall be remaineing and after paym[en]t of my sayd debts, and my will and meaneing is that the aforesayd Annuity and Legacy of fifteene pounds per Annum devised for the benefitt of the aforesayd poore of the parrish of All Saints in Hertford be soe sone as conveniently may be secured to be payd by some espetuall Rent charge or other valuable Estate of Lands of good Title to be purchased with the surplusage money aforesayd or some sufficient parte thereof in the names of my sayd Trustees or their heires or the heires of the Survivors of them or of such other persons as they shall nominate and appoint for that purpose hereafter is directed. Item I give and bequeath unto my sayd loveing sonne in lawe John Downes for an[d] dureing the Terme of his naturall life all that my messuage or tenement scituate in [document torn at this place]

Thomas Noble signed sealed and published
in the presence of Ralph Battell, Edward Tuffnell, Thomas Pratt, Richard Wilshire

Inventory Reference: 96HW15
Date of Appraisal: 13 October 1662

An inventory and a prasall of the gudes and chattels of Thomas Nobell gent lateley decesed tacken and made by us this 13 day of october 1662

warenreparall, Linninge, wollinge	10.00.00
Redey money	02.12.06
debtes	10.00.00
7 Cusshens	01.00.00
2 suines, one sow	02.00.00
a saddell and bridell	00.10.00
2 Trunckes	00.05.00
a Lukenglase	00.07.00

[Total] 26.10.06

[Appraisers]
Ed Lawrence, Edward Ambrose, Richard Wylding

Exhibited: 15 September 1662

WILLS AND INVENTORIES FOR HERTFORD, 1660-1725

7 William Nicholls   Grant of Probate: 9 January 1663   Will Ref: 4HR41
   Baker

In the name of God Amen the thirtieth day of October 1663 I William Nicolls of Hertford in the County of Hertford baker being, God be thanked, weake of body yet of perfect memory doe make and ordaine this my last will and Testament in manner and forme following. Imprimis I comitt my spiritt into the hands of him that gave it, hopeing that by the merritts of my Saviour Jesus Christ my soule and body at the last day shall be raised againe and reunited unto everlasting life. And for my body I leave it to be decently interred according to the discretion of my Executors hereafter to be named And for that estate wherewith God hath blessed me in this world I give and bequeath in manner and forme following vizt Imprimis I give unto my oldest sonne William Nicolls five and twenty pounds. Item I give to my other three children John Nicolls, Christopher Nicolls and Margarett Nicolls the sume of twenty pounds a peece. And my will and meaneing is that if my wife shall happen to marrie againe that my Executors take care to secure their respective legacies out of my estate; And that my wife receive the Interest of the legacies towards their maintainnance. And further my will is that my sayd children shall receive their respective legacies when they shall attaine to the age of one and twenty yeares without are charge or Incumbrance. And all the rest of my goods and chattles I give and bequeath unto my beloved wife Susan Nicolls . And lastly I doe hereby constitute and appoint my father John Nicolls and my father in lawe Cadwallinder Smith Executors of this my last will and testament desireing them to be carefull of my wife and children according to the true meaneing of this my will. In witnesse whereof I have hereunto sett my hand and seale the day and yeare first abovewritten the marke of William Nicolls sealed published declared and delived in the presence of John Downes [and] John Smith

Inventory Reference: 96HW19
Date of Appraisal: 7 January 1663

A true and p[er]fect Inventory of all the goods and Chattells of W[illia]m Niccolls of the p[ar]ishe of All Saints w[i]thin the Borough of Hartford Baker who deceased the 31th of October last past taken by us whose names are hereunder written this present 7th of Jan 1663

Impr[imis] **in the Brewhouse**	Copper, brewing vessels, other implements	06.00.00
In the pastry	boulting mill, flower, implements thereunto belonging	03.00.00
In the yard	4 Sheath Roundwood blocks and faggotts	15.00.00

16

WILLS AND INVENTORIES FOR HERTFORD, 1660-1725

In the Bakehouse	a kneding trough, 2 moulding bords	01.00.00
In the hale p[ar]lour	2 small tables, other implemts	01.00.00
In the Browne chamber	a bed, bedstead, curtaynes valents, Rug, blankett, feather bed	04.00.00
	a table, 3 joynt stooles, court cubbord	01.00.00
In the Kitchin	pewter, brasse, fireshovell, toungs, Jacke, spitts, 2 dressers, shelves, other Implem[en]ts	15.00.00
In the faulcon p[ar]loure	a table, 4 ioynt stooles, ii chayres, a little sidebourd	01.00.00
In the hall	ii tables, 9 ioynt stooles, 6 chayres, a court cubberd, a Jacke, Iron tonge, fireshovell, tongues, other implements	04.00.00
In the Browne Chamber	2 standing beds, curtaynes valence, rugs, blankits, feather beds, 2 trundle beds, beddings thereunto belonging	10.00.00
	a table, ioynt stooles, a chayre, cussions, 2 court cubbords, a chest, a payre of andirons, fireshovell, toungs	05.00.00
In the lion	a standing bed, valence and curtaynes, feather bed, beding thereunto belonging, a trundle bed, bedding thereunto belonging, a little table, 4 ioynt stooles, 4 chayres, fireshovell, toungues, other implements	08.00.00
In the Rose	a standing bed, valence and curtaynes, fether bed, bedding thereunto belonging, a trundle bed, bedding thereunto belonging, a halfeheaded bed, bedding thereunto belonging, ii chest, 2 truncks, other implem[en]ts	10.00.00
	linning belongin to the house	23.00.00
	his weareing appayrell, mony in purse	11.00.00

WILLS AND INVENTORIES FOR HERTFORD, 1660-1725

In the sellar	6 hogsheads beare, allefull w[i]th empty castes, other implements	09.00.00
	5 quarters of wheate	10.00.00
	20 sheepe	06.00.00
	hay in the barne	03.00.00
[Total]		**146.00.00**

[Appraisers]
Ed[ward] Bache, Henry? Herrick

Exhibited: 9 January 1663

8	**Mary Smith Widow**	**Grant of Probate: 2 June 1663**	**Will Ref: 4HR61**

In the name of God Amen this tenth day of January in the yeare of our Lord God one thousand six hundred sixty and two I Mary Smith of Hertford in the County of Hertford widdow being weake of body but, God be thanked, of perfect memory doe make and ordaine this my last Will and Testament in manner and forme following That is to say: first I Comend my soule into the hands of my Saviour Jesus Christ hopeing that by his merritts both my soule and body will be raised and united togeather at the last day unto eternall life. And for that estate wherewith it hath pleased God to blesse me in this world I will and bequeath in manner and forme following: Imprimis I give and bequeath to my sonne George Smyth one Bond with the Interest now due from William Fairman of Hertford brewer upon this Condition that he shall release his brother William and his brother John of that Legacy of money for the which their respective Estates of land given them by my husbands Will are charged. Item I give and bequeath to my sonne William Smyth one Bond with the Interest due from John Croft and William Carter towards the defrayeing of my funerall Charges which sayd sonne William Smyth I doe hereby constitute and appointe sole Executor of this my last Will and Testament. Item I give and bequeath to my sonne George all my wood and hay and all my stall geere out of doors the new wicker chaire, the shelves in the kitchin, the long and little table in the hall, the presse cupboard. Item I give to my sonne John the bedstedd curtaines and vallence in the little shopp chamber. Item I give to my grandchildren Mary and Elizabeth Porter the boxe of childehood lynnen with other things which was their mothers. Item I give one chest by the fire side in the great Chamber to Mary Porter and one trunck at the head and one Bond in which Edward Tuffnaile is bound. And for the rest of my goods I give to be equally devided amongst my children as they shall be [ap]praised by honest men, my debts being first payd and

WILLS AND INVENTORIES FOR HERTFORD, 1660-1725

funerall charges. In witnesse whereof I have sett my hand and seale to this my will the day and yeare abovewritten the marke of Mary Smith sealed and delive[re]d and published in the presence of John Clerke [and] John Downes

Inventory Reference: 119HW31
Date of Appraisal: 19 February 1662

An Inventory and Appraisall of the goods and chattells of Mary Smyth of hertford Widd[ow] made the nineteenth day of February 1662 By us whose names are underwritten

In the hall	Two tables and frames, one pres cubbard, one forme, three turnd chaires, two low stooles, one jack with a wait, two pot hangers, one gridiron, a fire iron	01.17.00
In the parlor	one drawinge Table, carpit, one standinge bedstead, 3 curtains rods with vallaines, a paire of creepers, five ioined stooles	01.14.00
In the greate chamber	one bedstead, cord, mat, one straw bed, one fether bedd, two fether bolsters, one fether pillow, one white blankett, greene rugg, five curtains w[i]th vallains, one trundle bedd, cord, matt, one fether bedd, blankett, one drawing table, carpitt, six ioine stooles, one court cubbard and cloth, two ioined chaires, a turnd chaire, two low stooles, one ioined chest, one bason and ewer, one paire of Andirons, creepers w[i]th brasses	11.00.00
In the Kitchin	Two bedsteads, cords, matt, two fether bedds, two fether bolsters, one blankett, rugg, one coverlidd, one trundle bedd, cord, mat, one flock bedd, one flock bolster, a pillow, one blanket, coverlid, one ioined pres cubbard, one table frame, formes, three chests, one settle, one chaire	08.00.00
A small roome	one halfe headed bedstead, some old beddinge	01.00.00

WILLS AND INVENTORIES FOR HERTFORD, 1660-1725

In the shop chamber	one halfe headed Bedstead, cord, mat, one fether bedd, two fether bolsters, pillow, one blankett, greene rugg, three curtaines and vallaines, a little Table, chest	04.00.00
In the new chamber	one bedstead, cord, straw bed, one fether bed, one fether bolster, two fether pillowes, two blankets, a rugg, five curtaines, three rods w[i]th the vallaines, one cort cubbard, cubbard cloth, one bason and Ewer, fower cooshin stooles, a chaire of the same, one little table, carpitt, two lether chaires, three cushions, two window curtaines, rods, one paire of creepers, one paire of Andirons w[i]th brasses, one paire of tongs, fireshovell, bellows	09.00.00
	Twenty paire of flexen and Towen sheets, fowre dozzen of flexen and towen napkins, Eight Table cloths, halfe a dozen paire of pillowbeers, adozen Towels	14.00.00
In the Kitchin and buttery	fine pewter twenty and five peeces, six chamber pots, six flagons, two posurts, an iron pott, a hangd pan, one paire of racks, a warminge pan, two pailes, three bras Kettles	04.05.00
In the barne	wood, hay	01.10.00
	Lumber in the garrett and other places	02.00.00
[Total]		**58.06.00**

[Appraisers]
John Downes, John Russell, William Smith

Exhibited: 20 May 1662

(A second copy of the inventory was exhibited 2 April 1663)

WILLS AND INVENTORIES FOR HERTFORD, 1660-1725

9   **Edward Tuffnell**   **Grant of Probate: 18 April 1665**   **Will Ref: 4HR172**
        Chirurgion

In the name of God Amen Edward Tuffnell of Hertford in the county of Hertford Chirurgion, being in perfect health and memory blessed be God yet well knoweing the uncertainty and frailty of mans life, doe this second day of February in the seaventeenth yeare of the Raigne of Charles the Second by the grace of God of England, Scotland, France and Ireland King defender of the faith etc Anno D[omi]ni 1664 make and ordaine my last Will and Testament in manner and forme following: Imprimis I comitt my soule into the hands of my gracious Redeemer Jesus Christ and my body to the earth to be decently interred according to the discretion of my Executor hereafter to be named, stedfastly beleveing that at the last day both soule and body shall againe be united unto everlasting life. And for my temporall estate wherewith God hath blessed me in this world I will and desire to my sonne Conor Tuffnell all that my messuage and Inn in Hatfeilde called the Swann with all and singular the appurtenances as they are now in the tenure of one John Brace. Item I devise and bequeath unto my sonne Thomas Tuffnell all that my messuage with Freehold and coppyhold lands and appurtences called Tunell in the Parrish of Bengeo in the tenure of one Ann Wood my sister wid[ow]. And allso I give and devise to my sonne Thomas Tuffnell all that my messuage in Hertford called the Maydenhead with all and singular the appurtenances as they are now in my occupacon. And my will and meaneing is that my sonne Thomas shall out of his estate pay to my daughter Ann Tuffnell the sume of tenn pounds within one yeare next after my decease. Item my will and meaneing is that if it shall happen either of my said sonns to die unmarried, the respective estate shall come to the other and yf they both dye unmarried both their estate shall come to my daughter Ann and her heires forever. And my will and meaneing is that yf my sonne Conor shall anywaies disturbe or trouble my sonne Thomas about any the coppie hold lands at Tunnell aforesayd that then my sonne Thomas shall have full power by vertue of this my will to enter upon the sayd Inn called the Swann and the same to have and keepe to him the sayd Thomas and his heires forever. Item I give to my sister Dorothy Scant twenty shillings and to my sister Wood twenty shillings to buy them rings. Item I give to John Wood five shillings and to Katherine Greeve five shillings and to Ann Wood five shillings. Item to Edward Cotton five shillings and I doe hereby make constitute and appoint my sonne Thomas Executor of this my last Will and testament. In Witnesse whereof I have hereunto sett my hand and seale the day and yeare abovewritten Edward Tuffnell sealed, signed, published and declared in the presence of John Mountfort, Robert Pile, Edward Ewanns

Inventory Reference: 132HW8
(undated)

A true invitory of the Goods and chatles of Edward Tuffnells

In the Little parlor	1 bedstid, Curtins and vallins, Curtin Rods, top peece, Cord	
	1 Fether bed, 3 Fether pillors, 1 bolsters wayes 40 pound	01.13.04
	1 straw bed	00.01.00
	1 chest	00.05.00
	2 trunkes	00.03.00
	2 blankets, 1 rug	00.03.00
	1 old Cubboord	00.05.00
	1 paire of Tongs	00.01.08
	1 pot shelfe	00.01.00
	1 Table, 3 Joynt Stooles	00.08.00
	2 Creepers, 1 porring pot	00.03.00
	1 warming pan, skillet	00.03.00
	sheets, table cloths, napkins, pillobeers, Towells	02.00.00
	pewter	00.05.00
[Total]		**06.12.00**

[Appraiser]
John Barfoot

10 Isabel Whison   Grant of Probate: 3 July 1663   Will Ref: 4HR75
**   Widow**

In the name of God Amen the xxiiiith day of May in the yeare of Our Lord one thousand six hundred sixty and thre, I Isabell Whison of the parrish of Allhallowes als[o known as] All S[ain]ts in Hertford in the county of Hertford widdow, being of perfect minde and memory praised be God, doe make and ordaine this to be my last will and testament in manner and forme following: First I comitt my soule into the mercifull protection of Allmighty God my Creator and my body to the earth (of which it was made) in hope of a glorious resurreccon at the last day to eternall glory through the only merritts and mediacon of Jesus Christ my only mediator and Redeemer. And for that portion of goods which it hath pleased God to bestowe uppon me I doe give and dispose them in manner and forme following: That is to say unto Mary Sanders the wife of Richard Sanders of Newgate Street in the parrish of Hatfeild, labourer, Elizabeth Feild of Stevenage the wife of Danniell Feild, Jane Myles of Stevenage, the

WILLS AND INVENTORIES FOR HERTFORD, 1660-1725

wife of John Myles saywer, Mary Elmer the wife of Elmer of new England, Thomas Heath of Stevenage, Carpenter, fifty shillings a peece to be payd unto them within twelve moneths next after my decease . And my will and meaneing is that my loveing freind William Carter shall pay noe use nor Interest for any money which he hath of mine in his hands. All the rest of my goods and Chattles whatsoever is due to me I give and bequeath unto my loveing kinsman Richard Sanders of Hatfeild aforesayd for the payment of my debts funerall charges and other expenses and I make and ordaine the sayd Richard Sanders sole Executor of this my last Will And doe utterly make voyd all other former Wills and make this my last Will and testament. In witnesse whereof I have hereunto sett my hand and seale the day and yeare first above written [the marke of] Isabell Whison signed, sealed, published and declared to be my last will and testament in the presence of the marke of Martha Widdowes, Jo. Best, John Pegg

Inventory Referenc: 140HW56
Date of Appraisal: 4 June 1663

A true Inventorie made the fourth day of June 1663 of all the moveable goods of Isubell Whison late of Hertford in the Countie of Hertford widowe deceased taken and aprized by us whose names are heerunder written

Imprimis in the Hall	one halfeheaded bed, Cords, two flock beds, one flock bolster, one fether bolster, two blankets, one Coverlid	00.17.00
	to wicker chaires, two cusshins	00.01.08
	two andirons, a frieinge pan, one paire of pothooks, a gridiron, bellowes, other small implements	00.05.00
It[em] in the parlor	one Cubord, one table and frame one chest, sixe stooles, a forme, a kneadingtrough	00.13.00
		01.14.00
	Linin of all sorts	01.10.00
	brasse of all sorts, pewter of all sorts, an iron pot	00.12.00
	a chest, a boxe, a bowle, parne, other Implem[en]ts	00.12.00
	her wearinge clothes linen and wolen, books, firewood	02.02.06
	good debts due to the testatour	13.00.00

WILLS AND INVENTORIES FOR HERTFORD, 1660-1725

£7.7.2 and £13
sum total

[Total]   20.07.02

[Appraisers]
Richard Carter, John Smith

Exhibited: 3 July 1663

11   **Francis Clarke**   **Grant of Probate: 3 August 1667**   **Will Ref: 5HR75**
      Chapman

In the name of God Amen. I Francis Clarke of the Burrough of Hartford in the County of Hertford, Chapman, being sicke in body but of good and perfect memory thankes bee to God, And considering with my selfe the Transitoryes of this present life doe make this my last Will and Testament in manner and forme following, That is say First I bequeath my soule into the hands of Almighty God and to Jesus Christ my Saviour through whose merritts and suffering I hope to have eternall life. And as for such worldly goods that God of his mercey hath lent unto mee, my will and desire is [they] shall bee thus disposed in manner and forme as followeth. Item I give and bequeath to my sonne Edward Clarke of the parrish of All S[ain]ts in Hertford in the County of Hertford, chapman, one shilling to bee payd unto him the s[ai]d Edward within one moneth next after my decease. Item I give and bequeath to my Grandchilde Robert Clarke, the sonne of Edward Clarke, the sume of one and twenty pounds of lawfull money to bee payd unto the sayd Robert Clarke out of one certaine Mortgage which I have of one Tenement scituate in the parrish of All S[ain]ts aforesayd in Hertford aforesayd, now in the tenure of one Mr William Edmonds to bee raised out of the sayd Tenement the last three yeares of the sayd Mortgage. Item I give and bequeath unto Francis Clarke, the sonne of Edward Clarke, the sume of one shilling to bee payd him within one moneth next after my decease. Item I give and bequeath unto my loveing sister Elizabeth Potter the wife of goodman Potter of Easingdon in the County of Hertford, Labourer, the sume of twenty shillings within three moneths next after my decease. Item I give unto my loveing sister Elizabeth Silverside of the parrish of London Colney in the County of Midd[lese]x, widdow, the sume of twenty shillings within three moneths next after my decease. Lastly All the rest of my Goods and Chattles, household stuffe, Bill, Bonds, dues, debts, p[ro]fitts and writeings whatsoever I doe give and bequeath unto my loveing wife Ann Clarke whome I doe make my full and sole Executrixe of this my last Will and Testament and to her heires and assignes forever, And I doe allso desire my loveing freind George Heath of the

WILLS AND INVENTORIES FOR HERTFORD, 1660-1725

Burrough of Hertford in the County of Hertford, Brewer, to oversee aide and assist my loveing wife in the performance of this my last Will and Testament. In Witnesse whereof I have hereunto sett my hand and seale the Thirtieth day of March in the Seaventeenth yeare of the Reigne of Our Sovereigne L[or]d Charles the second by the Grace of God of England Scotland France and Ireland King Defender of the faith etc Anno D[omi]ni 1665 The m[ar]ke of Francis Clarke sealed signed and delive[re]d in the presence of the m[ar]ke of William Greeve,   John Hill Sr

Inventory Reference: 23HW51
Date of Appraisal: 3 May 1667

An Inventory of the goods and Chattells of Francis Clarke of Hertford in the County of Hertf[or]d Chapman lately deceased w[hi]ch Inventory was taken the Third day of May Anno D[omi]ni 1667 Vizt

In the Hall	an old Table, five old stooles	00.04.00
	sixe old Chayres	00.02.00
	one press Cubboard	00.10.00
	Eleven pewter dishes	01.00.00
	sixe Flagons, two quarts, apynt pott	00.12.00
	Foure pewter Chamber potts	00.05.00
	one pewter salt, a fewe earthen drinking potts	00.01.00
	one litle brass porrage pott, Iron fier shovell, Andirons	00.06.00
	two kitles, three brass possnitts	00.16.00
	one warmeing pan, a brass Chaffing dish	00.02.06
	one pewter Candlestick, a bason, two old Candlestikes tyn and wire	00.02.00
	two old Fryeing pans, a gridiron	00.02.00
	one litle Table w[i]th drawers, a pott shelfe, a old Cubboard, with some other Lumber	00.05.00
	two old pott Hangers	00.01.00
	two Hampers w[i]th Chapman wares in them	14.00.00
	3 spitts, a old Jack, a dripping pan	00.04.00
In the Buttery	one bedsted, bedding	01.06.08
	an old boxe, a baskett, a Quarter of a barrell of beare, with some other Lumber	00.15.00

In the Chamber over the Hall	one old Table, Seven stooles	00.08.00
	a bedsted, bedding, a trundle bedd, bedding	02.00.00
	two Chests w[i]th weareing Cloaths and some Lynen	02.00.00
	one Trunck with some Lynen	01.00.00
	a wicker Chayre, a litle forme, foure old Cushions with some Lumber	00.06.08
In the Chamber over the Buttery	a Standing bedd, bedding, a Trundle bedd, bedding	02.00.00
	an old Chest, a great Chayre	00.02.06
	one litle Chayre, a Table, a Joynt Stoole and a litle Lumber	00.05.00
In the Garrett	an old trundle bedd, bedding and some old things	00.04.00
In the Barne and yard	two Load of wood, a fewe Tubbs and some Lumber	01.05.00
	It[em] halfe a Load of Hay	00.15.00
In the Stable	one horse, a rack, Mainger	02.00.00
	Debts oweing to the s[ai]d Francis Clarke	06.00.00
[Total]		**39.00.04**

These goods and Chattells was valued and praysed the day and yeare above written by us George Heath, John Hill, Praysors

Exhibited: 3 August 1667

12   Joane Baker   **Grant of Probate: 21 May 1695**   **Will Ref: 7HR151**
       Widow   **Estate valued at: £115.12.10**   **[nuncupative will]**

Memorandum that Joane Baker of Hertford in the County of Hertford Widow being sick of the sicknes whereof she dyed and being of sound and disposeing minde and memory on or upon the sixth day of Aprill one thousand six hundred ninety five at or in the dwelling house of her the said Joane Baker situate in Hertford aforesaid where she had lived for the spane of her days and upwards, being asked by our Mary Rooding the wife of John Rooding of Hartingfordbury in the presence and hearing of

WILLS AND INVENTORIES FOR HERTFORD, 1660-1725

Margarett the wife of Francis Page of Hartingfordbury and Elizabeth the wife of Marke Brace of Hertford, to whome she did intend to give what she had to, whether to her sister Mary the wife of Robert Clarke or not, to whom she answer'd and did nuncupate and declare these words following. Vizt, Yes she did give all she had to her said sister Mary, to whome shou'd she give it else, or used words to the like effect, and the said words were declared in the presence and hearing of the Witnesses abovemencond who have hereunto set their hands.

Mary Rooding,   Margarett Page,   Eliz[abeth] Brace.

Inventory Reference: 14HW14
Date of Appraisal: 10 April 1695

A True and perfect Inventory of all the goods and Chattells of Joane Baker widdow Late of the parish of St Johns in Hertford in the County of Hertford dowager as they ware Taken and Apprized the 10 day of April 1695 by uss whose Names are here subscribed

The Goods in the Hall	06.07.06
The goods in the buttery	02.16.06
The Linin	02.19.04
In the Yard	09.09.06
	(unclear)
Money owing in good and bad depts	100.00.00
her Wairing Apparrill	03.00.00
[Total]	**115.12.10**

[Appraisers]
John Barfoot, The marke of Marke Bran

Exhibited: 21 May 1695

WILLS AND INVENTORIES FOR HERTFORD, 1660-1725

13   William Halfhead;Halfhide   Grant of Probate: 17 June 1692   Will Ref: 7HR48
     Bachelor   Estate valued at: £40.17.00

In the name of God amen! The thirtyth first day of May 1692 according to the computacon of the Church of England, I William Halfehead of Hertford in the County of Hertford Batchilor, being of perfect memory and remembrance praysed be God doe make and ordaine this my last Will and Testam[en]t revokeing all other Wills by me made in manner and forme following vizt. First I bequeath my soule into the hands of Almighty God my maker and Redeemer hopeing through the merritorious death and passion of Jesus Christ my only Saviour and Redeemer to receive free pardon and forgiveness of all my sins, and as for my body to be buried in Christian buryall at the parish Church at Hartingfordbury at the discretion of my Executors hereafter nominated. Item it is my will and mind and I doe give and bequeath unto my eldest sister Susanna Purcell ten pounds, the wife of Thomas Purcell to be paid one whole yeare after my decease. Item I give and bequeath unto my eldest brother Thomas Halfehead the sume of ten pounds to be paid one whole yeare after my decease. Item it is my will and mind and I doe give and bequeath to my second brother Edward Halfehead the sume of ten pounds to be paid one whole yeare after my decease. Item I give and bequeath unto my youngest Sister Mary Halfehead the sume of ten pounds to be paid one whole yeare after my decease. Item it is my will and minde and I doe give and bequeath unto my youngest brother John Halfehead the sume of ten pounds to be paid one whole yeare after my decease. Item all the rest of my household goods both quick and dead I give to my father Robert Holyoake my father in law: to Mary Holyoake my owne Mother, and doe make them Robert Holyoake and Mary Holyoake my whole Executor and Executrix of this my last Will and Testament revokeing all other wills and Testaments, they paying all my debts Legacies and funerall expenses as far as the goods will pay and noe farther. In Witnes whereof I have hereunto set my hand and seale the day and yeare first abovewritten W[illia]m Halfehead, [witnessed by] William Nash, John Hall, Henry Willson.

Inventory Reference: 59HW17
Date of Appraisal: 14 June 1692

The Inventory of the Goods and Chattles of Will[ia]m Halfhide of Stevenage lately Deceased was made the 14th of June 1692

Imprimis Buttery	1 Bed in the Chamber, Curtains vallens, ruggs, Blanketts	03.10.00
In the Hall Chamber	18 Rush Chairs, 1 Table, A pair of Andirons, fire shovle, tongues	01.04.00

WILLS AND INVENTORIES FOR HERTFORD, 1660-1725

In the Parlour Chamber	1 Flock bed, Boulster, Pillow, 1 Blanckett, an old Coverlet	00.10.00
In the Parlour	A pair of Andirons, fire shovell, Tongues, 1 Table, a joynt stoole, 2 chairs, a case of Rasors	00.12.00
In the Halle	Brass	01.00.00
	Pewter	02.13.00
	Plate, 1 pint Tankerd, 2 spoones	04.00.00
	1 Table, 4 Joynt stooles, 5 Rush chairs, 1 jack, 2 spits, 1 pair of Andirons, fire shovell, Tongues, 1 Gridiron	00.12.00
	A Mare, 2 Piggs	03.00.00
	Moneys	03.11.00
	Debts Sperate	11.00.00
	Debts Desperate	04.00.00
	Wearing Apparrell	05.00.00
	Dung	00.05.00
[Total]		**40.17.00**

[Appraisers]
The day and year above written these goods were Apprised by us wittness our Hands Fra[ncis] Pratt *(possibly the vicar of Stevenage at this time)*, Tho[mas] Pusey

Exhibited: 17 June 1692

14   Sarah Runnington   Grant of Probate: 24 May 1694   Will Ref: 7HR111
      Widow   Estate valued at: £56.04.00

In the name of God amen! I Sarah Runnington Widow in the towne of Hertford in the County of Hertford being of perfect memory, praised be God for the same, doe make and ordaine this my last Will and Testament in manner and forme following vizt First I bequeath my soule into the hands of Almighty God my maker hoping that through the merritorious death and passion of Jesus Christ my only Savior and Redeemer to receive free pardon and forgiveness of all my sins and for my body to be buried in Christian buryall at the discretion of my executor hereafter nominated. Item I give and bequeath to my Grandson Henry Runnington twenty shillings. Item I give unto my Grand-daughter Elizabeth Runnington, daughter to my Son Henry deceased, the sume of five pounds to her and to her heires to be paid by my Executor. Item I give unto Sarah Runnington, daughter to my Son Henry, deceased, the sume of five pounds to her or to her heirs to be paid by my Executor. Item I allsoe give unto Mary Runnington daughter of my Son Henry deceased the sume of five pounds to be paid to her or to her heirs by my Executrix. Item I leave unto my daughter Sarah Throwgood all that my Copyhold house with all and every the appurtenances thereto belonging situate lying and being in West Streete in the parish of All Saints Hertford which I have Surrendred to use of my last Will during the terme of her naturall life and after her decease I give to her foure sons (that is to say) to Henry Thorowgood, Robert Thorowgood, John Thorowgood and Davied Thorowgood, to hold to them their heires and Assignes for ever, all that my aforesaid house with all the appurtenances thereto belonging. Item I allsoe give unto my Son John Runnington twenty shillings to buy him a Ringe. All that I have not already bequeathed I give unto my daughter Sarah aforesaid whome I make sole Executrix of this my last Will and Testam[en]t revokeing all other Wills formerly by me made. In Witnes whereof I have hereunto set my hand and seale the twenty third day of February in the yeare of our Lord God 1691 in the second yeare of our Sovereigne Lord and Lady William and Mary, King and Queen over England Scotland France and Ireland defenders of the faith. The marke of Sarah Runington Signed, sealed, deliver'd and published in the presence of James Taylor, the marke of John Perin, Thomas Arnold, Ralph Battell senior.

Inventory Reference: 111HW87
Date of Appraisal: 21 May 1694

An invetarey of the Goodes of Sarah Runenton widow Late of Hartford desesed taken and apraysed this 21 day of May in the yeare of ower Lord of 1694

In the Kittchen	one litell Copper, one warmen pan, a pare of Iron Rackes, a fender, 3 spittes, a fier shovell, tonges, 8 pewter dishes, 18 pewter plates, a cheese plate, 12 pewter flagons, a pewter tankard, 10 pewter saltes, a screene to sett before the fiar, a Iron drippenpan, a Jack and waigt, a clever, 3 skiletes, a Brass fryen pan, to Bordes, a chafer, a Baston barell, a slise, a fleshforke, to pare of potthangers, a forme, to dressers, shelfes, a Bread Grate, other od implements in cluded	06.18.06

WILLS AND INVENTORIES FOR HERTFORD, 1660-1725

In the Brew Howse one Coper, Irones, wooden pumpe,
to tunnes, a Sydor Cask, one cooler,
a shorte trof, a wine pipe, to bearen tubbes,
a pare of slinges, a sturor,
other odd implements in cluded   18.00.00

In the Hall a table, 4 Joynd Stowles, a Jack, to pott shelfes,
a bras pott lid, a hand candell stik,
a cole shovell, tonges, fier forke,
a Iron candell stik, to flower potts,
a owld chayer,
a Iron Grate for the ashes to fall throw   01.02.06

In the Parlor one Bedsteed, cord, Matt,
fether bed, bolster, a side table,
5 turkey work chayeres, a Greene chayer,
a Stowle, to owld Rugges   03.16.06

Linen, plate, 6 pare of corse sheetes,
9 ould napkines, 3 pare of pillobeares,
to silver spownes   02.06.06

In the Litell Hall a table frame, a Long forme, a Bench bord, 00.05.00

In the Greate Chamber a Bedsteed, cord, matt, a flock Bed, Rood,
curtaines, one Blankitt, to Rugges,
one fether Bolster, one flock Bolster,
one pare of Bras andirons,
a pare of creeperes, one Livery cobbard,
one Long table, 4 turkey worke chayeres,
4 shelfes in the closett, 3 window curtaines,
roodes   [04.00.06]
                          (*sum obscured by ink blot*)

In the Long Chamber one Bedsteed, one fether bed, bolster, pillow,
one coverlid, one flock Bolster,
three more fether bolsters, a straw Bed,
a other flock Bolster, a Blankitt,
to pare of Greene curtaines, to tables,
one sid bord, 4 chayeres, to stowles,
other od thinges   03.14.06

WILLS AND INVENTORIES FOR HERTFORD, 1660-1725

Item in the Hall Chamber	one hey beedsted, one trundell Bedsted, one fether Bed, Bolster, a flock bed, Bolster, one Blankitt, a old Rugg, a chest, a case of drawers, a box, a trunke, a old stowle	02.18.06
In the Garatt	3 old Bedsteedes, cordes, to flock Matreses, a straw Bed, one fether bed, 3 bolsters, one blankitt, one Rugg, one coverlid, to par of old curtaines, 9 old chayeres, stowles, a chest, a flock bed, to table chayeres, a pare of creeperes, other Lumber	03.05.06
In the selere	8 hogesheads, one pipe, a funell, to old troues, old drink stalls, other od thinges	04.06.00
In the yard	f[o]r the halfe of a Cow, a Scafold, a Lav, to hoog trofes, a old forme	02.10.00
	hur waren aparill, money in hur purse	03.00.00
[Total]		**56.04.00**

[Appraisers]
apraysed by us Will[ia]m Guyse *(who wrote the inventory - the other signature is illegible)*

Exhibited: 24 May 1694

15   Grace Smarte   Grant of Probate: 12 July 1697   Will Ref: 7HR260
     Widow   Estate valued at: £38.00.00

In the name of God amen! I Grace Smarte of the towne of Hertford in the County of Hertford widd[ow] being sicke and weake in body but of sound mind and memory (praised be Almighty God for the same) doe make publish and declare this to be my last will and Testament in manner and forme following. Imprimis I commend my Soule into the hands of Almighty God my Creator hopeing through the merritts of my Saviour and Redeemer Jesus Christ to receive perfect remission and forgiveness of all my sins, and as to the temporall Estate which it hath pleased Almighty God to blesse me with I give devise bequeath and dispose thereof as followes First I give and bequeath unto Daniell Smarte, son of Ralph Smarte, one payre of sheets and twenty shillings in mony the said sheets and money to be paid and delivered to the said Daniell Smarte by my Executor herein after named within twelve Months after my decease. Item I give and bequeath unto Elizabeth Smarte, daughter of the said Ralph Smarte, one flockbed, one payre of greene curtains, one rugg and blankett, one payre of sheets and twenty shillings in money to be paid and delivered to the said Elizabeth Smarte by my Executor herein after named within twelve Months after my decease. Item I give and bequeath unto my son William Smarte of the towne of Hertford aforesaid Webster one silver spoone to be deliver'd to him by my Exec[uto]r hereafter named within three Months next after my decease. Item I give and bequeath unto my Son Stephen Smarte of Stevenage in the said County of Hertford Butcher one silver spoone to be deliver'd to him as is last above mencon'd and directed. Item I give and bequeath unto my son Jonathan Smarte of the towne of Hertford aforesaid Webster my biggest Silver cupp and two payre of sheets. Item all other my goods Chattells mony's and householdstuffe whatsoever not herein before given and bequeathed after all my debts and funerall expences are fully paid and discharged I give and devise unto my daughter Mary the wife of Harmer Offley of the towne of Hertford aforesaid Webster to be paid and deliver'd to my said daughter Mary at such time and place and in such manner and forme by my Exec[uto]r hereafter named, as to my said Exec[uto]r shall seeme most meete and convenient. Lastly I doe hereby make nominate ordayne constitute and appointe my said Son Jonathan Smarte Sole Exec[uto]r of this my last Will and Testament hereby revokeing all Wills by me formerly made I doe make publish and declare this to be my last Will and Testam[en]t. In Witnesse whereof I the said Grace Smarte have hereunto set my hand and seale this three and twentieth day of Aprill Anno D[omi]ni one thousand six hundred ninety and seaven. The marke of Grace Smarte Signed Sealed published and declared to be the last Will and Testam[en]t of the said Grace Smarte in the Presence of us Adlord Bowde, William Rayner, W[illia]m Browne.

Inventory Reference: 121HW29
Date of Appraisal: 12 July 1697

The Inventory of Grace Smart Widdo Deceased taken this 12 Day of July 1697 In the Parrish of Allsts Hartford

In the Hall	04.00.00
In the Best Chamber	07.00.00

WILLS AND INVENTORIES FOR HERTFORD, 1660-1725

In the Hall Chamber		04.00.00
	2 Chest of Lining	08.00.00
	plate, money, waring aparll	15.00.00
[Total]		**38.00.00**

[Appraisers]
Ad[lord] Bowde, John Barfoot

Exhibited: 12 July 1697

16   Robert Mariott   Grant of Probate: 2 November 1692   Will Ref: 7HR64
      Joiner

In the name of God amen! I Robert Mariott of Hartford in the County of Hertf[ord] Joyner being very sicke and weake but of good and perfect memory thanks be to God doe make and declare this my last Will and Testament in manner and forme following, that is to say, First I bequeath my Soule unto Almighty God my Creator and to Jesus Christ my Savior and Redeemer through whose merritts after this mortall life is ended I hope to have everlasting joy in the world to come. And for my worldly goods that God of his mercy hath lent me I give and bequeath as followeth: Imprimis I doe give and bequeath unto my brother George Mariott of Watton Stone in the County of Hertf[ord] Husbandman, all that my working tooles belonging to my trade of a Joyner. Item Whereas I bought the reversion of a Messuage or Tenement scituate in the parish of Tocester in the County of Northampton with Forty acres of Land be it more or lesse with barnes stable and Cowhouse and killhouse Orchard yard and appurtenances thereunto belonging now in the tenure of Richard Mariott of the same husbandman for and during his naturall life, I doe give and bequeath unto my brother George Mariott aforesaid and to his heires for ever after the decease of the said Richard Marriott Provided always and upon that condicon that my said brother George Marriott doe pay or cause to be paid unto my brother William Marriott the sume of twenty pounds of lawfull money of England after the decease of my father Richard Marriott, and allsoe two years more to be expired after those Legacies are paid to my brothers and Sister according to the Deeds Will of my Brother Richard Marriott. Lastly I doe make and ordaine my brother George Marriott full and sole Executrix [sic] of this my last Will and Testam[en]t. Witnes my hand and seale the one and thirtyeth day of October Anno D[omi]ni 1692. The marke of Robert Marriott Signed, Sealed, published and declared to be the last Will and Testam[en]t of the said Robert Marriott in the presence of us Zach: Feild, Roger Dancer, John Hill.

WILLS AND INVENTORIES FOR HERTFORD, 1660-1725

17 John Bach   **Grant of Probate: 9 ? 1699**   **Will Ref: 8HR73**
    Alderman   **Estate valued at: £454.18.6**

Mem[oran]dum that I John Bach one of the Aldermen of the Borough of Hertford in the County of Hertford, doe make publish and declare this to be my last Will and Testam[en]t. And I doe hereby devise and give unto my loveing wife Anne Bach all and singular my stocke of corne Graine and hay now in the barnes or on the ground belonging to my Farme at Hertingfordbury and the seale, allsoe all my household goods plate, Lennen hay Corne moneys and other things in my dwelling house, and Outhouses belonging, alsoe all other my goods and chattells whatsoever desireing her that all my debts may be paid thereout, and that she would be kind to all my children, and I doe hereby constitute and appointe my said wife full and sole executrix of this my Will and doe request my loveing friends Mr Israell Keynton, Mr William Hurrell, Mr Henry Marson and Mr Jonathan Smart jun[ior] to advise and direct my said wife in the execution of the said trust, thus revokeing all former wills by me heretofore made have hereunto sett my hand and seale this one and thirtieth day of December Anno D[omi]ni 1698. I Bach signed sealed published and declared to be the last Will and Testam[en]t of the said John Bach in the presence of us (and the seale) being first interlined. Benja[min] Wall, Mary Kingitt, Anne Potts her marke, Bos[tock] Toller

Inventory Reference: 14HW38
Date of Appraisal: 20 September 1699

A true and perfect Inventory of the Goods and Chattels of John Bache of the towne of Hertford in the County of Hertford Gentleman late deceased belonging to Anne Bache widdow relict and sole Exec[utri]x etc of the last Will and testament of the said John Bache taken and appraised by William Guise and Adlord Bowd the twentieth day of September Anno D[omi]ni 1699 as followeth and the value etc

In the Hither Garretts	one Flock bed, boulster, two blanketts, two Feather beds, two boulsters, three blanketts, two Ruggs, one Counterpaine, three bedsteds, ten dozen trenchers	03.10.00
In the undder Garretts	Two Feather beds, two boulsters, two blanketts, two Ruggs, two Setts Curtains, two bedsteads, one side cupboard, one chaire, one stool, two close stools, two other beds, boulsters, two other blanketts, Ruggs,	

35

WILLS AND INVENTORIES FOR HERTFORD, 1660-1725

	one other sett Curtains, two other bedsteads, one chaire, stand	09.00.00
In the Great Garrett	One dough trough, two Benches, Four Spinning Wheeles	
In the further painted Chamber	one bed, boulster, two pillows, one blankett, one Rugg, one sett of Curtains, one cupboard cloth, one side cupboard, one bedstead, one window curtaine, five chaires, one table, the room hung with paper	06.00.00
In the hither painted Chamber	one bed, boulster, two pillows, two blanketts, one Rugg, one Sett of Curtains, one window curtaine, one paire Andirons, five chairs, one table, one bedsted, the room hung with paper	06.00.00
In the white bedded Chamber	Two beds, two boulsters, four pillows, six blanketts, two Ruggs, two setts of curtaines, two bedsteads, four window curtains, two tables, six chaires, one paire Andirons, fyershovell, tongs, the room hung with Druggett	13.00.00
In the Gatehouse Chamber	one bed, one boulster, two pillows, two blanketts, one Rugg, one Sett of Curtains, one window Curtaine, one table, four chairs, one Bedstead	02.18.00
In the greene Roome	one Bedd, one boulster, two pillows, two Blanketts, one Rugg, one sett of Curtains, one bedstead, one window curtaine, one table, six chaires, the room hung Bayes	05.10.00
In the yellow Roome	one bed, one boulster, two pillows, three blanketts, one Quilt, one sett of curtains, one bedstead, one table, one paire Andirons,	

WILLS AND INVENTORIES FOR HERTFORD, 1660-1725

	fyershovell, tongs, one Couch, four chaires, two window curtains, one looking glasse, the room hung with yellow	11.00.00
In the Blew Roome	one bed, one boulster, two pillows, three blanketts, one Quilt, one sett of curtains, one bedstead, two window curtains, one paire Andirons, fyershovell, tongs, one looking glasse, one table, six chaires, six cussheons, the room hung with Blew	15.00.00
In the Magpy	one bed, one boulster, two pillows, three blanketts, one Quilt, two setts of curtains, one pare Andirons, fyershovell, tongs, one lookinglasse, one table, five chares, the Roome hung with Blew	02.00.00
In the ? *(stamp obliterating the word)*	one bed, one boulster, two pillows, two blanketts, one Rugg, one Counterpayn, two setts of curtains, one paire Andirons, fyershovell, tongs, one table, five chaires, the room hung with Druggett	07.10.00
In the Chamber over the Store Roome	one bed, one boulster, two pillows, three blanketts, one Quilt, two setts of curtains, one bedstead, window curtaine, one paire Andirons, fyershovell, tongs, one lokkinglasse, one table, one chest, one trunck, one chest of drawers, six chaires, three pictures, the room hung with Druggett	12.00.00
In the Chamber over the Dolphin	one bed, one boulster, two pillows, two blanketts, one Rugg, one sett of curtains, one bedstead, one trundle bedstead, one table, two chaires, one hanging presse	04.00.00

WILLS AND INVENTORIES FOR HERTFORD, 1660-1725

In the Great Roome	Four great tables, two Spanish tables, two dozen Rush Leather Chaires, two pair Andirons, two paire tongs, two Fyershovells, one large Carpett, eight sconces for candells	10.00.00
In the Parlor	one large table, one side table, ten chaires, one paire Andirons, Fyershovell, tongs, the room wainscoated	02.15.00
In the Stoor roome	Two tables, six chaires, six pictures, one paire tongs, one Stove, the iron to hang before the greate	02.00.00
In the shipp	one table, six chaires, one stove, the iron to hang before the greate, the room wainscoated half way	01.00.00
In the Dolphin	one table, one Bench, one Forme, one settle, one paire Andirons, two chaires, the room wainscoated half way	00.10.00
In the Groom	one table, Benches round the roome, wainscoated halfe way, two paire of tables	00.12.00
In the Ankor	one table, benches round the roome, wainscoated halfeway	00.02.06
In the Hall	Three tables, two settles, two Formes, one Bench wainscoated, two shelves, Five stools, Four chaires, one fyershovell, tongs, one Grate to lett asshes downe, one sconce	03.05.00
In the Barr	one Chaire, two cupboards, two shelves, thirty glasses, one Lanthorne, the Bell in the Barr	00.10.00
In the Bottle Room	one great board, twelve paire slippers, one Candlebox, five quart potts, fifteen pint potts, five halfe pint potts, one quarten pott, two Copper potts	

WILLS AND INVENTORIES FOR HERTFORD, 1660-1725

	one gallon pott, one pottlepot,	
	one large copper Tummill, two tin Tummills,	
	four tankards, four and twenty Flaggons,	
	three large white muggs, five double muggs,	
	twelve muggs, one paire of Gold scales,	
	six grose bottles, twelve cans, one Rubbinbrush,	
	two hand brushes, one scraper, one Cote Rack,	
	one Reell, two dozen custard cupps,	
	three dozen patty pans,	
	three dozen bisskett pans	28.00.00
In the Kitchin and Scullery	Forty pewter dishes, thirteen dozen plates,	
	four pye plates, one cheesplate,	
	four Rings to sett dishes on, porringers,	
	three dozen spoons, eighteen saltsellars,	
	one Bason, two monteths, two sesterns,	
	two graters, two warmingpans, two Fryinpans,	
	two Coverpans, one Fish plate, one Culinder,	
	two pasty pans, one Sawcer, one tin drippinpan,	
	one large iron and copper drippinpan,	
	one iron drippinpan, eight spitts, one Jack,	
	three weights, one sugardrawer,	
	six smoothirons, two irons, two warm plates,	
	one box iron, two sconces, one grate,	
	one fyershovell, tongs, one Fender,	
	one Grate to lett the asshes in, two racks,	
	four porridge potts, four bottles,	
	two skilletts, three saucepans, two brasse potts,	
	two skimmers, one brasse slice, one brasse ladle,	
	one saltbox, one choppinblock, one Forme,	
	one Chest, six leather chaires, four rush chaires,	
	dressers with drawers and cubords,	
	three store Frames, one large Chaffindish,	
	three gridirons, four paire bellows,	
	one Bason Rack, fifteen brasse Candlesticks,	
	tin Candlesticks, twelve iron Candlesticks,	
	one iron mortar and pestle, six crewetts,	
	one pepper box, one drudgin box, six sawcers,	
	twelve mint glasses, one lokkinglasse,	
	twelve Chamberpotts, shelves, one dresser,	
	one vessell of vinegar, one stewpan,	

WILLS AND INVENTORIES FOR HERTFORD, 1660-1725

	one bedpan, one choppin knife, one Cleaver,	
	two trencher Racks, two Racks,	
	three wooden platters six trays, six gallypotts,	
	two pipkins, six butter potts, six millk potts,	
	one Forme, two Fleshforks,	
	two paire potthooks, four pailes	33.05.00
In the Buttery	one dresser, five shelves, one dow trough,	
	three jarrs, one pouderintubb,	
	three sives, one chest, three pitchers,	
	one paire brasse scales,	
	eight brasse weights, one paire Stillyards,	
	four dozen knifes, three dozen Forks	01.10.00
In the Brewhouse	Two coppers, irons, a copper pump,	
	two tins, jack, two double coolers,	
	Frame, a wooden pump, one great Husktubb,	
	two Kimneles, one Ladder, one hopbaskett,	
	three shutes, one jett, one drink stall, lumber	42.10.00
Linnen	Forty paire sheets, two dozen pillowbers,	
	eighteen boardcloths, eliven dozen napkins,	
	twelve towells	36.00.00
In the small Beere Buttery	three hogsheads, three kilderkins,	
	two hampers, one beere stall	01.10.00
In the Wine Cellar	three stalls, eight hogsheads,	
	three halfehogsheads, eight Runletts,	
	two Strikers, two tilters, odd things,	
	Halfe an hogshead of sack,	
	two Hogsheads of Red and White port	42.10.00
In the Little Cellar	one beere stall, one Kilderkin,	
	nineteen bottles of sider	00.10.00
In the Beere Cellar	Fourteen beere Stalls, fourteen pipes,	
	fourteen Hogsheads, three halfehogsheads,	
	three small vessels, three Kinnells,	
	one beereintubb, Ten hodgsheads of stale beere,	
	four hogsheads of mild beere	37.00.00

WILLS AND INVENTORIES FOR HERTFORD, 1660-1725

	Six silver spoons, silver taster	09.00.00
	Wearing Cloths, money in his pockett	14.00.00
	two paire of pistolls	02.00.00
In the yard stable and Barn at the Seale	one ashbinn, two hoggtubbs, one Kilderkin, one Washblock, one Wheelbarrow, five great Ladders, one beerintubb, one hoggpaile, thirtyfive loads Hay, one thousand Jack Faggotts, Six Load Roundwood and blocks, twelve busshells Coal, six piggs, six busshells oates, two Ladders, Dung in the yard, one Henpen, one hogshead, Lumber	97.05.06
[Total]		454.18.06

[Appraisers]
Ad[lord] Bowde, Will[ia]m Guyse

Exhibited: 9 August 1699

**18   John Moores   Grant of Probate: 14 July 1701   Will Ref: 8HR159
        Turner**

I John Moores of Hertf[ord] in the County of Hertf[ord] Turner enjoying the mercye of health both in minde and body Doe make this my last will and Testam[en]t: in manner and forme following First and principally I comitt my soule to Allmighty God my body to the earth to be buried. And for such outward substance as I shall leave behinde me I give and dispose thereof as followeth I will that all my Debts and Funerall charges be paid and discharged. Item I give unto my loveing wife Ann Moores all my household goods whatsoever to be wholey at her dispose. Item I give unto Benjamine Smart the younger son of Benjamine Smart of Digswell in this County of Hertford Brickmaker the sume of Five pounds to be paid unto him within twelve months next after the decease of my wife. Item I give unto Thomas William and Joseph Smart sons of the aforesaid Benjamine Smart Twenty Shillings apeece to be paid to every of them within one year next after the decease of my wife. Item I give unto Elizabeth daughter of the said Benjamine Smart Twenty Shillings to be paid to her within one year next after my wifes decease. Item I give unto Ann, Susanah, Mary and Sarah, daughters of the said Benjamine Smart, the sume of Forty shillings apeece to be paid unto ev[er]y one of them within one year next after the decease of my wife. Item I bequeath unto the poore Friends belonging to Hertford meeting Five pounds to be distributed among them within three months next after my wifes decease. Item I give and bequeath five pounds to remaine in the hands of my Executors to be distributed or disposed of to any poore Ministring Friends that travells this way for the service of Truth as my Executors hereafter named shall think Fit after the decease of my wife. And allso bequeath to my wife such money as shall be in my hands att the time of my decease saveing only what will pay my Debts (if I shall owe any at my departure) and discharge the reste of my Buriall All the rest and residue of my estate and money out att use vizt the rent or income of an House with the appurtences w[hi]ch I and my wife have att Wellwyn in this County of Hertf[ord] dureing our lives to the value of Ten pounds by the year (more or lese) Taxes excepted and also Fifty pounds out att interest out of which Fifty pounds I will the legacyes above bequeathed be paid And I will after they are so paid that the remainder be equally divided betweene my two Executors hereafter named. And lastly my will is that imediately from and after my decease my Executors see after and received the yearly income of my house and money before menconed and dispose of all the same to the maintaineing of my wife and if that be not sifficient will wt also I leave my wife I desire so much of the principall money beforemenconed be called in and disburst for her as will do itt and all the legacyes before given out of it to be proporconably so much the lese. And I doe nominate and appointe John Curlis the younger of Hertford afores[ai]d Cordwainer and Williams Addams of Hertford abovenamed Tanner full and wholy joynt Exec[uto]rs of this my last will and Testam[en]t and I doe hereby utterly revoake and annull all and ev[er]y other former Testam[en]t wills and Legacys Bequests and Executors by me in any way before this time named willed and bequeathed ratifieing and confirmeing this to be my last will and Testam[en]t

In Wittnesse whereof I have hereunto sett my hand and seale this seaventeenth day of the Twelfth month called February Ann[o Domini] 1698 And in the Eleaventh year of the reigne of William the third King of England etc John Moores Testator his marke signed sealed and published pronounced and declared by the said John Moores as his last will and Testam[en]t in the presence of us John Nutting, Thomas Webb, Arthur Thomas, W[illia]m Jenkins

Inventory Reference: 91HW28
Date of Appraisal: 11 June 1701

An Inventory of the Goods and Chattles of John Moore of the parish of St Andrews Hertford deceased

WILLS AND INVENTORIES FOR HERTFORD, 1660-1725

Impr[imi]s **In the Hall**	Five stools, 6 Chaires, two Tables, one Cupboard, four dishes, one Warming pan, three sawcers, one Cup, five Iorns	01.15.00
The backroome	One bed, beding, a kneeding trough	00.15.00
The Buttery	Three Kettles, skelletts, one Table, kemnells, some other ware	01.10.00
The drinkhouse	four vessels, one kettle, a drink stall	00.10.00
Buttery Chamber	One bed, bedstead,bedding, small Chest	00.10.00
The Hall Chamber	One Bed, bedstead, Bedding, three Chests, one Box, six Chaires, linnen	04.00.00
The back Chamber	beehives, a Flaskett, Cloaths Wearing Cloaths, linnen Withoutdoores Wood, Bees	00.05.00 01.10.00 01.05.00
	Money at Interest	50.00.00
[Total]		62.10.00

[Appraisers]
John Child, the mark of William Kene

Exhibited: 14 June 1701

19   James Pendred   Grant of Probate: 13 December 1698   Will Ref: 8HR38 31
         Maltster   Estate valued at: £468.08.10

I James Pendred of Hertford in the County of Hertford Maltster being sicke and weake in body, but of sound mind and remembrance doe make this my last will and Testament in manner following. First I commit my soule to God, my body to the earth to be buried, and as for such outward substance and Estate as it hath pleased the Lord to lend me I give and dispose thereof as followeth I will that all my debts and funerall charges be paid and discharged. Item I give unto my brother John Pendred of Wotton in this County of Hertford the sume of thirty pounds to be paid unto him within six Months next after my decease by my Executors hereafter named, and whereas my said brother John hath foure Children (all whose names I cannot remember) my mind and Will is and I doe hereby give unto every one of them the sume of twenty five pounds to be paid to every one of them by my Executors hereafter named within six months next after my decease (that is) to soe many of them as shall then have accomplished the age of one and twenty years [omission in left hand margin] and to those that are younger not only at six months after my decease but as or when they shall severally have accomplished the age of one and twenty years, but if either of those foure children shall happen to dye before their Legacy or Legacies hereby given shall become due and payable, my Will is that then such Legacy or Legacies be equally divided betweene the other of my brother Johns Children who are now and shall be then liveing, but in case they should all dye before their Legacies become due, then their Legacies hereby given to be equally divided betweene my three brothers John, Robert and Samuell Pendred or betweene soe many of them as shall be than liveing. Item I give and bequeath unto my brother Robert Pendred of Datcher als[o known as] Datchworth in this County of Hertford the sume of Forty pounds to be paid to him by my Executors within six months next after my decease, and whereas his my said brother Robert alsoe alsoe [sic] hath foure Children (all whose names I cannot justly nominate) I give unto every one of them the sume of twenty five pounds to be paid to every one of them by my Executors within six months next after my decease if they shall then have accomplished the age of one and twenty years, and to them that have not as soone as they shall have attained unto the said age of one and twenty years and if either of them dye before their Legacy or Legacys hereby given shall become due, then such Legacy or Legacys to be equally divided betweene the other of my brother Roberts Children who are now and shall be then liveing, or if all dye, then to be divided betweene my brothers afores[ai]d or betweene soe many of them as shall be then liveing. Item I give and bequeath unto my brother Samuell Pendred of Burralls Greene in the parish of Sacombe and County of Hertford the sume of twenty pounds to be paid to him within six months next after my decease by my Executors hereafter named. Item I give and bequeath unto the three children of my brother William Pendred deceased (late of Hatfeild in this County of Hertford) the like sume of twenty five pounds to be paid to every one of them within six months next after my decease if they shall then have accomplished the age of one and twenty years, if not then to be paid to every one of them severally soe soone as they shall have accomplished that age, but if either of them dye before their Legacy or Legacies hereby given shall become due and payable, then such Legacy or Legacys to be equally divided betweene the survivors of them, or if all dye, then to be equally divided betweene my three brothers aforesaid or among soe many of them as shall be then liveing. Item I give and bequeath unto Elizabeth the wife of Humphry Brittain of Barnet the sume of ten pounds to be paid unto her within six months next after my decease. Item I give and bequeath unto the poore friends belonging to the meeting at Hertford the sume of ten pounds to be paid unto them within one Month next after my decease, And I appointe

WILLS AND INVENTORIES FOR HERTFORD, 1660-1725

Richard Thomas, John Stout, Henry Sweeting and Henry Marson to distribute the same amongst them. Item I give and bequeath unto John Child of Hertford Maultster the sume of five pounds to be paid to him within six months next after my decease. Item I give and bequeath unto the poore Widows belonging St. Johns parish soe called in Hertford the sume of twenty shillings to be paid to them within one Month next after my decease. All the rest and residue of my personall Estate goods and Chattells whatsoever I give and bequeath unto my brother John Pendred of Wotton and John Child of Hertford Malster joyn Executors of this my last Will and Testament, and I doe hereby revoke disannull and make voyd all former Wills and Testaments by me heretofore made. And whereas I give unto the foure Children of my brother John to the foure Children of my brother Robert, and to the three children of my brother William deceased the sume of twenty five pounds a peice to be paid as abovesaid (I not knowing all their names) desire all their names may be taken as soone as may be and set downe in this my last Will and Testament in the presence of the Winesses hereunto, And Lastly whereas the Legacies of severall of these my brothers Children will remaine in the Executors hands dureing their minority I desire that the Income or Interest of the said Legacies soe remaining shall be rendred and paid unto every one of them not exceeding the rate of foure pounds per Cent per annum Interest. In Witnesse hereof I the said James Pendred to this my last Will and Testam[en]t have set my hand and seale the one and thirtieth day of the eighth Month Anno D[omi]ni 1698 and in the tenth yeare of the reigne of King William the third over England etc James Pendred his marke. Signed sealed published and declared by the said James Pendred as his last Will and Testament in the presence of us W[illia]m Jenkins, Thomas Kemson his marke, Sarah Sibley.

John Pendreds Children, Edmund, James, Samuell, Joseph Brother Roberts Children, William, Mary, James, Elizabeth Brother Williams Children, Mary, William, Elizabeth

Inventory Reference: 104HW84
Date of Appraisal: 24 November 1698

An Inventory of the Goods Chattells and Creditts etc of James Pendred of the Parish of St Johns Hertford Maltster deceased as followes viz

Barley	277.17.06
his part of the Kilnewire	02.00.00
his part of the Faggotts	07.00.00
his part of the Maltdust	00.15.00
Debts outstanding etc	180.16.04
[Total]	**468.08.10**

WILLS AND INVENTORIES FOR HERTFORD, 1660-1725

Debts [owing by testator to be debited from estate]

Owing for Barley	debit	10.00.00
Owing to Liddy Draper	debit	10.00.00
[Total debit]		**20.00.00**
[Total]		**448.08.10**

In all (when the Debts which were owing are paid, and the Debts outstanding are received, there remaines Foure hundred fourty eight Pounds eight shillings and tenne Pence)

[Appraisers]
Peter Crook, John Stout

Exhibited: 13 December 1698

20   John Randall   Grant of Probate: 4 June 1701   Will Ref: 8HR168
       Mealman

In the Name of God Amen. I John Randall of the parish of St Johns in the County of Hertf[ord] Mealman being sick and weake in body but of sound minde and memory (praised by Allmighty God for the same) Doe make Publish and declare this my last Will and Testam[en]t in manner and forme following. Impr[imi]s I comend my soule into the hands of Allmighty God my Creator hopeing through the Merritts of my Saviour Jesus Christ to receive remission. And as for the worldly estate w[hi]ch it hath pleased God to blesse me withall I give devise and dispose thereof as followeth (that is to say) I give unto my loveing Sister Ann Randall of Pulloxhill in the County of Bedford Spinster the sume of Fifty and five pounds to be paid her by my Exec[uto]r hereafter named within six moneths after my decease. Item I give unto Elizabeth, Ann and Mary the Three children of my sister Elizabeth, the wife of John Stoakes, the sume of Five pounds apeece to be paid them at their sev[er]all ages of Eighteene years by my Exec[uto]r in manner following (that is to say) Twenty Shillings every year till the same be fully paid. Item I give unto my Cozen Thomas Randall Son of Samuell Randall the sume of one hundred pounds to be paid when he shall attaine the age of one and twenty yeares. Item all other my Goods chattells jewells plate and money whatsoever not hereinbefore bequeathed I give and bequeath the same unto the said Samuell Randall my brother. And I doe hereby make nominate ordaine constitute and appointe my said brother Samuell Randall sole Executor of this my last will hereby

46

WILLS AND INVENTORIES FOR HERTFORD, 1660-1725

revoakeing all wills by me formerly made I doe publish and declare this to be my last Will and Testament

In Wittnesse whereof I have hereunto sett my hand and seale this six and twentieth day of May Anno D[omi]ni 1701 The marke of John Randall Signed, sealed, published and declared to be the last will and Testam[en]t of the said John Randall in the presence of Jonathan Smith, the marke of James Berry, W[illia]m Browne

Inventory Reference: 111HW98
Date of Appraisal: 3 June 1701

A True and perfect Inventory of all the Goods and chattels of John Randall of the parrish of Saint Johns in Hertford, Batchelor, Late Deceased, the twentie sixt day of May in the yeare of our Lord God 1701 made and Apraised by us whose names are under written the Third day of June 1701,

	Purs, Apparrell	15.00.00
in the flower shop	one flower mill with cloths, Bushellment	15.00.00
in the wheat shop	one screen, weights, scailes, Bushellment	02.00.00
in the Bran shop	Bran fine and course	03.00.00
	one horse, bridle, saddle	05.00.00
	Hay	00.15.00
[Total]		**40.15.00**

[Appraisers]
Jonathan Smith, George Hodgson

Exhibited: 4 June 1701

21   John Richardson   Grant of Probate: 13 January 1699 /70   Will Ref: 8HR87
       Yeoman   Estate valued at: £577.08.06

Mem[oran]dum that I John Richardson of Brickendonbury in the County of Hertford doe make and publish this to be my last Will and Testament, and doe revoke and make voyd all other Wills, and I doe hereby give and bequeath unto my loveing wife Mary all my goods and Chattells whatsoever and I desire her to pay my debts and funerall

WILLS AND INVENTORIES FOR HERTFORD, 1660-1725

charges and to be kind to my Children. And I doe make my loveing wife sole Executrix of this my last Will. Witnesse my hand and seale this foure and twentieth day of June Anno D[omi]ni 1699 John Richardson Signed, sealed, published and declared to be the last Will and Testam[en]t of the said John Richardson in the presence of us, Joseph Marshall, James Scigges his marke, Thomas Richardson

Inventory Reference: 111HW96
Date of Appraisal: 31 July 1699

An Inventory and appraisement of the goods and Chattles of John Richardson in the liberty of Brickendon in the parrish of all saints in the county of heartford yeoman deceased taken this 31 day of July 1699

Inprimis in the kitchin	goods that are in it	06.10.00
	goods in the hall	04.00.00
	goods in the parlour	06.00.00
	goods in the brew house	06.02.00
	goods in the litle buttery	03.05.00
	goods in the quarn house	05.00.00
	goods in the seller	01.18.00
	goods in the milk houss	02.13.06
	goods in the cheespress houss	01.10.00
	goods in the pantry	00.15.00
	goods in the chamber over the parlour	13.00.00
	goods in the Read chamber	16.00.00
	goods in the chamber over the hall	03.03.06
	goods in the chamber over the bin houss	12.10.00
	goods in the chamber over the kiching	24.06.00
	goods in the chamber over the quarn houss	18.07.00
	goods in the garrots	16.02.06
	fyer wood	09.18.00
	carts and waggins	18.03.00
	plows and harrows	06.10.00
	hay	34.00.00
	forks, a ladder	00.03.00
	cow cribs	00.17.06
	a fork, a shovell	00.01.06
	a horss and harniss	36.00.00
	cows and bullocks	43.10.00
	laders, troues, grinstone	00.19.00
	hoggs, piggs	10.00.00
	wheat	73.00.00

WILLS AND INVENTORIES FOR HERTFORD, 1660-1725

barly	111.05.00
oates, peass, tearss	87.00.00
waring apparill, money in purss	05.00.00
[Total]	**577.08.06**

[Appraisers]
John Palmer, Josiah Hale

Exhibited: 13 January 1699/70

22 Will[iam] Catlin   Grant of Probate: 1 March 1700   Will Ref: 8HR136
   Yeoman   Estate valued at: £781.00.00

In the Name of God Amen. I William Cattlin of Ducketts in the p[ar]ish of St Johns Hertf[ord] in the County of Hertf[ord] Yeom[an] being ancient and crazy in body but in sound minde memory and understanding (praised be Allmighty God for the same) Doe make publish and declare this my last will and testam[en]t in manner and forme following (that is to say) Impr[imi]s I comend my soule into the hands of the Eternall God stedfastly beleiveing that through the Merritts of his son and my Saviour Jesus Christ I shall receive remission of all my sins. And as for the Temporall Estate which it hath pleased God to endue me with I bequeath give and dispose of the same as Followth. Impri[mi]s whereas my daughter Mary now the wife of William Hawkins of the Towne of Hertford Pattenmaker and formerly the wife of one James Runninton Did dureing her widowhood to witt the sixth day of November 1690 by the name of Mary Runnington widow Surrender Certaine Copyhold Messuages or tenem[en]ts holden of the Mannor of Brickendon to me the said William Cattlin and my heirs upon Condicon that she should pay to me the sume of one hundred and sixty pounds with interest att such days times and place as are menconed in the said recited surrender as by the said surrender more att large may appeare Twenty pounds, part of which said money I doe acknowledge my selfe satisfied from my said daughter Mary. That soe there then remaines due to me only the sume of one hundred and forty pounds. I doe therefore give and bequeath unto my said daughter Mary Hawkins the sume of one hundred pounds part of the sume of one hundred and forty pounds which she now owes me upon the surrendeer aforesaid to be paid and allowed unto her by my Exec[uto]r hereafter named within two months next after the decease of Mary my loveing wife and not sooner in case she shall happen to survive and overlive me the s[ai]d William Cattlin. And I doe desire and my will and meaneing is that the said one hundred poundes part of the s[ai]d one hundred and forty pounds be continued and doe remaine in the hands of my s[ai]d daughter Mary Hawkins upon the surrender aforesaid as a security for the same Provided that she my said daughter doe pay or cause to be p[ai]d to my Execr hereafter named the sume of Five pounds ev[er]y year by equall quarterly paym[en]ts for and dureing the naturall life of the s[ai]d Mary my loveing wife. The first paym[en]t to begin and be made on the next usuall or genrall quarter day after my decease To be for and towards the provision and maintenance of the s[ai]d Mary my wife. Item I give and bequeath unto the five children of my s[ai]d daughter Mary Hawkins to witt Mary Runnington, Henry Runnington, Sarah Runnington, Melitabell Runnington and Elizabeth Hawkins the sume of Twenty shillings apeece to be paid to them by my executors hereafter named within two yeares next after my decease But in case any of them shall depart this life before the s[ai]d time of paym[en]t Then the said sume or sumes of money intended to be paid as afores[ai]d to him her or them soe dyeing shall goe to and be equally divided amongst the survivors of them. Item I give and bequeath unto the seaven Children of my daughter Alice, the wife of William Poole of Ducketts afores[ai]d yeom[an], to witt to Mary Poole, Alice Poole, Ann poole, William Poole, John Poole, Susan Poole and Richard Poole the sume of Twenty Shillings apeece to be p[ai]d to them by my Exec[uto]r hereafter named within two yeares next after my decease but in case any of them shall happen to depart this life before the said time of paym[en]t then the s[ai]d sume or sumes of money intended to be paid as afores[ai]d to him her or them soe dyeing shall goe to and be equally divided amongst the survivors of them. Item I give and bequeath unto my Son in Law Thomas Pavett of Naseing in the County of Essex and to my Grandaughter Mary Pavett the daughter of the s[ai]d Thomas the sume of Twenty Shillings apeece to be paid to them by my Exec[uto]r hereafter named within two yeares next after my decease but in case either of them shall depart this life before the s[ai]d time of paym[en]t then the sume of sumes of money intended to be paid as aforesaid to him or her soe dyeing shall goe to and be paid to the survi[v]our of them. Item I doe earnestly desire and request my Son in Law William Poole to take care and provide for my loveing wife Mary with all convenient and decent necessarys which she shall have att any time hereafter any occasion or need for, for and dureing soe long time as she shall happen to live. And in consideracon thereof I doe give and bequeath unto my said Son in Law William Poole all my goods moneys debts and Chattells and psonall estate whatsoever not herein before bequeathed and given. And I doe make constitute and appointe him the said William Poole sole executor of this my last Will and Testam[en]t thus revoakeing all former wills by me heretofore made, I doe hereby publish and declare this to be my last will and testam[en]t. In Wittnesse whereof I the s[ai]d William Catlin have hereunto sett my hand and seale the fourth day of May in the fifth year of the reigne of our Soveigne Lord and Lady William and Mary by the grace of God of England Scotland France and Ireland King and Queene Defenders of the Faith etc Anno D[omi]ni 1693 [the words 'the marke' are then crossed out] William Cattlin his mark signed, sealed, published and declared to be the last will and Testam[en]t of the s[ai]d William Cattlin in the presence of us James Beecher, Bos[tock] Toller, William Browne

WILLS AND INVENTORIES FOR HERTFORD, 1660-1725

23 Joseph Saward   Grant of Probate: 10 December 1709 Will Ref: 10HR27
     Yeoman   Estate valued at: £665.12.00

In the name of God Amen. I Joseph Saward the Elder of the parrish of AlSaints Hertford in the County of Hertford due make declare and ordain this my last will and testament in manner and forme folloing. Imprimis I give and bequeath unto my Dafter Ann Saward and to hur heirs for ever All that my Messuage or tenement with all the appurtenances thereunto belonging which is now in the Tennor and occopation of James Clapham knowen and called by the name of blackefeild or otherways Great and Little blackfeild containing by estemation twenty acres more or less. And also All that my Close of land called the Grove bought of William Collins containing by estemation fouer acres. And also All those my three closes or feilds of arable land which I latly bought of Richard Lawson knowen and called by the name of the underwood containing sixten acres which said fouer lastmentioned feilds and also in the tennor and occopation of James Clapham and all are lying and being in the parrish of St Johns Hertford in the County of Hertford. Secondly I give and bequeath unto my son William Saward and his heaires for ever All that my two closes or feilds of arable Land called and knowen by the name of Allings containing by estemation eaight acres which I latly bought of Phillip Bridgman. And also All that my feild or those of ground called Sprats feild which is latly devided into two feilds and both the two fields containe by estemation nyne acres. And also All that my Close or feild of arable land knowen and called by the name of Edwards Lands containing by estemation five acres And also All them my three fields of arable Land which I latly bought of Richard Lawson two of them are knowen or called by the name of Peas Croft or Peas feilds containing by estimation nyne acres the other feild is knowen and called by the name of Wilkins feild containing by estemation four acres all which Lands and premeses are in the Tennor and occopation of mee Jos[eph] Saward the elder and Thomas Spencer and are lying and being in the parish of St Johns Hertford in the County of Hertford. And also further I give unto my said William Saward All my wright and title to the house barne yard and outhouses with all the appurtenances therunto belonging with two p[ar]cels of Land all which are in the Tennor and occopation of Thomas Spencer and which I hold by Lease from my Cozen Elezebeth Dawes duering hur life, but the Revertion therof belongeth to my said son William Saward after the death of the said Elezebeth Dawes. Thirdly I give and bequeath to my said daughter Sarah Saward the sum of four hundred pounds of good and lawfull money of Great Britain to be paid unto hur one yeare after my decease by my son Joseph Saward out of the Lands and tenements free and Coppi which I shall hearin give and bequeath to my son Joseph Saward. And my son Joseph Saward shall pay my daughter Sarah Saward Intrest for the said four hundred pounds for the first year after my decease tell the principall becomes payable not exceding five pounds in the hundred. Fourthly I give and bequeath unto my loving wife all the furneture or goods in any one of the upper roomes of my house she shall have the Liberty to chouse which roome she will. Fifthly I give and bequeath unto my cosen Elizabeth Whittaker five pounds to be paid her within one year after my decease by my son William Saward out of the lands and tenements which I have given to my son William Saward, but if it shall so happen that shee shall be dead before this gift becoms payable then this gift shall be void and of no effect to hur heirs or executors. Sixthly I give and bequeath unto my son Joseph Saward and to heirs for ever All the rest and resedue of my Lands both free and Coppi which I have not before in this my will given and desposed of to som of my children nevertheless it is my mind and will that all the Lands and tenements herby given to my son Joseph Saward shall be chargable with the payment of the abovesaid four hundred pounds to my Daughter Saward. Lastly I nomenate and appointe my said Son Joseph Saward my whole and Sole Executor of this my Last Will and testament to whom I give all my goods and chattels or personall estate which I have not before in this my will disposed of to pay my debts and to discharge my funerall charges. In Witness hearof I have set to my hand and seale this Twenty third day of December In the year of our Lord God one thousen Seven hundred and Eaight. Joseph Saward. Signed, sealed, published and declared to be my last will and testement in the presents of the underwrighten Jonas Thurrowgood, Henry Harbutt Yungar, George Nash junor, the mark of Sarah Thurrowgood, the wife of Jonas Thurrowgood.

Inventory Reference: 122HW11
Date of Appraisal: 29 November 1709

November, the 29th 1709 A True Inventory of the Goods and Chattles of Mr Ioseph Sawerd of Late, decased in the Libberty of Brickendon in the Parish of All Saints, Hertford, in the County of Hertford, aforesaid. Valued or Appraised by Iohn Palmer and Daniell Nash as followeth

Imprimis The Goods in the Dwelling hous

In the Parler	2 Tables	01.08.00
	A looking glass, 17 Chaiers, severall other things	06.01.00
In the Hall	2 Tables, stools, 8 Chares	01.02.00
	A Clock, a Iack, a Looking glass, severall other things	04.14.00
In the Kitchin, and Brewhous	Pewter, Brass	16.00.00
	A Iack, a powdering trough, Spits, Brewing vessels, severall other things	10.10.00

WILLS AND INVENTORIES FOR HERTFORD, 1660-1725

In the Sellers	Hogheads, Barrels, Bottles, several other goods	11.15.00
In the Darrey	2 Cherns, a Stan, a Cheestub, Milkvessils, a Cheespres, som other things	05.04.00
In the Clossets	Plate, Books, som other things	24.07.00
In the Hall Chamber	A Beadsted, Curtains, valants, beding	12.00.00
	Linnin	20.00.00
	a Chest, Chairs, som other things	02.16.00
In the Kitchin, Darrey, Chambers	2 Beadsteds, Curtains, beading to them, a Looking glass, 2 Chests, som other things	13.05.00
In the Garrits	4 Beadstids, Beading to them, severall other things	22.10.00
	the Armes	05.00.00
	wearring Apparill, pockit money	25.00.00
In the Yard and Outhouse	6 Horses, 4 Cows, 4 Hogs	33.04.00
	firniture for the Horses, a Waggon, 3 Carts	30.03.00
	Plows, Harrows, Dragrakes, Ladders, Wood, Bricks, Rouls, Straw, Hame, Grass seed, Plowtimber, severall other things	61.11.00
In the Barns	Wheate	128.00.00
	Barly	72.00.00
	Ooats, Peas	61.06.08
	Chaff, Hay	19.03.04
In the Feelds	Tilage and dunging	53.12.00
	Debts good and Bad	25.00.00
[Total]		**665.12.00**

[Appraisers]
Dan[iel] Nashe, John Palmer

Exhibited: 10 December 1709

WILLS AND INVENTORIES FOR HERTFORD, 1660-1725

24   Daniel Smith   Grant of Probate: 3 July 1712   Will Ref: 10HR149
     Baker   Estate valued at: £291.06.00

In the name of God Amen. I Daniell Smith of the Town of Hertford in the County of Hertford Baker being of sound mind memory and understanding (I praise God) though indisposed in body, doe make publish and declare this my Last will and Testament in maner following (vizt) Impr[imi]s I resign my Soule into the hands of my heavenly Creator assuredly trusting to receive remission of my sinns through the meritts, death and passion of his sonn and my blessed Redeemer. And my body I comitt to the Earth to be decently buried as near my Brother Thomas as may be in All S[ain]ts parish Church hertford with such charge and expence as my Hon[oure]d Mother and all my sisters (or the greatest part of them) shall think fitt and direct. And I do of this my Will nominate constitute and appoint my said Mother Martha Smith and my Sister Martha Smith to be Joint Executrices. Item as to the temporall Estate with which it has pleased the Almighty to bless me, I give devise bequeath and dispose thereof as follows (vizt): My will and meaning is, And I do hereby order, that my said Executrices do in the first place pay of and discharge all my debts and funerall charges out of my personall estate. Item I doe hereby give and devise All that my Mesuage or Tenem[en]ts Scituate and being in the po[se]ssion of William Bucket Woollstapler, his Assignes or Undertenants, between a lane leading into Porthill feilds and the Queens Highway Leading from Cowbridge to Porthill. Also All that Close or Feild of ground thereto adjoining and belonging now in my occupacon lying between the said house, Queens Highway Porthill feilds and the Quakers burying place, together with all the houses, outhouses, barns, stables, yards, gardens, orchards, priviledges, advantages and app[ur]tences w[ha]tsoever to the same belonging unto my Sister Anne Smith and to the heirs of her body Lawfully begotten. And for want of such Issue unto my Sister Martha Smith and to the heirs of her body Lawfully begotten, And for want of such Issue to my sister Mary Smith and to the heirs of her body Lawfully begotten, And for want of such Issue to my Sister Sarah Smith and to the heirs of her body Lawfully begotten, And for want of such Issue To my Sister Elizabeth Hillock and to the heirs of her body Lawfully begotten or to be begotten for ever And I doe hereby earnestly charge desire and entreate all and every of my said Sisters not to act or doe any thing with intent to defeat or destroy this my devise, but that they do permitt and suffer the said premisses to be held occupied and enjoyed pursuant to the true awaiting of this my Will. Item I give unto Joseph Hillock Sonn of my sister Elizabeth Hillock the sume of tenn pounds to be paid unto him by my said executors at the age of one and twenty yeares. And I do hereby Order my said Exectors that they putt place and continue out at interest the said tenn pounds on some good Security or Securitys untill such time as the said mony shall become payable And the interest, proceed and profitt thereof pay and apply towards his educacon, bringing up and maintenance. And In case the said Joseph Hillock shall happen to dye before the age of one and twenty yeares, Then I do give the said tenn pounds with all interest for the same which shall be then due and unpaid and applyed to the s[ai]d Joseph Hillock unto and amongst all my beforenamed Sisters and to their respective Executors, Adm[inistrato]rs and assignes equally to be devided between them share and share alike. Item I give unto my S[ai]d Mother Martha Smith and Uncle Mr Benjamine Turner and to each of them a broad peice of Gold of the value of three and twenty shillings and six pence a peece. Item all other my goods stock of all sorts ready mony at interest or on Securities, chattles and personall Estate whatsoever I give and devise unto all and every my beforenamed sisters Mary, Martha, Sarah and Anne Smith and Elizabeth Hillock and to their respective Exec[uto]rs Adm[inistrato]rs and assignes equally to be divided between them share and share alike, And my will and meaning is that such part of my personall estate and Effects which I have not at present by me shall be gott in with all convenient Speed and paid and divided between all my said sisters within twelve months at the furthest next after my decease. Item I doe appoint my said Uncle Mr Benjamin Turner to be overseer of this my Will and desire him to advise and direct my said Exec[uto]rs in all things relateing thereto, And that they would take his directons therein. Thus revokeing all former Wills by me heretofore made, I the said Daniel Smith have hereunto set my hand and seale this sixteenth day of May in the eleaventh yeare of the reigne of our Sovereign Lady Anne over Great Britain etc Queen Anno D[omi]ni 1712. Daniell Smith. Signed, sealed, published and declared by the said Dan[ie]ll Smith to be his Last Will and Testam[en]t in the presence of us who have subscribed our names in his presence: Joshua Downes, Bos[tock] Toller, Edw[ard] Heath

Inventory Reference: 122HW32
Date of Appraisal: 26 June 1712

An Inventory of all and singler the goods and Chattells of Daniel Smith late of the towne of Hartford in the County of Hartford, Baker Deceased, taken and Vallued and Appraised the twenty sixth day of June in the eleventh year of the Reign of Queen Ann, Over Great Brittan France and Ireland, Anno Dom[ini], one thousand seven Hundred and twelve, by James Browne and Joseph Barfoot as followeth viz

Mault in a shop	30.00.00
Oates in a shop	22.10.00
money due uppon bills and depts	56.19.06
money in hand	168.16.06
Wareing Apparrell	05.00.00

[Total] **291.06.00**

Appraised by us whose names are hereunto affixed
James Browne, Joseph Barfoot

Exhibited 3 July 1712

WILLS AND INVENTORIES FOR HERTFORD, 1660-1725

25   John Babb   Grant of Probate: 7 April 1725   Will Ref: 12HR67
       Mealman

In the name of God Amen. I John Babb of the Town of Hertford in the County of Hertford Mealman being of sound mind and memory, praised be God for the same, Do make this my last will and testament in manner and form following. Imprimis after all my Debts and funeral Expences are first paid and discharged, I Give Devise and Bequeath all my Goods Chattells reale and personal Estate of What kind or nature soever (an Inventory of my said Goods being annexed unto this my Will) unto my Daughter Sarah Bowd of Hertford afores[ai]d, widdow, for and during the terme of her natural life. And after her Decease I Give Devise and Bequeath the same Goods Chattells reale and personal Estate unto Sarah Bowd, Lidia Bowd, Susannah Bowd, Daniel Bowd, John Bowd and Ann Bowd, children of my said Daughter Sarah Bowd, to be equally divided between them Share and Share alike, Each of them to take and receive their respective Share when they Shall attain to their respective ages of one and twenty years. And if any of them dye before they come to the age aforesaid, then the share and proporcon of him or her so dying before that time to be equally divided between the remainder of them. Item I do hereby nominate and appoint my said Daughter Sarah Bowd and my loveing friend James Man of Hertford aforesaid, Brasier, Executors of this my last will and testament. And I do hereby intreat and desire my said Executor James Man to See this my last will duly performed. And I do give unto the said James Man the Sum of Five pounds for his trouble therein. And I do hereby utterly release and make void all former Wills by me heretofore made or declared. In Witness whereof I the said John Babb have hereunto set my hand and seal this first day of June in the ninth year of the Reign of our Soveraign Lord George By the Grace of God of Great Britain, France and King, Defender of the Faith etc Anno D[omi]ni 1723. John Babb Signed, Sealed, delivered, published and declared by me the abovenamed John Babb as my last will and testament in the presence of those whose names are underwritten and Subscribed by them in the presence of me the said Testator, John Stout, Susana Holte, Fran[cis] Feilde

Inventory Reference: 12HR67
Date of Appraisal: 7 April 1725

An Inventory of the Goods of John Babb of Hertford Mealman

Pooles Annotacons two Vollumes, Ar[thu]r Perkins Works three Vollumes, a Great Old Bible, 40 Bookes, a Wainscott Box in my Closett, two Gold Rings in the box, two Silver Spoons, Silver Tea Spoon

WILLS AND INVENTORIES FOR HERTFORD, 1660-1725

In the Chamber　　　One Chest, one Clock and Case,
where I lye　　　　　a Chest of Drawers,
　　　　　　　　　　　my Bed blanketts and Rugg,
　　　　　　　　　　　Feather Bed, Curtains and Vallance

In the Kitchen above　a Fire Shovel, tongs, Warming Pan,
　　　　　　　　　　　a Nest of Drawers, little Table,
　　　　　　　　　　　Two New holland Shirts

In the Garret　　　　One Chest of Drawers, Feather Bed
　　　　　　　　　　　a Breadth being added to it, a halfe Bed

In the little Garret　Flock Bed and Bedding where the maid lyes

In the lower Kitchen　One Great Brass Kettle, a Dish Kettle,
　　　　　　　　　　　Seven pewter Dishes, fifteen plates,
　　　　　　　　　　　a pull up Jack and Spitt, two dripping panns,
　　　　　　　　　　　a Frying pan, Gridirons, two brass porridge potts,
　　　　　　　　　　　a Wind up Jack and Waites,
　　　　　　　　　　　One Skillet at M[istres]s Crows

In the Shop　　　　　One Counter, a Binn, Tinn Scales and Beame,
　　　　　　　　　　　and all sorts of Small waites and measures

at the Mill　　　　　my Horse, All my Wood, Hay, All Sorts of Corn,
　　　　　　　　　　　a Screene, Great Scales and Beam,
　　　　　　　　　　　All my Waites and Bushell and Small Measures,
　　　　　　　　　　　Sacks in the Millhouse, Copper Mashing Fatt,
　　　　　　　　　　　Coolers, two Cooling tubs, four Kilderkins,
　　　　　　　　　　　Brass paile, Scimer

　　　　　　　　　　　(no money values were provided for this inventory)

26　Josiah Adams　　Date of Appraisal: 27 Sept 1690
　　　　　　　　　　　Inventory Ref: H22-41

Ann Addams Invintary [of] Josiahs Goods appraisers, the 27th of Sept 1690, Rob[er]t Smith and John Humberstone Lawfull Appraisers

　　　　　　　　　　Sold to Georg Cater goods which come to　　　07.10.00

WILLS AND INVENTORIES FOR HERTFORD, 1660-1725

his wareing Clothes	04.00.00
The bed	03.00.00
The flock bed	01.00.00
One Chest, table	01.00.00
One table and chares	00.10.00
[Total]	**17.00.00**

[Appraisers]
Robert Smith, John Humberstone

27 Mary Barber Date of Appraisal: 13 June 1662
    Widow   Inventory Ref: H22-137

The originall Inventory of the goods of Mary Barber of Hartford
Inv[entory] t[he] 13 June 1662

A tru and parfict Inventarey of All the Goods of Marey Barbor Leate of Hartford Widow deceased taken by us whose neames are under writen this 13 of Anno 1662

2 fether beds, one bollster, 3 pillowes, 4 blanckets, 2 coverlids	04.00.00
a chest with linen in it	01.00.00
A trunck with hur wareing linen in it	01.00.00
the rest of hur waring aparill	04.00.00
redy mony	05.00.00
[Total]	**15.00.00**

[Appraisers]
Will Carter, Isaac Heath

28 William Bennett Date of Appraisal: 16 Oct 1704
    Currier   Inventory Ref: H22-171

A true and perfect Inventory of all and singular the Goods, Chattells, Implements, houshold stuff and things in and belonging to the dwelling house of William Bennet Currier of Hertford lately deceased taken and appraised by us whose names are hereunto subscribed the sixteenth day of October 1704

WILLS AND INVENTORIES FOR HERTFORD, 1660-1725

Imprimis **In the hall**	one press Cubboard, 2 tables, 2 skilletts, a Warming pann, brass Mortar and pestle, one chafeing dish, one Jackwaite, 2 spits, one dripping pann, 2 brass Candelsticks, 2 iron Skewers, one brass Skimmer, one pyeboard, one brass Ladle, one pewter quart pot, five chaires, 5 stooles, 2 potthangers, one iron pair Andirons, 2 pair Tonggs, one fireshovel, 2 Cushings, one pair of Bellows, 20 peeces of Earthen Ware, 3 Fryer Candlestiks, and other odd things	04.00.09
In the Buttery	2 porridge Potts with Covers, 2 skilletts, one Kettle, 2 brass Ladles, a pair of brass Seales, 2 brass Saucepanns, brass fryer, 2 brass pudding panns, one powdering tubb, one dripping pann, 2 tinn pudding panns, one Colleder, one Iron frying pann, 7 pewter dishes, 2 Sarvers, one Candlebox, 2 Dozen Trenikers, 5 Glass bottells, 100 peices of Earthen Ware, 3 formes, one Flower Tubb, one bason, one Gridiron, one box Iron, 3 beakers	02.12.04
Item in the Shop	2 Boards, one Tubb of Lamblack, one Lanthorne, 2 brass basons, pine blockbeam, one Strawe form	00.13.06
Item in the **Best Chamber**	one Beddstead, Corde, Straw bedd, Curtaines, Vallens, Rodds, tes terehead Cloth, one Feather bedd, bolster, 2 pillows, 2 blanckets, one Rugg, one Chest, one box, 2 tables, one stoole, one Cupboard, 3 chaires, one pair of bellows, one pair of Tonggs, one fireshovel, a pair of Doggs, 2 Window Curtains and Rodds	07.07.00

WILLS AND INVENTORIES FOR HERTFORD, 1660-1725

Item in the Maids Chamber	One Beddstead, Corde, Matt, Curtains and Vallens, Rodds, one flock bed, feather bedd, bolster, 3 pillows, one Rugg, one Trundlebeddstead, one Flock bedd, one bolster, 2 Blanckets, one Rugg, 2 Chests, one Cupboard, 4 Chaires, and other odd things Vallued all at	05.13.00
Item In the Garrett	2 Beddsteads, 2 Cordes, 2 Straw bedds, one flock bedd, 2 bolsters, 2 blanckets, one Coverledd, 2 Chests, 2 Hairlines?, 2 Flaskets, one Clock	03.00.06
Item In Linnen	6 pair sheets, 6 pair pillowbeers, 6 Table Clothes, one Dozen Napkins, one Dozen Towells	04.05.00
Item In the Wash House	one Copper Cover, 2 Kittles, Tubbs, one Wheelbarrow, one Shovel, and other odd things	03.10.00
Item In the back Shop	3 boards, 2 Chests, 5 Strawes, 2 beams	01.10.00
Item In the other Shop	one Dresser, one Iron Kettell, 5 Kilderkin, 3 Stalls, 6 oyle vessells, One Horspenn, One Bricking Tubb, one pine block, 2 Ladders, Settells, a parcell of Hay, one Hoggshead of Oyle, 30 Hides, one Down and half of Skinns, 2 pattyhides, 2 Collermakers hides, one Tubb of Vargis, One horse, 5 loades of Wood, one Hogg	35.07.06
	In Wareing Apparell	03.00.00
	In Good and badd Debts	53.00.00
[Total]		**123.19.07**

[Appraisers]
Will[ia]m Guyse, Will Smitheman

Exhibited: 20 October 1704

WILLS AND INVENTORIES FOR HERTFORD, 1660-1725

29 George Boyce   **Date of Appraisal: 6 May 1703**
   Plumber and Glazier   **Inventory Ref: H22-168**

Inventory of the goods and Chattells of George Boyce of Hartford in the County of Hertf[or]d, Plomer and glasier, lately deceased taken the Sixth day of May Anno D[omi]ni 1703

In the hall	Severall goods	01.07.00
In the Forchamber	Severall goods	01.19.08
In the best Chamber	Severall goods	04.09.02
In the Garrett	It[em] Severall goods	02.00.00
In the Shopp	Severall goods	04.00.00
	Wearing Cloaths	02.00.00
	Saperat and desperat debts	02.00.00
	Ready money	02.00.00
[Total]		19.09.10

Those goods now valued and aprised the dates First above written by us John Hill, John Gurney

Exhibited: 8 May 1703

30 Benjamin Bradney   **Date of Appraisal: 23 Feb 1664**
                Inventory Ref: H22-141

A true and perfect Inventory of the goods of Baniamin Bradney of Hartford in the County of Hartford lately deceased taken by us whose names are underwritten

Imp[rimis]		
in the hall and buttery	in pewter	02.10.00
	one brasse Kittle, one warming pan, and other goods	00.12.00
	one Cubbard and Tobacco	00.15.00
	one Table, Forme, nine chairs	01.00.00
	two Iron grates, two spits,	

	one drippinge pan, one paire of Andirons,	
	one gridiron	01.10.00
	one jack and weight	00.10.00
	one paire of scales, beame and weights	01.10.00
	and other goods	00.05.00
In the shop	Fue mill cloths and sacks	05.00.00
	one Trough, Tubs, other goods	01.00.00
In the Bakehouse	One copper, other brasse	02.00.00
	two Troughs, two moulding boards,	
	And other goods	01.15.00
In the yard buttiry	In beers	03.00.00
	Five hogsheads, other goods	01.10.00
In the Chamber over the hall	One Fether bed, two pillowes, one bolster, two blankets, one Coverlid, Curtaines And Valiants, a hy bedstead, one trundlebed	06.00.00
	One Chest, one Coverlid, Curtaines, valyants, Carpets, two Cushings	04.10.00
	One chest of drawers, linnen	03.00.00
	One silver bole a Cup and a spoon	03.10.00
	One Chest, 3 dossen and a halfe Napkins, 4 paire sheetes, 3 pillow beeres, Foure table cloths two tables	04.00.00
	nine stooles, six chaires	02.05.00
	One paire of Andirons, fire shovell, tongs	00.05.00
	A cubbard with glasses and pots	00.10.00
	A pot shelfe and goods in it	01.10.00
	A shelfe, bookes	01.10.00
In the Closett	Butter, cheese, spices, other goods	03.00.00
[Subtotal]		**53.05.00**
In the Chamber over the shop	One Fether bed, foure bolsters, three pillowes, Foure blankets, one rug, Curtaines and valyants, one hy bed, trundle bed	05.00.00

WILLS AND INVENTORIES FOR HERTFORD, 1660-1725

	one Chest, eight paire sheetes, and other linnen	05.00.00
	one Trunke, one dussen and a halfe Napkins, two paire sheetes, one Towell	01.10.00
	In yarne	02.00.00
	One presse	00.15.00
	One table, four stooles, and other goods	01.00.00
In the Chamber over the Bake House	One flocke bed, two bolsters, 3 blankets, one bedstead	01.10.00
	One chest, other goods	00.10.00
In the Garruts	One Flocke bed, 3 bolsters, two blankets, one bedstead	01.00.00
	One settlebed, one Chest, a box of candles	01.05.00
	In hops	01.10.00
	One still, one wateringe pot, other goods	01.16.00
In the brew house	One Copper, brewing vessell	10.00.00
	In Coles	05.00.00
	In wood	02.00.00
In and out shop	In wheat, ry, meale, and other goods	02.00.00
In the yard	Three hogs	02.00.00
	A barne upon pattings and wood in it	15.00.00
	In basons	01.00.00
	In debts	0.02.05
	In wearinge parrell	05.00.00
[Subtotal]		**122.18.05**
	carried forward	53.05.00
[Total]		**176.03.05**

[Appraisers]
William Gardiner, ? Clark, Will Carter

Exhibited: 14 ? 1665

WILLS AND INVENTORIES FOR HERTFORD, 1660-1725

31 William Bridgman   Inventory Ref: H22-160
    Mealman   Date of Appraisal: 7 March 1670 ?

A true Inventorie of all Goods and Chatells of William Bridgman Late desiced march the 7th 1670

	His waring Aparill	05.00.00
	and in his purs	00.10.00
In the Hall	An bord great tabell, some stoles, 4 pewter dishes, with other lumber	01.01.06
In the Ketchen	3 Ketels, one pote, and litle other th[i]ng	01.10.00
In the Chamber over hall	one bedsted, furniture to chest	02.00.00
	one chest with sume linen	01.00.00
In the next rome	to servants beds and beding	01.00.00
In the next rome to that	a quarter pease	01.00.00
In one other rome	to quarter oats and other lumber	01.16.00
In the garett	to servants beds and furniture	01.00.00
In the Dary	cheese tubs, milke vesels	00.10.00
In the stabel	4 hors, harnis, carts, Harrows, plowes	25.00.00
	Cowes fourteene	35.00.06
	Two sows	01.10.00
In the barne	apart of bay of wheat	05.00.00
In the moate barne	one litle quantitie of oate mowe	02.10.00
	Sheepe sume to cowe	13.00.00
	Some poltery	00.02.00
	tenn eakers of tilt wheat one growne	10.00.00
	sume tilte for barly	05.00.00
[Total]		**113.10.00**

[Appraisers]
Prasieerys: William Catlin, Hosiah Pratts

Exhibited: 12 January 1679

WILLS AND INVENTORIES FOR HERTFORD, 1660-1725

32 William Edmonds Inventory Ref: H22-372
    Gentleman   Date of Appraisal: 21 July 1680

An Inventory of the Corne and Hay and Horses and Carts and plows and harrows and *(word obliterated by ink blot)* with sum other goods an Chattells of William Edmonds of Hartford in the County of Hartford Gentl[eman], Lately deseased, taken this 21th of July 1680 by John Browne of Hartinford Bury in the County of Hartford And Richard Pooly of Eassendon in the aforesayd County of Hartford

	17 Acres of Ry	17.00.00
	17 Acres of Wheat	59.00.00
	28 Acres of Barly	69.00.00
	4 Acres of peas	06.00.00
	30 Loads of hay	34.10.00
	2 hogs, 4 pigs	02.15.00
	4 Horses	15.00.00
	fower Cartts, f[o]wer pare of wheels, harrows, sum ould Harnis	10.00.00
	wood	10.00.00
[Total]		**223.05.00**

[Appraisers]
Richard Pooley, John Browne

33 James Chamberlain   Inventory Ref: H22-1320
                    Date of Appraisal: 30 June 1682

A True Enventory of the Goods and Chattell of James Chamberlin Late of Hertford in the County of Hertford Deceassed Taken and Appraised June the 30th Anno Dom[ini] 1682

Ittem in the Hall	a Cubbard, little Table, 5 old chairs	01.15.00
Ittem in the Parler	a Bedsted, Bedding, 6 chaires	02.00.00
Ittem in the Buttery	4 old vessells, 4 Earthen Dishes	00.10.00
Ittem in the outward Chamber	a Bedsted, Bedding, 2 chests	00.10.00

65

WILLS AND INVENTORIES FOR HERTFORD, 1660-1725

Ittem in the Inner Chamber	a Bedsted, bedding a chest of Drawers	01.00.00
Ittem in the Barn and the yard	Timber, Boards	05.10.00
Ittem in the Shop	working-Toolls	01.10.00
Ittem in the outward Buttery	Brass, Pewter	01.05.00
	Wareing Apparell, Money	11.01.04
[Total]		**25.01.04**

Appraissed by us whose names are hear under Written
John Pratt, John Chamberlain

Exhibited: 1682

34 Andrew Bray   Inventory Ref: H22-1373
**   Tanner   Date of Appraisal: 1 March 1683**

A True Iventory of the Goods and Chattells of Andrew Bray of Hertford in the County of Hertford Tanner lately deceased, Taken the First of March Anno Dom[ini] 1683 Vizt

In the Hall Imp[rimi]s	Severall goods	01.08.00
In the Parlor	Severall goods	01.00.00
In the Kitchin	Severall goods	05.08.06
In the Seller	Severall goods	00.14.06
In the Kitchin	Severall goods	06.02.06
	The lynnen	03.02.00
In the Chamber over the Parlor	Severall goods	04.17.00

WILLS AND INVENTORIES FOR HERTFORD, 1660-1725

Debts Sperat and desperat	07.18.00
The lease of the houses, severall goods in the yard	179.18.00
His weareing Apparrell	02.00.00
His money in pockett	02.00.00

[Total] 214.08.06

These goods was valued and [ap]prized by us John Hill, John Barfoot
Praysors for the houshold goods Will Hurrell, Hen[ry] Marson Praysors for the yard

Exhibited: 7 Mar 1683

35   Alice Dyer   **Inventory Ref: H22-1269**
                              Date of Appraisal: 4 May 1663

May 4 1663 An Envintory off the goods off Alice Dyer off the parrish off all s[ain]ts Hertford, Lattly disseased

In the Hall	a bench settle, a litle table, tin fire shovlle, 2 ould chaires, andirons,	
	a Carpett, 3 Cushins, some other Lumber	00.18.00
In the kitching	2 spitts, two drippinge pannes, 1 Hare cubberd	00.05.00
	pewter	01.00.00
	brasse severall peeces	00.17.00
	in tubbes and bowlles and brasses	00.05.00
	a cruett, smotheing iron, other lumber	00.05.00
In a Rome next	the sheetes, 3 p[ai]r Handles, an old Cheste, and other lumber	00.05.00
In the Chamber over the Hall	one standinge bedstead, trundlebedsted, Curtins and vallance	00.30.00
	two fether beds, one fether bolster, one Rugge, one Coverlett, two blanketts, two straw beds, 2 mattes	07.00.00
	two Lether Chaires, two Leather stoulles, one table, 3 twine stoulles, a Chest of drawers, one Carpett, 2 Curtines, 2 Cushines, Andirons, fire shovell, tonges, a setle bench	01.13.04

67

WILLS AND INVENTORIES FOR HERTFORD, 1660-1725

In the Chamber over the kitching	one standeinge bedstead, Curtins and vallens, rods	01.00.00
	4 Chestes, 3 boxsses, a Close stoulle and pann	01.10.00
	one fether bed, bolster, 4 pillowes, straw bed, a cuverlett, blankett	05.00.00
	4 Chaires, Andirons, one forme, 4 twine stoolles, Fire shovell, tonges	00.13.04
		08.03.04
In the Chamber over the entry	an old bedstead, one fether bed, bolster, a flocke bolster, one Rugge, blanketts	02.00.00
	and other Lumber	00.02.06
		02.02.06
	In Lynning of all sorttes	04.00.00
	In wood and bordes	00.10.00
	Upon bond From John Kinge	60.00.00
	In Ready money	31.17.00
	Her warreinge aparrel	03.00.00
[Total]		**123.11.02**

Praysed by us Will Carter, Robert Stothard

Exhibited: 10 June 1664

---

36 John Goodman   Inventory Ref: H22-1261
    Tanner   Date of Appraisal: 25 Sept 1663

(damaged document - details incomplete)

Sept 25 1663 An Inventory off the goodes off John goodman off the parrish of St Andrewes in Hertford and in the County of Hertford Latly disseassed

In the Halle	1 table, 3 Joine stooles, som ould Chaires, 1 setle, 1 fire Iron, and some other old thinges	01.00.00
In the Buttery	pewter, brasse, Iron ware and som other ould Lumber	03.06.08

WILLS AND INVENTORIES FOR HERTFORD, 1660-1725

In the parller	1 bedstead, 1 fether bed, boulster, 1 Coverlett, two blanketts, 2 pillowes, Curtin and vallens, 1 side bord, Chaires, Cushions, 1 p[ai]r fire Irons	06.06.08
In the Chamber over the Hall	1 bedstead, 1 bedstead, 1 fether bed, 1 Coverlett, Cartins and vallens, 1 trundlebed, fether bed, two Fether boulsters, 1 ould Coverlett, tow pillowes, tow Chestes	06.00.00
In the Chamber over the parler	1 Halfheaded bedstead, 1 floke bed, boulster, blanket, 1 Chest, 2 [document torn] Chestes, 1 litle table, 10 p[ai]r of sheetes, 3 p[ai]r Slap?, 18 napkins, pillow beares, 8 table Cloths, some towells, beare vessells	
In the yard	nine ? and Cakes of Leather [torn] twentysix Hides, three Dossen Calve skins, 1 Horse Hide, tow Tubes, 26 Fattes, severall shades, 1 mill, workeing toulles, shovles, 1 barow, wood, Hog, Cowe [torn],	
	1 Cow	03.00.00
	1 Horse	04.00.00
	money oweing in good debts [torn] wareinge aparrell money in perse	08.00.00
[Total]		**363.00.00**

praised by us whose names are under written W[illia]m Turner, Hen[ry] Marson, Samuell Pondman

Exhibited: 14 April 1664

69

WILLS AND INVENTORIES FOR HERTFORD, 1660-1725

37 Arthur Randolph   Inventory Ref: H22-968
    Tobacconist   Date of Appraisal: 13 March 1677

An Inventorye of the Goods and Chattells of Arthur Randolph of the parish of St Andrews in Hertford Tobacconist, Lately deceased, taken and apprized the 13 day of March 1677-8 by J[oh]n Barfoote and J[oh]n Martin of Hertford as followeth

Imprimis
In the Garrett   Bedsteads, bedds, and other goodes   05.00.00

In the Chamber   p[ar]cell brasse, pewter, Tables, fire Irons
                          and other Lumber   03.17.04
                          6 sheetes, napkins, Towells   00.15.02

In the Shopp   p[ar]cell tobacko, pipes, engine   07.01.05

                          in debts and money   12.10.00
                          his weareinge apparell   02.10.00

[Total]   31.13.11

Apprized by us
John Barfoot, John Martin

Exhibited: 30 Mar 1678

38 Grace Spratt   Inventory Ref: H22-1080
                     Date of Appraisal: 15 February 1689

Feb[ru]ary the 15th 1689 An Imnartory of the goods and Cattle of grace Spratt latley Deceased

In Primmus in the hall   one table, 5 Stouls   00.06.08
                             Six old Chiriss, little table, one board   00.02.06
                             Tow Andirons, two Spits,
                             one pare of tongs, fire Shuvel,
                             one dripingpan, 2 pare pot hangers   00.03.06
                             A dusen putter Dishes, one flagon,
                             one putter pot, one Candlestick,
                             two porenger   00.18.00

70

WILLS AND INVENTORIES FOR HERTFORD, 1660-1725

Itum in the kittin	one brass pan, 4 kittle, 3 brass pots, three skileits, two warminpans, Amorterandpesel, one Chafindish, one prass Skimerss	03.10.00
	Seven Drink vesels, four Tubes, one kimnele, three payle	00.12.06
I tum in the milcuss *(milk-house)*	six trays, six bouls, one Stan, one Charne, one Cheesepress, one poundering tub, one poudering troufe, four formes, Six Shuffes, Seven Cheese metes, two Cheese breds, three tunels, one pare of Catse and wats	01.00.00
I tum in the paler	linine in the paler, one fether bed, one straw bed belonging to it, two boulsters, six pilours, one rug, two blankets belonging to it, one little Cobberd, one little table, three Chairese, two Stooles, one Clothes pers with her wareing Clothes, one peyre of ?, one Cloth	05.00.00
Itum in the Chamber over the paler	two feathers beds, one straw bed, two fethers boulsters, two Coverlids with A rurg, three blankets, A Chest, box, settle, two bare Currtuans and valants, one Joynet bedsted, A halfe bedstead, twelfe pare Shitees, and other linens	06.00.00
Itum in the Chamber over the milcus	one old flock bed, two bed steds, one fethers boulster, one flock boulster, three old huches, ther or four pound of woole, one fethears pillors	01.00.00
Itum In the butery	botles, earthen ware dishes, Spones, trenches	00.01.06
	A Cart, plow, pare of harrows	02.00.00
	for the Corne in the barne and wheat and barly	10.00.00
	for the wheat in ground	07.10.00
	for the Ech Corn in the ground	03.11.00
[Subtotal]		**38.15.08**

	for the horse	10.00.00
	for the Cows and Cafe	09.00.00
	for the pidge	01.10.00
	for Sheep	04.10.00
Itum in the Stable	for herhose, Colleres, paneles	01.00.00
[Subtotal]		**26.00.00**
[Subtotal]		**38.15.08**
[Total]		**64.15.08**

Ap praised by us
Phillip Bridgman, William Pryer

Exhibited: 11 February 1690

39   Robert Stothard   Inventory Ref: H22-1069
     Innholder   Date of Appraisal: 28 January 1672

(document has a thick black mark along foldline making some words illegible)

An Inventorye of the Goodes and Chattels of Robert Stothard late of Hertford in [the county of] Hertford, Innholder, taken and appraized the 28th day of Januarye 1672 vizt Imprimis:

In the Hall	one longe table, 1 shorter table, 2 formes, 1 presse Cupboard, cloath, 6 woodden chairis, 2 Joint stoolis, 1 little table, 1 glass, 5 old Cushions, a Jacke, 2 leaden weights, p[ai]r bellowes, p[ai]r andirons, fire Iron, fire shovel, tonges, 2 pot hangers, a salt ben	02.16.06
In the parlour	1 table, 4 Joind stooles, 3 chaires, p[ai]r andirons, fireshovell, tonges	01.04.00
In the kitchin	16 pewter dishes, 24 flagons, 11 poring, 2 basons, 7 chamber potts, 12 saucers, 3 Candlesticks, 4 pewter salts	06.02.01

WILLS AND INVENTORIES FOR HERTFORD, 1660-1725

	4 brasse Kittles, brasse pann, 3 skillets, 1 brasse pott, 2 brasse Ladles, Skimmer, a warmeinge panne, Iron drippinge pan, 2 Iron potts, 1 Jacke, 2 p[ai]r pothookes, 2 p[ai]r hangers, 2 racks, andirons, 1 fire Iron and heatt?, cleaver 3 spitts, gridiron, chafindish, tostinge Iron, shredinge knife, miatt forke,	03.06.08
	3 joint stooles, and other old Lumber	02.18.04
	p[ar]cille bottles, canns, tin plate, drippinge pan, puddinge pann cullinder	00.12.00
In the Hall Chamber	1 longe table, 1 shorter table, 11 Joine stooles, 2 high hayer chaires, 2 low hayer chaires, 1 court Cupboard etc, 2 cushions, p[ai]r Andirons, Creepers, p[ai]r bellowes, fire shovell, tonges,	03.10.06
	1 bedstead, cord, curtaine, rods, matt, straw bed, straw boulster feather bed, feather bolster, 2 pillowes, 2 blankets, 1 rugge, curtanes and vallance	05.17.00
In the garett	2 flock beds, 2 bolsters, 2 Coverlids, 3 blankets, 1 bedsted, halfheaded bed, curtaines and vallance, stools, tables, curtaine rods	01.12.04
In the Gatehouse chamber	1 bedsted, cord, and matt, curtaine rods, trister cloath, 1 feather bed, boulster, 4 pillowes, 1 greene rugge, blankit, curtaines and vallance	04.01.04
	1 trundlebed, cord, matt, feather bed, feather boulster, straw bolster, 1 Coverlid, 1 blanket	01.12.08
	1 trundlebed, cord, matt, flocke bed, flocke bolster, 1 blankit, 1 Coverllid and some other old lumber	01.00.00
	2 forme Chests, 13 doz[en] 4 p[ar]t flexen and part towin Napkins at 7s p[e]r doz	05.02.06
	1 diaper table cloath	00.16.00

WILLS AND INVENTORIES FOR HERTFORD, 1660-1725

In the parlour Chamber	1 bedstead, cord, matt, tester cloath, Curtaine rodds, straw bed, flock bolster, Feather bed, feather bolster, 2 pillowes, 2 blankets, 1 red rugge, curtaines and vallance, a table, 4 stooles, 2 chaires, a chest, p[ai]r andirons, fireshovell, tonges, bellowes, carpitt	06.08.00
	25 p[ai]r sheetes p[ar]t flexen and part towin	14.06.08
In the Kitchin Chamber	bedstead, cord, matt, straw bed, feather bed, bolster, 2 pillowes 1 red rugge, blanket, curtaines and vallance, 1 longe table, carpit, 6 stooles, 2 chaires, 1 chest, 1 trundle bed, cord, p[ai]r andirons	05.19.03
In the Sellar	14 hoghds, 1 barell of beere w[i]th the vessell	18.10.08
In the Brewhouse	a copper, and all the brewinge vessells	14.00.00
In a shopp in the yard	12 bushell oates and some other old lumber	01.10.00
In the yard	a wooden horse, washinge blocke, 3 ladders, 24 hurdles, 18 tresells	01.19.08
	a nagge, maire	03.06.08
	a p[ar]cill hay	10.00.00
	wood	10.00.00
	4 sowes, 3 barrow hoges, 4 piggs	05.10.00
	debts	01.10.00
	his weareinge cloathes	05.01.04
[Total]		138.06.06

Appraised by us
Ad[lord] Bowde, John Barfoot

Exhibited: 22 November 1673

WILLS AND INVENTORIES FOR HERTFORD, 1660-1725

40   John Gurrey   Inventory Ref: H22-489
         Grocer   Date of Appraisal: 23 April 1671

A Inventory of the Goods and Chattells of John Gurrey of Hertford in the County of Hertf[or]d Grocer Lately deceased, made the 23th of Aprill Anno Dom[ini] 1671

Impr[imis] **In the shopp** **and Stoarehouse**		65.00.00
It[em] in the Parlor	table, chayre, stooles and other things	02.00.00
It[em] in the kitchin	pewter, brass and other things	04.00.00
It[em] in the Buttery		01.10.00
It[em] in the Chamber over the Shopp	abedd, furniture and other things	02.05.00
It[em] in the Chamber over the kitchin	two bedds w[i]th Furniture, one Chest, w[i]th other things	12.00.00
It[em] in the Chamber over the Parlor	one bedd with Furniture, table and other things	07.00.00
It[em] in the Brewhouse	two coppers w[i]th Coolers	05.00.00
It[em] in the yard	wood and Some other things	01.06.00
	Earthen Ware	01.10.00
	Severall Sorts of Lynen	05.00.00
	his Wearing apparrell	02.00.00
[Total]		**108.11.00**

These goods were valued and a praysed by us the date abovewritten W[illia]m Turners, Richard Martin

Exhibited: 16 Sept 1671

WILLS AND INVENTORIES FOR HERTFORD, 1660-1725

41   John Johnson   Inventory Ref: H22-667
Date of Appraisal: 12 August 1673

25th July 1672 allegation of intestacy made by Susanna Johnson of Hertford All S[ain]ts before David Budd

An Inventory of the Goods and Chattells of John Johnson, late of the parish of Allsaints Hertford, in the County of Hertf[or]d, deceased, taken and appraised by us Thomas Herricke and James Goodman this twelveth day of August in the yeare of our Lord 1673

	his wearing apparell, ready money	10.00.00
Item in his Parlour	One Bedsted, Coard and Matt, Curteynerodds, Curteynes and Vallance, One feather bedd, two blanketts, a coverlid, two feather bolsters, two pillowes	09.04.00
	One Trundle bedd, cord and Matt, one feather bed, two Blanketts, a bolster, one pillowe	03.16.00
	One Table, forme, a Livery Cupboard, a Glass case, Looking glasse, a small deske, Box, baskett	01.11.00
Item In the hall	one long Table, six joint stooles, a presse cupboard, one Forme, four chaires, a Linen Wheele and Reele, three spitts, one paire Racks, two paire Andirons, a fire shovell, tongs, one Jacke	04.13.00
Item In the Little Parlour	one Settle, one haire cupboard, a Little Table, forme, one chaire	01.03.00
Item In the best Chamber	One bedsted, Curteynes and Vallence, one feather bedd, one Straw bedd, two feather bolsters, two pillowes, a Rugg, blankett	10.00.00
	One Trundlebedd, feather bedd	03.00.00
	One drawing Table, two joint stooles, a Cupboard, two chaires	03.08.00

76

WILLS AND INVENTORIES FOR HERTFORD, 1660-1725

	a paire Racks for Coales, fire shovell, tongs, a paire creepers, bellowes, six cushions, a small Table, Couch	04.00.00
It[e]m In the Chamber over the Hall	One Bedstead, feather bedd, bolster, two pillowes, one coverled, curteynes and vallance, two chests, one chaire, one Box, one Table, Forme, one Tapistry carpett	10.04.00
Item In two other Roomes above staires		02.10.00
Item In the Kitchin	Brass, pewter and other things	08.00.00
	Nine pairs towen sheetes	05.08.00
	Napkins, Tablecloths, pillowbeeres and other linen	06.04.04
	Bynn, poudring trough	00.06.06
	Sixteene dozen Bottles	02.08.00
	Seaven Butchers Stalls	04.00.00
	Fifteene Loads Faggotts, Blocks and Roundwood	11.05.00
	two acres hey	06.00.00
	A horse	02.00.00
	An hovell wherein the hey lyes	06.00.00
	Three fouling pienes, a hooke and carbine	03.10.00
	Three drinke Stalls	00.10.00
[Total]		**130.10.10**

Debts and Charges owing by the Intestate at the time of his decease

	For hey	debit	10.00.00
	for Wood	debit	08.00.00
	for beare	debit	08.00.00
	In money	debit	16.00.00
	funerall charges	debit	08.00.00
	Admin[istrati]on and charges therein	debit	01.00.00
	for apraysing the goods and Inventory		00.10.00

	debit	00.00.10
	debit	00.01.04
	debit	00.01.00
	debit	00.03.04
	debit	00.02.06
	debit	00.05.00
	debit	08.10.04
	debit	00.10.00

[Total debts to be subtracted from previous total sum of 130.10.10] [debit] 53.04.04

[Total] **77.06.06**

Tho[mas] Herrick, James Goodman Appraysers

Exhibited: 9 Dec 1673

42   Richard Kerby   Inventory Ref: H22-702
      Cordwainer   Date of Appraisal: 3 May 1672

An Inventorye of the Goodes and Chattells of Richard Kerbye late of Hertford in the Countye of Hertf[or]d, Cordwainer decesd, taken and apprized the 3d day of May 1672 Imprimis

In the hall	1 drawinge table	00.18.00
	4 chaires	00.03.00
	1 wooden chaire	00.02.00
	1 round table	00.04.00
	1 cushion	00.00.04
	1 p[ai]r doggs	00.02.06
	2 spitts	00.02.06
	1 gridiron	00.01.06
	fireshovell, tonges	00.02.06
	3 stooles	00.07.06

(the following line is indistinct)

	1 pewter bason	00.03.00
	1 chamberpott, 2 poring ?	00.09.00
	1 p[ai]r canlesticks, 1 pewter flaggon,	

WILLS AND INVENTORIES FOR HERTFORD, 1660-1725

	1 plate, 3 pewter dishes	10.19.09
	1 Tyn drippinge pan	00.02.00
	1 kettle, skillett	00.15.00
	skimmer	00.01.04
	1 p[ai]r andirons, 1 racke, barr Iron	00.02.06
In the hall Chamber	1 p[ai]r flaxen sheetes	00.17.00
	2 p[ai]r Towen sheetes	01.03.00
	1 doz napkins	00.07.00
	2 table cloathes	00.03.06
	1 Towell	00.00.04
	a bedstead, Tester, cord and Matt, curtaine rodds	00.13.00
	1 red curtaines and vallance, window curtaines, rodd, syde board cloath	01.10.00
	a red rugge, 7 chaires, stooles, 3 side tables	02.10.00
In the shopp Chamber	wrought chaire, 2 stooles	00.10.06
	side table, cloath	00.02.06
	feather bed, 2 bolsters, 2 pillowes	00.00.08
		02.15.04
	2 blankets	00.05.00
	flocke bedd, boulster	00.13.05
	bedstead	00.07.00
	brasse Andirons	00.08.00
[Subtotal]		**05.01.11**
In the shopp	2 doz lasts [at] 0.0.3	00.06.00
	1 doz lasts [at] 0.0.2	00.02.00
	30 lasts [at] 0.0.2	00.05.00
	shopp hammer	00.01.00
	shopp tubb	00.01.06
	rails and shelves	00.00.10
	3 seales	00.04.00
	a Tubb and Dy	00.00.11
[Subtotal]		**00.04.11**

	upper leather	00.12.00
	sole leather	00.13.00
	leather	00.01.00
[Subtotal]		**01.06.00**
	1 doz weomens shoes [at] 0.2.6	01.10.00
	10 p[ai]r shoes [at] 0.1.8	00.16.08
	7 p[ai]r mens shoes [at] 0.3.4	01.03.04
	baskett	00.02.00
	his wareinge cloathes vizt 1 suite and coate and hat	01.10.00
	In debts	02.10.00
[Total]		**09.16.03**

appraised by Richard Martin, Ad[lord] Bowde, William Hurrell
(*various arithmetical workings at bottom of page:*
'goods come to 9.16.3 plus 17.13.10 making total credit   27.09.1
oweinge by Rich Kirby about £31')

Exhibited: 6 May 1672

William Hurrell testified with widow Anna Kerby that Richard Kerby of Hertford St Andrews had died intestate

43   Tymothy and Sarah Miles Inventory Ref: H22-806
                       Date of Apprsial: 7 July 1699

An Inventory of the goods and chattells of Tymothy Miles and Sarah his wife lately deceased of the parrish of St Johns Hertford in the County of Hertf[or]d taken the 7th day of July Anno Dom[ini] 1699 vizt

In the Hallroome	severall goods	00.17.04
In the Buttery	Severall goods	01.10.00
In the best Chamber	Severall goods	04.05.02

WILLS AND INVENTORIES FOR HERTFORD, 1660-1725

In the old Chamber	Severall goods	02.10.00
It[em] in the shedd		00.01.00
It[em] in the yard		00.03.02
	A pigg	00.10.00
	The Lynen	02.02.00
	ready money	17.10.00
	sperat and desperat debts	04.14.00
	Wearinge Cloaths	00.18.00
[Total]		34.03.02

These goods was valued and prised by us the day and date above written with a double stamp John Hill, John Woolmer, Praysors

Exhibited: 8 July 1699

44   Thomas Kirbey   **Inventory Ref: H22-700**
                     Date of Appraisal: 8 April 1670
                     Bond of Administration H23-1429 [the bond is damaged]

An Inventory of the Goods and Chattells of Thomas Kirbey of Hertford lately deceased made the 8th of Aprill Anno Dom[ini] 1670

In the Hall	goods	01.10.00
In the Parlor	goods	00.10.00
In the Kitchin	goods	03.00.00
In the Brewhouse	Tubb, wood	00.10.00
In the litle Buttery	severall small goods	00.06.08
In the Chamber over the Shopp	2 litle tables, five Joynt stooles, forme, litle chayre, bedsted, trundle bedd, bedding and some other small things	06.10.00

WILLS AND INVENTORIES FOR HERTFORD, 1660-1725

In the litle Chamber over the Buttery	severall goods	01.10.00
In the Chamber over the Hall	a litle table, Four stooles, bedsted, trundle bedd, bedding, with some other things	08.00.00
In the Chamber over the Parlor	table, stooles, bedsted, bedding, with some other goods and lynen	20.00.00
In the Chamber over the Kitchin	a bedsted, trundle bedd, bedding, Court Cubbord, Chests, and some other goods	04.00.00
In the great and litle Garrett	a Halfe headed bedsted, bedding and some other goods	02.10.00
In the yard and abroad	Wood, Hay	07.00.00
	2 hoggs	02.00.00
	Speratt and desperat debts upon bond and otherwise, ready money	40.00.00
	his wearing apparrell	05.00.00
[Total]		**102.06.08**

These goods and Chattells was valued and praysed by us the day and date First written James Goodman, Will[iam] Bigge Praysors

Exhibited: 8 April 1670

45 John Axtell   Inventory Reference: H23-38
   Shopkeeper   Date of Appraisal: 21 December 1698
               Bond of Administration: 31 December 1698

Granted to Mary Axtell, widow of the deceased at Hertford. A true Inventory with a double Stamp of the goods and Chattells of John Axtell of the parrish of All S[ain]ts Hartford in the County of Hertf[ord], Shopkeper, lately deceased taken the one and twentyeth of December Anno Dom[ini] 1698 Vizt

In the Hall	pewter, brass, dressers, Jack, Chayres, Cote racks and other lumber	08.00.00

WILLS AND INVENTORIES FOR HERTFORD, 1660-1725

In the best Chamber	Foure bedds, bedsteds and bedding, two Chest of drawers, two little tables, severall Chayres and some other lumber	25.00.00
	the plate in the s[ai]d chamber	20.00.00
In the Hall Chamber	one bedd, bedsted and bedding, eight cane chayres, a trunck, the Hangings and some other lumber	07.00.00
In the passage roome	A Couch	00.16.00
In the worke house	Two Coppers, a candle mole with the materialls, brewing tubbs, a cooler and other lumber	05.00.00
In the outward shopps	a boulting mill with materialls thereunto belonging	02.05.00
In the shopp	severall sort of goods belonging to a Shopkeeper	40.00.00
In the yard	A horse and the Hay	03.05.00
	Two cowes	08.00.00
	The Lynen in the House	20.00.00
	Debts Sperat and desperat	0.00.00
	His wearing Cloaths	05.00.00
	Money in pockett	10.00.00
[Total]		**194.06.00**

Those goods were valued and appraysed by us the day and date above written John Gurney, John Yardley Appraysers

Exhibited: 31 December 1698

WILLS AND INVENTORIES FOR HERTFORD, 1660-1725

46   John Bayford   Inventory Refe: H23-178
Husbandman   Date of Appraisal: 12 August 1684
Bond of Administration: 16 August 1684

Granted to Susan Bayford, widow of the deceased, by Thomas Ince

A true Inventory of the goods and chattells of John Bayford of Hartf[ord]d in the County of Hertf[ord] husbandman, lately deceased, taken the 12th day of August Ann Dom[ini] 1684 vizt

In the Hall	a table, two Joynt Stooles	00.04.06
	another long old table	00.04.00
	an old press Cubbord	00.02.00
	3 pewter dishes, 3 porringers,	
	a pewter cupp, 2 litle dishes	00.06.00
	2 pewter Chamber potts,	
	two earthen fruit dishes	00.01.10
	two doz trenchers	00.01.06
	3 old kitles	01.00.00
	6 bass chares	00.02.00
	a drippin pan, a pudding pan, two litle spitts	00.02.06
	Jack and the weight	00.05.00
	3 skilletts	00.03.00
	an old Forme, dresser board	
	and some lumber	00.01.00
	Fryeing pan	00.02.00
	warmeing pan, two Flagons, bellowes,	
	Andirons, Fyer shovell old	00.02.06
In the Buttery	3 drinke tubbs, 2 old tubbs, beare stall with some other odd things	00.05.00
In the milke house	a store, 3 milke pales	00.05.00
In the best Chamber	an old bedsted, Cord and Matt, Curtaines and valance, a Feather bedd, bolster, two pillowes, a sad coller rugg, 2 blancketts	02.10.00
	Halfeheaded bedsted, Cord and Matt, Flock bedd, Flock bolster, greene rugg, two blancketts	01.00.00

84

	an old table, stoole	00.02.00
	a pare of old streack Curtains and valance	00.06.08
	a old Chests, halfe a doz pare course sheets, 2 table Cloaths, towells	01.06.08
	a boxe, two old Chayres	00.01.08
In the old Chamber	an old chest, 2 bibles and some lumber	00.05.00
In the yard	3 old carts, an old wagon	04.00.00
	a load of round wood	00.15.00
	4 litle mares and their Furniture	07.10.00
	8 Cowes	14.00.00
	one pigg	00.08.00
	two plowes old	00.10.00
	a pare of harrowes	00.05.00
	a litle old hay	02.00.00
	Sperat debts	02.00.00
	Desperat debts	04.00.00
	Money in hand	01.00.00
	Weareing apparrell	01.00.00
[Total]		**46.07.10**

These goods and chattells was prised and valued the date First written by us John Hill, Georg Barnes Praysors

47   Edmund; Edward Bickerton   Inventory Ref: H23-151
                                    Date of Appraisal: 20 August 1668
                                    Bond of Administration: 19 Dec 1668

Granted to Audrey Bickerton, widow of the deceased, at Hertford. An inventory of the Goods and Chattells of Edward Bickerton late of the parrish of AllSaints in Hertford in the Countye of Hertf[or]d, deceased, Taken and appraised by Thomas Herricke and Adlord Bowde the 20th day of August 1668

In the Hall	7 flaggons, one Cupboard, 4 brass Candlesticks, one Jacke	02.02.00
In the kitchyn	2 brasse potts, 2 skillitts, saucepan,	

WILLS AND INVENTORIES FOR HERTFORD, 1660-1725

	kettle, potlyd, 2 pewter dishes, pewter plate, chambrepott, 2 drippinge panns	02.00.00
In the shopp Chamber	1 feather bed, blanckett, rugge, Curtaynes and vallance, 1 chest, 1 chest drawers, 1 table, 1 carpet, 4 stooles, 4 chaires, brasse Andirons, one paire creepirs, lookinge glasse	15.00.00
In the Closett	1 chest, lynnen, silver Tumbler, 2 silver spoones, 5 large pewter dishes, 1 pewter bason, 6 plates, 1 pewter pott, 2 chamberpotts, 1 warmeinge pan, 1 pewter salt, 2 candlesticks	37.00.00
In the Kitchin Chamber	1 feather bed, 1 blanckett, 1 rugge, bedsted, curtaynes and vallance, bolster	06.00.00
In the greate Chamber	1 longe Table, 1 little Table, 3 stooles, 1 chaires, 1 flocke bed, bolster, 2 blancketts, rugge, bedsted, Curtaynes and vallance, Andirons	05.01.04
In the Garrett	flocke bed, bolster, Coverlitt, blanckitts, bedsted	01.00.00
	2 p[air] pillowes and other houshouldstuffe	03.00.00
	Wood and hay in the yard	30.00.00
	3 Hoggs	03.10.00
	one horse, Coult	06.00.00
	new and old Iron, steele, coales, workeing tooles in the shopp	36.00.00
	In debts, ready money and Bonds	50.00.00
	His weareinge Apparell	05.00.00
[Total]		**201.13.04**

Taken and appraised by us Tho[mas] Herrick, Ad[lord] Bowde

Exhibited: 19 December 1668

WILLS AND INVENTORIES FOR HERTFORD, 1660-1725

48 Emery Bradney Inventory Ref: H23-169
     Widow Date of Appraisal: 30 January 1671
                              Bond of Administration: 2 March 1671

Granted to Joseph Bradney, baker, of Hertford All Saints, at Hertford

An Inventory of the goods and chatells of Emery Bradly [sic], widdow, in the Town of Hartford, lately deceased, taken and praysed by us whose names are heare under writen

In the halle	one tabell, one prese coubart, brasse, pewter and other lumber	08.10.00
In the shope	dresing mell, clothes, sackes and sum other lumber	05.10.00
In the Bakehouse	one coper, moulding bords and other goods	03.10.00
In the seler	Beare, barels, hogesheds and other goods	05.10.00
In the Chamber over the halle	bedsted, Fether bed, Coverlet, pelowes, blankets, chest of drawers, ten small tabells, great Chare, fower lether chares	10.00.00
In the Chamber over the shope	bedsted, fether bed, ruge, curtaines and valincs, a chest of linen, hanging prese	15.10.00
In a chamber over the bakehouse	Ten Flocke beds, ruge, blankets, curtaines and valancs, tabell, sum other goods	05.15.00
In the Garetts	still, chest and other goods	03.10.00
In the Brewhouse	coper, coulers, sume other vesells belonging to thim	12.00.00
In the yard	wood, coles	0.00.00
	a parcill of hoges 5 in number	03.10.00
	In dettes for wares	43.00.00

WILLS AND INVENTORIES FOR HERTFORD, 1660-1725

In money and plate	11.00.00
Her waring Apparill and waring lenen	08.00.00
[Total]	**165.05.00**

[Appraisers]
William Gardner, James Goodman, William Carter

Exhibited: 2 March 1671

---

49 Richard Churchman Inventory Ref: H23-470
    Innholder   Date of Appraisal: 5 October 1694
                           Bond of Administration: 20 October 1694

Granted to Susanna Churchman, William Mills and Thomas Clarke

The Inventory of the Goods and Chattills of Richard Chirchman late of Hartford, Inholder, deceased, taken and apraysed this 5 day of October 1694 by us whose names are heerunto subscribed

In the Hall and parlor	3 tables, 15 bass chaires, 3 p[air] Andiorns, fier shovle, tongs	01.00.00
In the Kiching	One Jack and waight, Cole grates, shovle, tongs, 1 tab[le], 2 dressers, shelves, 10 chaires, stooles, 3 spitts, 5 kittles, warming pan, 2 skillitts, 2 poots, 12 Candlesticks, bellows, 20 dishes, 3 pye plates, 4 sawsers, 2 salts, 22 flaggons and poots, 3 chamberpoots, tinn ware	04.00.00
In the Best Chamber	one bedsted, fether bed, bolster, 4 blankits, 1 quilt, Curt and vall[ance], 6 chaires, andiorns, shovle, tongs, fender, bellows, table, hanging, glass, window curtins	05.00.00
In the Sho: Bord Rowm	2 tables, 6 stooles, formes, one bedsted, fether bed, bolster, 2 blankits, 1 rugg, Curtins and vall[ance], 4 chaires, window Curtins	02.00.00

WILLS AND INVENTORIES FOR HERTFORD, 1660-1725

In the Garroots	2 bedsteds, curtins and vall, bed, bolster, 2 chaires, 2 Cobberts, 2 ruggs, 2 blankits	01.10.00
In the Parlor Chamber	One bedsted, Curt and vallans, bed, bolster, quilt, 4 blankits, 2 pillows, 6 chaires, 2 chest, 2 glass in window, Curtins, roods, Iorns, shovle, tongs, fender	03.00.00
In the Gatehowse Chamber	One bedsted, bed, bolster, pillos, rugg, blankit, Curtins and vall[ance], 6 chaires, 1 tab[le], window Curt[ain], roods, glass	02.05.00
In the Parlow Chamber	One Bedsted, bedd, bolster, 3 blankits, one rugg, Curtins and vall[ance], 6 ould chaires, one table, window Curtins, roods, 2 p[air] doggs, shovle, tongs	02.10.00
In the Longe Garrot	3 bedsteds, 4 bedds, 7 bolsters, 3 ruggs, 5 Ould blankits, 3 old Curtins, 7 chaires, 1 table, 3 window Curts	04.00.00
	Two Chest with Lining In them	04.10.00
In the Bewhowse and Seller	one Copper, 2 Cowlers, brewing Vessells, 26 beer vessills, Beer In the Seller	15.00.00
	Hay, wood, Coales	10.00.00
	His Wareing aparrell, mony, alhis Deats, plate	08.00.00
[Total]		**60.15.00**

Adlord Bowde, Humphrey Clarke Apraysors

Exhibited: 20 October 1694

WILLS AND INVENTORIES FOR HERTFORD, 1660-1725

50   **Mary Cornell**   **Inventory Ref: H23-499**
         Spinster   **Date of Appraisal: 6 July 1714**
                           Bond of Administration: 21 August 1714

Granted to sister Sara Bradley, Joseph Sanders of Hitchin and John Willis, cordwainer
A Inventory of the Houshould Goods of the late Deceased Mary Cornell; and Appraised By me as Followeth etc.

1 old Chest, 1 old trundell bedsted, Corde and matt, 3 boxes, 1 dessk, a p[ai]r of old virgenalls, 1 old bellmettell pott, 2 brass kettells, 1 Chest of Drawers, 1 littel pottshelf, earthen war, Glass, bottells, 7 putter dishes, 2 litel plates, 1 litel basson, 1 putter ?, 1 putter salt, 1 putter porringer, 5 flexen sheetts, 5 flexen napakins, 2 towells, 1 pillow bear, 1 feather bed, bolster, 2 pillows, 1 Coverlide, 1 blankett, 1 old Chest	47.10.00
In moneys	05.08.08
[Total]	**52.18.08**

Wittness my hand the Day and date Above written John Barfoot

Exhibited: 7 October 1714

51   **Luke Clisby**   **Inventory Ref: H23-459**
                          Bond of Administration: 4 October 1684

Granted to Isabell Clisby, Ralph Gore and John Crouch at Hertford

An Inventory of the goods of Mr Luke Clisby Deceased of the p[ar]ish of Hert[ford] All S[ain]ts

Imprimis in the Chamber 1 Bed stead, 1 feather bed, 1 Rug, 1 Blankett, Curtaines, Bolster	03.00.00
In the kichen 4 old Chaires, A paire Andirons, firshovell, tonges, A table, 5 pewter dishes, A porige pot, skillit of terase	00.18.00

90

WILLS AND INVENTORIES FOR HERTFORD, 1660-1725

	Linnen	00.05.00
In the Celler	1 kilderkin , 2 firkins	00.05.00
	Malt	05.00.00
	In Money	40.00.00
[Total]		**49.08.00**

[Appraisers]
Daniel Clarke, John Crouch

52 John Briden   Inventory Ref: 13HW38
   Tailor   Date of Appraisal: 19 August 1684
                 Bond of Administration: 12 August 1684

Granted to Richard Martin and Edward Perkins

A true and perfect Inventory of all and singular the goods and Chattells of John Briden of the p[ar]ish of St Johns in the County of Hertford Taylor, deceased, Taken, vallued and Apprized the Nynteenth daye of August Anno D[omi]ni 1684 By us whose names are Subscribed

His wareing Ap[ar]ell, money in his purse	02.15.00
14 Acres of land that he held by Lease lyeing in wide Feild and in a Close Called new Close	70.00.00
Due and oweing upon Specially and w[i]thout Specially for in Sheep and money	20.15.00
Tubbs , barrells and other lumber	01.05.00
[Total]	**94.15.00**

[Appraisers]
Thomas Dearmer, The marke of Nicholas Birdsey

WILLS AND INVENTORIES FOR HERTFORD, 1660-1725

53 John Catlin   Grant of Probate: 24 Dec 1687   Will Ref: 24HW71
    Bricklayer

In the Name of God Amen. The eighteenth day of January in the yeare of our Lord God one thousand six hundred eighty and five, I John Catlin of Hertford in the County of Hertf[ord], Bricklayer, being of sound and perfect memory I thanke God therefore doe make this my Last Will and Testament in manner following (that is to say): First and pricipally I resigne my Soule to God Allmighty believeing for Salvation through the meritts of my Saviour Jesus Christ and my Body I comend to the earth from where it was formed to be decently buryed according to the discretion of my Executrixes herein after named. And as to my temporall Estate I doe dispose of it as followeth (that is to say): I doe give and bequeath all my personall estate, debts owing to me, money, Goods, Howsholdstuffe, Cattell and Chattells whatsoever to my loveing Wife Mary Catlin and my daughter Susanna Catlin equally to be devided amongst them share and share alike. And also I make my said Wife Mary Catlin and my said daughter Susanna Catlin joint Executrixes of this my Last Will and Testament. In Wittnesse whereof I have hereunto sett my hand and Seale the day and yeare abovewritten John Catlin [his own hand] Subscribed, Sealed, declared and delivered in the presence of William Craven, ? Prichard

Inventory Reference: 24HW71
Date of Appraisal: 26 December 1687

An Inventory of the goods and Chattles of the Late deceased Jo[hn] Catling of Hartford in the County of Hartford Brickloyer Taken and Appraised by us whose names Are under Ritten this Twenty and sixt day of desem[ber] 1687

In the Chamber **over the Litle parlor**	03.18.00
In the Rombe **over the Litle howse**	01.00.00
The Litle parler	03.10.00
In the Litle Rombe	01.10.00
In the Kitching	07.18.06
In the hall	00.15.00
In the Siller	04.13.00

WILLS AND INVENTORIES FOR HERTFORD, 1660-1725

In the Barne		00.10.00
In the Best Chamber		06.05.00
	The Linning	12.19.00
Long Chamber		08.10.00
In the Toe Clossets		01.10.00
In the yarde outt howse		16.02.00
In the Stayer head		00.10.00
	In good deebts	38.00.00
	Wareing Apparrell	05.00.00
	Reedy mony	02.00.00
[Total]		114.10.06

[Appraisers]
John Barfoot, Will[iam] Smitheman

**54   Elizabeth Churchman   Grant of Probate: 2 Feb 1688   Will Ref: 24HW77
       Widow**

In the name of God Amen. I Elizabeth Churchman of Hertford in the County of Hertf[ord], Widdow, being in p[er]fect minde and memory praysed be God therefore doe make and ordaine this my last Will and Testam[en]t in manner and forme following (that is to say): First and most principally I bequeath my Soule unto God that gave it and my Body to the Earth from whence it came to be decently buryed at the discression of my Execut[o]r hereafter named. And and [sic] as for those worldly goods and estate w[hi]ch God hath bless[ed] me w[i]th, I give and bequeath as followeth (that is to say): First I give and bequeath unto my Loveing Daughter Elizabeth Baker, the Wife of Thomas Baker, the sume of Thirty pounds in manner and forme following (that is to say): I will give and bequeath unto my said Daughter Elizabeth Baker one debt or sume of Tenn pounds due to me from Adlord Bowd; also I give and bequeath unto my said Daughter the sume of fower pounds and seaven shillings w[hi]ch is due to me from Humphrey Clarke upon bill; also I order and appoint my Execut[o]r hereafter named to pay unto my said Daughter the full sume of Fifteene pounds and Thirteene shillings w[hi]ch makes up the inst[ant] sume of Thirty pounds as aforesaid w[i]thin six moneths after my decease. Item I give and bequeath unto my said Daughter The Feather Bedd and Bolster and Greene Rugg w[hi]ch now are in the Greene Chamber. Item I give and bequeath unto Elizabeth Baker my Grandaughter the sume of five pounds w[hi]ch is left in the hands of Mr Robert Bull to be p[ai]d her at her age of one and Twenty years or day of Marriage w[hi]ch shall first Happen w[i]th reasonable Interest for the same, and incase the said Elizabeth should dep[ar]te this life before the respective ages as aforesaid, then my will and meaneing is that the said five pounds shalbe to and for the use of the childe my Daughter Elizabeth goes w[i]th. Item all the rest of my goods and estate I give and bequeath unto my Sonn Richard Churchman, who I make and appoint to be full and whole Execut[o]r of this my last will and Testam[en]t, Chargeing him to be aydeing and assisting to my said Daughter for the Recovery of the said debts before menconed and likewise payeing the legacy by me given to her according to the time before menconed. In Witnes whereof I have hereunto set my hand and seale this Fifteenth day of December 1688 the marke of Elizabeth Churchman, Sealed, Signed, published and declared in the pr[e]sence of Ro[bert] Bull, Edm[und] Lathbury, John Stave

Inventory Reference: 24HW77
Date of Appraisal: 7 February 1688

An Inventory of the Goods and Chattles of the Wido Churchman Deseased of the Bourough of Hertford Taken and Appraised by us whose names are here under written the seaventh day February 1688-9

Imprimis in the Kitchen	12 pewter Dishes, 15 plates, 16 Flagons, pott, 6 Chamber potts, od peeces pewter, 2 Brass Kettells, 2 Skilletts, fower pan 1 iron Dripin pan, 2 Iron porrage potts, 2 pare of Andirons, feireshovell, Tongs, forke, Bellows, 3 pott hangers, Gridiron, Chaving Dish, Jack with waites, 3 spitts, 2 tabls, 6 Joynd stooles, 6 flag bottoms Chairs, 2 Brass Candle stikes, 6 fine Candle stickes, 1 Brass Morter, 2 winder Curtains	06.10.00
In the Buttery	1 Cubbord, frying pan, other odd things	00.10.00
In the Hall	1 Table, 2 stoole, 1 forme, 6 Flag Bottom Chaires, 1 pare of Andirons, Tongs, 3 pare of pott hangers, 1 Glass Shelfe	00.14.00

WILLS AND INVENTORIES FOR HERTFORD, 1660-1725

In the parlor	2 Tables, 1 Forme, 1 stool., 6 Leather Chares, 1 pare of Tongs, 1 pare of Andiroons, 1 Glass Shelfe	01.10.00
In the Seller	Bere in the seller, twenty hogsheads, stalls	10.00.00
In the Garritt	1 half headed Bedstead, 1 Cord, 1 Matt, 1 Feather bed, 1 feather Bolster, 1 old Rug, 1 old Coverled, 2 Tables, 1 forme	02.15.00
In the Chamber over the gate house	1 Bedstead, Cord, Matt, hed Cloath, Teaster, Curtain Rod Vallence and Curtaines, 1 Feather bed, 2 Bolsters, 1 pillow, 1 Rugg, Blankett, 1 Livery Cubbord, Cloath, 2 Chares, 1 stoole	02.15.00
In the Chamber over the hall	1 Bedstead, Cord, Matt, headCloath, Curtaines and Vallence, 2 feather Beds, 2 Bolster, 1 pillow, 1 Blankett, Rug, 3 Leather Chares, 2 Turkeywork Chaires, 1 Table, 1 Table Cloath, 1 Joyned stoole, 1 par of Andirons	05.15.00
In the Chamber over the parlor	1 Bedstead, Cord, Matt, tester Cloath, 1 Feather Bed, 2 bolsters 2 pillows, Vallence and Curtains, 1 Rugg, 1 blankett, 1 Round table, Livery Cubbord, 3 Leather Chaires, 2 par of Brass Andirons, 1 pare of Tongs	05.10.00
In the Garrett over the Kitchen	2 old half headed Bedsteads, 1 Trundle Bed. Cords. Matt. 1 Flock bed 4 feather pillow, 1 old Chest	01.08.00
In the Chamber over the Kitchen	2 Bedsteds, Cords, Matts, Curtain Rods, 2 feather Beds, Bolsters Vallence and Curtaines, 2 blanketts, 2 Ruggs, window Curtain, Rod, 2 Chests, Case of Drawers, 1 Looking Glass	07.10.00

WILLS AND INVENTORIES FOR HERTFORD, 1660-1725

In the Chamber over the Buttery	1 Bedstead, Cord, Matt, feather Bed, Bolster, Rug, blankett Vallence and Curtaines, 4 Curtain Rods, 2 Tables, 1 Carpett, 6 Joynd stools, window Curtain, 1 Little Chest, Iron Spitt, Rack	04.12.06
	All the Lynning in the house Namely 20 par of sheetes, 12 dozzen of Napkens, 8 table Cloaths	08.00.00
In the Brewhouse	Copper, Brewing vessells	10.00.00
	The hay and wood in the yard	08.00.00
	2 Cowes	06.00.00
	6 hoggs	04.00.00
	Wearing Appareall	03.00.00
[Total]		**88.09.06**

Appraised by us: Robert Warner, Will[iam] Guyse

**55 James Chamberlain   Grant of Probate: 20 April 1680   Will Ref: 24HW17
Carpenter**

I James Chamberlain of the Parish of All S[ain]ts (so calld) of Hartford in the County of Hartford Carpenter, being outwardly weake of Body Howbeit of good Memory God be thanked, Doe this Ninth Day of the 1st Mo[n]th commonly calld March 1678 Make and appoint this my last will and Testam[en]t in Manner and form following: Impr[imi]s I give and Bequeath unto James Chamberlain my Eldest Son the Sum of Fourty Shillings of lawfull money etc to be paid him w[i]thin One half Yeare next after my Decease by myne Exec[uto]r hereafter herein nominated and Appointed. It[em] I give to my Daughter Mary now wife of [Geo Wade?] of London Weaver the sum of Thirty Shillings of Lawfull money of England to be paide her by my Exec[uto]r as aboves[ai]d. It[em] I give to my Daughter Sarah One Cedar Table standing in the Hall; Also to the s[ai]d Sarah my Daughter I give and bequeath One halfe of my Household-stuffe or Goods portionably to be devided. Also I give and bequeath unto her my s[ai]d Daughter Sarah the sum of Seven pounds of good and Lawfull English Money to be p[ai]d her by my Exec[uto]r hereafter nominated when shee shall Accomplish the Full Age of 21 yeeres or at her Day of Marriage, which shall first happen. It[em] I give and bequeath unto John Chamberlain my other Sonn the other halfe of my s[ai]d household Goods portionably to be devided w[i]th All my Stock, Tools, Tember and w[ha]tsoever within Doores or w[i]thout, w[i]th All other my Goods and Chattles and w[ha]tsoever herein before unbequeathed [*in left hand margin the words:* 'enterlined before the ensealing the word Tember']. He my s[ai]d Son John Chamberlain first paying and discharging All my Debts, Funerall Charges, and and above written Legacyes, whom hereby I also make and Appoint Sole Executor of this my last Will and Testam[en]t; Desiring my Loving Freinds and Neighbours Richard Thomas and Arch Palmer both of Hartford abovesaide as Supravisors to See and take the Oversight of the Due and true intended Execution of the same, Lastly Revoking, Disanulling and and [sic] making voide all and all other wills and Testmts whatsoever by mee heretofore made I ordain and appoint this as my Last will and Testam[en]t Conteining one whole Sheet of paper folded; In witnes hereof I have hereunto set my hand and seale the Day and Yeere first above written Sig[ned] James Chamberlain. Declared, Sealed and Subscribed In the presence of us A Palmer, Will[iam] Clark, John Yardley

Inventory Reference: 24HW17

(date of appraisal omitted)

The Inventarie of James Chamberlain of the parish of All S[ain]ts of Hertford in the County of Hertford Carpenter

In the Kitchen	One Cedar table	00.05.00
	A Cup-board	00.04.00
	A Little table with a Drawer	00.01.06
	Six Pewter dishes	00.03.00
	Two plates	00.00.06
	Two pewter Candelsticks	00.01.00
	Two tankards	00.01.00
	A salt sellar	00.00.06
	A warming-pan	00.02.00
	A looking-glass	00.01.00
	A Jack, spit, tin dripping-pan	00.02.06
	A pair of bellows, fire-shovel, tongs, End-irons	00.01.06
	A fender-iron, grate-iron, tosting-iron, 2 pot-hangers	00.02.00
	Four candel-sticks, four chairs	00.01.00
	Three pottingers, 3 Sausers, A glass-case	00.01.00
	A spice-box, 3 smoothing-irons	00.01.00

WILLS AND INVENTORIES FOR HERTFORD, 1660-1725

In the Buttery	Two brass kettles, a copper Kettle,	
	a little brass ladle	00.15.00
	Four brass skillets, one brass Scummer	00.04.00
	One frying-pan,	
	2 iron pottage pots with hoaks	00.05.00
	Four peeces of tin,	
	half a dosen alchymie spoons	00.00.06
	Other wooden [ware], a little earthen ware	00.02.00
	A kneading trough	00.01.00
	A standing copper meal tub,	
	pewter chamber pot	00.16.00
In the Parlor	A beds-stead, flock bed, bolster,	
	3 coverlets, blanket	01.00.00
	An old Chest, three chairs	00.01.00
	A hanging cup-board	00.00.06
In the first Chamber	A beds-stead, feather bed, bolster,	
	coverlet, three blankets,	
	striped curtains and vallance	01.15.00
	A pair of iron end-irons, fire-shovel	00.01.00
	A table with a drawer	00.01.00
	Two chests, one box	00.02.00
	Two little join'd stools, a chair	00.01.06
The Inner Chamber	A beds-stead, feather bed, bolster,	
	green rugg, 2 blankets,	
	green sarge curtain and vallance	02.00.00
	A chest of Drawers, another chest	00.06.00
	Two chairs, four join'd stools	00.01.06
	Linnen Thirteen pair of Sheets	02.00.00
	Six napkins	00.03.00
	Two table-clothes	00.03.00
	Two course table-clothes	00.00.06
	(the shilling column is unclear)	
	A dozen odd peeces	00.02.00
Stock In the Loft	Oaken boards	02.12.00
	Elm boards	02.00.00
	Deal boards	02.05.00
In the Shop	Elm boards	00.18.09

WILLS AND INVENTORIES FOR HERTFORD, 1660-1725

In the Yard	Wood	02.00.00
In the Street	Timber, sawn stuff, 2 ladders	02.10.00
	Tools	01.00.00
[Total]		**24.16.09**

Surveyed and apprized By Us Arc: Palmer, John Pratt, Thomas Robarts, Rich[ard] Thomas

56   Thomas Cooke   Grant of Probate: 6 August 1673   Will Ref: 23HW88

In the name of God Amen. I Thomas Cooke of the p[ar]ish of all Saints Hartford in the County of Hartford being weake in Body, but of good and perfect remembrance praised be God therefore, Doe make and ordaine this my Last Will and Testament as followes, that is to say, First of all I bequeath my Soule into the hands of God who gave it and my Body to be buryed in place convenient. Item I give and bequeath unto my two daughters Mary and Margarett Cooke to each of them two paire of Sheetes and halfe a dozyn of Napkins, to be delivered to them by mine Executrix at the day of each of their Marriages. Item I give unto my said two daughters a Pottage Pott and a Bedstead to each of them: and likewise to each of them a Skillett, and to each of them a paire of pillowbeeres, to be delievered to then as afores[ai]d at the days of yir Marriages. Item I give unto my loving Wife Ann Cooke All those my two Coppihold Tenements with the Appurtennances Scittuate lying and being in a streete called backe streete in the parish of All Saints in Hartford afores[ai]d To have and to hold the s[ai]d Tenements to my s[ai]d Wife dureing the terms of her naturall life And after her decease to My s[ai]d two daughters Mary and Margarett, to them and their heires for ever: Lastly, All the rest of my goods and Chattelles in this my Will unbequeathed I freely give and bequeath unto my Said Wife, whom also I make nominate and appoint to be sole Executrix of this my last Will and Testament, and I desire and apoint my loving Freinds, my Brother Nicholas Tuffnall and John Burton, of Hartford to be Overseers of this my Will to see it performed and I utterly revoke all former Wills by mee made whatsoever and appoint this only to be my last Will and Testament. In witnes whereof I have hereto set my hand and Seale this Nineteenth day of July in the Five and Twentieth yeare of our Soveraigne Lord King Charles the Second over England, etc in the yeare of our Lord God 1673, the marke of Thomas Cooke, Witnesses to this Will, John Burton, the marke of James Cooke, John Reeve

Inventory Reference: 23HW88

(date of appraisal omitted)

WILLS AND INVENTORIES FOR HERTFORD, 1660-1725

An Inventery of the Goods and Chattels of Tho[mas] Cooke of Hartford late deceased appraised by John Burton and Robert Nicholls

In the Hall	Goods belonging thereunto	04.00.00
In the parlor	*(£ column very indistinct)*	03.00.00
In the Celler		02.00.00
	The roof abroad	02.00.00
	A little nagg	02.00.00
In the Chamber over the Entrey		01.10.00
	Linning	02.00.00
In the Kitchin and Chamber over it		01.10.00
In the Chamber over the Hall		02.00.00
In the Chamber over the parlor		02.10.00
[Total]		18.10.00

The marke [of] John Burton, Robert Nicholls, Ann Cooke

Exhibited: 6 August 1673

**57   Judith Day   Grant of Probate: 9 June 1688   Will Ref: 34HW1
        Widow**

In the name of God Amen: The eighteenth day of May 1688 and In the fourth year of the Reign of King James the second over England etc, I Judith Day of the parish of St Andrews In Hartford In the County of Hartford, Widdow, being sick of body butt of sound and perfect mind and memory, praised be God for the same, Considering the uncertainty of the time of my abode here on earth and the shortness of my Journey on this side of the Grave: to prevent all Trouble thatt might otherwise arise amongst my survivers: do make and ordain this my Last Will and Testament In maner and form following: hereby Revokeing all other wills and Testaments by me formerly made. Imprimis I give and bequeath unto my Daughter Mary Kent the sum of Thirty pounds of good and Lawfull money of England to be paid to her within six months after my

WILLS AND INVENTORIES FOR HERTFORD, 1660-1725

Deceace by my Executor hereafter named.. Item I give and bequeath to my daughter Margarett Thurston the like sum of Thirty pounds of good and lawfull money of England to be paid to her by my Executor within nine months after my Deceace.. Item I give and bequeath unto my Daughter Hannah Kent the like sum of Thirty pounds of Good and lawfull money of England to be paid to her by my Executor within twelve months after my Deceace.. Item I give and bequeath unto my Grandson Nathaniell Bray and my Granddaughter Mary Bray the sum of five pounds apeece of good and Lawfull money of England to be paid to them by my Executor within twelve months after my Deceace. Item I give and bequeath to my son In Law John Thurston the sum of ten pounds of good and lawfull money of England to be paid to him within four months after my deceace In Condition thatt he will take my grand Daughter Sarah Bray and keep her till she shall be Capable of getting her own Livelyhood. Item I give and bequeath unto poor people calld quakers the sum of twenty shillings and to the poor of the parish where I now live the sum of ten shillings both of them to be paid Within on month after my Deceace.. Item I give unto my son John Goodman all my household goods thatt I shall Leave att my Decceace. Item I ordain and make my son John Goodman my sole and only Executor of this my Last Will and Testament hoping he will Carefully perform the same According to this my plaine mind and meaning and I give unto him all whatsoever else is mine thatt is nott herein before bequeathed to enable him to pay my Debts and Legacys above mentioned and funarall Charges and lastly this my will hath been Read unto me and I have sett my mark and seall to the same and published it to be my very Last Will and Testament the Day and year herein first above mentioned.

The marke of Judith Day Widdow

In the presense of James Saban, Joseph Prentis, Matthew Sake [possibly Seale]

Inventory Reference: 34HW1

(date of appraisal omitted)

A True Inventory of the household goods and stock of Judith Day of the Parish of St Andrews In Hartford: Widdow Lately Deceased

Imprimis In The Hall   1Table, 2 forms, 3 Joynt stoolls,
1 setle Bench, 5 Chaires, 5 Cushions,
1 pair of fire Irons, 1 pair of tongs,
2 Brass Ketles, 3 Brass Skelletts,
2 brass Scumers, 1 Brass Chaffing Dish,
Brass pottage pott, 1 Iron pottage pott,
1 pair of pott hooks, 1 pair of pott hangers,
1 grid iron, 1 pott Iron, 1 Chopping Knife,

WILLS AND INVENTORIES FOR HERTFORD, 1660-1725

	1 Tin Dripping pan, 1 tin puding pan,	
	1 flower box, 1 paper box, 2 pair of Bellows,	
	1 pair of Snufers, 1 Aple Roaster,	
	4 Smoothing Irons,1 spitt, 3 Iron scewers,	
	1 Iron frying pan, 1 Jack and weights,	
	1 spice box,1 parcell of earthen ware,	
	1 brass Cake pan, 2 Brass Candlesticks,	
	1 bras morter and pestle, 34 peeces of Pewter,	
	1 bible, 1 parcell of glasses, 2 Iron Candlesticks,	
	1 brass warming pan, 1 tin Lanthorne,	
	1 perfuming pott	07.00.11
Item In the Parlour	2 Tables, 1 form, 1 wooden Elbow Chair,	
	4 Leather Chaires, 4 Searge Chairs,	
	1 hanging Cuboard, 1 pair of Andirons,	
	1 fender, 1 pair of tongs, eleaven pair of sheetts,	
	23 Diaper napkins, 6 Flaxen napkins,	
	1 Diaper table Cloth, 1 Diaper towell,	
	3 pair of pillowbeers, 3 window Curtains,	
	1 Rod, 6 Course towells, 2 table Cloaths	05.10.00
Item In the Stair Casse	1 Clock	01.05.00
Item In the Parlour Chamber	4 old Chests, 3 Boxes, 1 Turkey workchair,	
	1 stooll box and pan, 2 stoolls,	
	1 Leather Chair, 1 Cushion, 1 Table topp,	
	1 suit of Curtains	01.02.00
Item In the Hall Chamber	1 bedsted, cord, straw bed,	
	1 suit of curtains and vaillens, 2 Chests,	
	2 boxes, 1 Joynt stooll, 1 Chest of Drawers,	
	1 Looking glass, 1 feather bolster,	
	1 Coverlidd, 1 green Rugg, 2 old blanketts,	
	1 flock bedd, 1 pillows, 1 pair of Andirons	03.05.00
In the litle Chamber	1 bedsted, 1 flock bed, 1 bolster, 2 blanketts, and other Lumber	00.12.06
Item In the Cellar	3 hogsheads, 1 barrell, 1 Kilderkin,	
	1 old bedsted, 5 tubs, 1 Copper,	
	18 glass Botles, and other Lumber	02.15.06

WILLS AND INVENTORIES FOR HERTFORD, 1660-1725

Item In the other Room	1 feather bed, 2 feather bolsters, 2 flock bolsters, 3 blanketts	02.15.06
	1 Silver Cup, 2 silver spoons	02.05.00
	her wearing aparrell, money In the house	10.00.00
	on horse, on Cow	10.00.00
	Crop of Corn & grass on the ground	06.00.00
	a parcell of wood In the yard	
	a parcell of Turfes, Tann	02.00.00
	a parcell of hair	01.00.00
	a parcell of horns	01.00.00
[Subtotal]		**58.12.02**
In The Tann Fatts	18 Dicker of Backs att 10 £ a Dicker	180.00.00
	4 Dicker & a halfe of hides	30.00.00
	9 Dozen Calve Skinns	10.00.00
	The Tann and ouses In the Fatts	02.00.00
	The Mill and Mill Lake, Riddle, horse Coller	02.00.00
	The shave and shave block	00.01.00
	1 wheelbarrow, 1 Cowlbarrow, 1 tan fork, 1 Shovell, 1 wooden horse	00.10.00
	2 shootts, 1 Geat	00.08.06
	2 working Knives, 1 flesher, 1 shearing Knife, 1 sawing Knife, 1 Beam, Beam Apron	00.10.00
	28 Fatts, 5 scourings, 3 Tubs, 1 Pump	20.00.00
	1 graine Tubb	00.02.06
	12 Loges and Timber Bark att £4.3s a Load is	49.16.00
	2 Loads Slabb Bark att £3.2.6d a Load	06.05.00
	4 Shedds, 1 Killhouse, 1 Barn	12.00.00
	4 Sheep, 3 Lambs	02.00.00
	Book Debts	23.17.06
[Subtotal]		**339.10.06**
[Subtotal]		**58.12.02**
[Total]		**398.02.08**

These Goods were Apraised by us William Hurrell, Will[iam] Guyse

WILLS AND INVENTORIES FOR HERTFORD, 1660-1725

58 Judah Lea   Grant of Probate: 9 March 1662   Will Ref: 80HW29
Widow

In the name of God Amen. I Judah Lea of the p[ar]ish of St Andrews in Hartford in the County of Hertford widd[ow] beeing sicke and weary in body but ofe good and p[er]fect memory, thanks bee to God, and considering the frailty and uncertainty of this naturall life, doe make this my last will and Testam[en]t in maner and forme followeing, That is to say: First I bequeath my soule unto Almighty God and Jesus Christ my Saviour, through whose merritts and sufferings I hope to have eternall life, and my body to bee burried att the discretion of my Executor hereinafter named. It[em] I give and bequeath unto Elizabeth Finch, the wife of Thomas Finch of the Burrough of Hartford, one great Joyne Chest that now is standing in my Lodging Chamber. It[em] All the rest of my goods householdstuffe whatsoever, lynen and Wollen, I doe give and bequeath unto Susan Harbor my Grandchild to her and her heires forever, provided the s[ai]d Susan shall demeane and behave her selfe well and to that end doe desire my well beloved Freind Thomas Lane of Bromfeild in the County of Hertf[or]d yeoman to bee overseere and Gaurdner for the s[ai]d Susan and to dispose and give these things unto the s[ai]d Susan as hee shall see her have occasion, onely the s[ai]d Thomas Lane to bee satisfyed his charges. And Lastly I doe make my s[ai]d Freind Thomas Lane my full and sole executor of this my Last will and testament. In witness whereof I have heerunto sett my hand and seale the Sixth day of July in the yeare of our Lord 1662, The marke of Judah Lea, Sealed, Signed and declared in the presence of us, The marke of Mary Casely, Sarah Allen, John Hill Jun[ior]

Inventory Reference: 80HW29
Date of Appraisal: 21 November 1662

An Inventory of the goods and Chattells of Judith Lea of the p[ar]ish of St Andrewes in Hertf[or]d in the County of Hertford wid[ow] deceased made taken and appraised by us whose names are hereunto subscribed, the xxith day of November 1662

a Table, frame	00.10.00
three stooles, a forme	00.04.00
a Cupboard	00.14.00
a kettle, an Iron pott, pot hookes	00.10.00
a pot hanger, a grate Iron	00.02.00
a little brass morter and pestle	00.01.00
earthen ware in the Cupboard and other lumber	00.05.00
a bedsted in the Lower roome	00.03.00
two old Flock beds, two old boulsters,	

WILLS AND INVENTORIES FOR HERTFORD, 1660-1725

two old pillowes	00.15.00
bedstedd, Trundell bed above staires, Cords	00.18.00
a Court Cupboard	00.08.00
a petticoate, wastcoate, a yeallow petty Coate	00.08.06
a greene apron, a Cushion	00.02.06
two Lynnen apruns, two old pillowbeers	00.04.00
a short table Cloath, three towells,	
a pare of new Cushions	00.06.00
a box, a little stoole table	00.04.06
an old hutch, a little stoole forme	00.02.06
an old Chest	00.04.00
five old sheetes, two old shifts	00.10.00
a smoothinge Iron	00.00.08

[Total]   **07.00.08**

Exhibited: 11 December 1662

(an identical inventory was exhibited 9th day of March 1662/3. Neither inventory shows the names of the appraisors)

59   Robert Nicholson   Grant of Probate: 15 November 1688   Will Ref: 96HW66
     Yeoman

I Robert Nichollson of **Hartford in the County of Hartford** yeoman doe make and ordaine this my last **will and testament** revoaking all wills by me formerly made. Impr[imi]s I give and **bequeath** unto my son Matt Nichollson one flockbed, two pare of the best towing sheets **and two blanketts** and bedsteed and twelve pence in mony. Next I Give unto my Granddaughter Frances Bond one feather bed and two blanketts and her Grandmothers **truncke and one paire of andirons made by R: Greene.** Next I give unto my Daughter **An Nichollson** twenty pence to be paid when she comes to age. Lastly I make my lo[ving] **wife** An Nichollson full and wholle Executrixe of this my last will and testament **unto which I have doe** set my hand Robart Nichollson this 7th of July 1686 in the presence of Joshua Downes, John Clowes, Esais Omans

Inventory Reference: 96HW66 *(very faded document)*
Date of Appraisal: 3 October 1688

An inventory of the Goods of Robert Nicholes deceased taken the thurde of October 1688 as follows

WILLS AND INVENTORIES FOR HERTFORD, 1660-1725

It[em] in the Kitchen	one Jacke, spites, 6 pewter dishes, to brass kittells, a table, a forme, other of thinges	02.10.00
In the litell palor	one table, one old cubbord	00.05.06
In the ?	one long Table, to old formes, old Bedsted, a trundell bedsted, to old flock Beds, to old blanketes, to Ruges, a pare of old andirons,	
In the Chamber over the Kitchen	one Long Tables, 6 Joynd stoules, a old Bedsted, old fether Bed and Bolster, a old Rug, to old Blankitts, a Livery cubbord	03.10.00
In the Chamber over the enterey	one bed stead, cord, matt, curtaines and vallens, to fether beds, to Bolsters, to Blankitts, a Rug, one trundell Bedsted, flock bed, Bolster, old Rug, to old Chests	04.10.00
In the old Chamber	to old Bedsteds, a old cubbord pres, a old flock Bed, Bolster, trundell bedsted, other odd thinges a Bowte the Rome	04.00.06
In the wood howse	all the wood and ?	01.15.04
In the stable	a parcell of hay	02.03.00
	a parsill of ?	00.10.00
In the seler	a Bere stall, Boxe, od thinges	03.04.06
	ewes and lame	05.00.00
	his waren aparill, money in his purse	01.10.00
[Total]		**28.06.10**

apraised By Mee Will[iam] Guyse

WILLS AND INVENTORIES FOR HERTFORD, 1660-1725

60   Mary Pettit   Grant of Probate: 14 July 1690   Will Ref: 104HW51
Widow

In the name of god Amen: The twenty eight day of May one Thousand six hundred and ninty Accordinge to the Comp[ut]attion of the Church of England: I Mary Pettett of St Andrewes: Hertford and In the County of Hertfordsheir Widdow: Beinge of perfeitt memory and Remembrance praised bee to god Doe make and ordaine this my Laste Will and Testamentt in manner and Forme Followinge viztt: Firste I bequeath my soule Into the handes of Allmighty God my maker: Hopine that through the merittorious Death and pasion of Jesus Christe my onely saviour and Redeemer to Receive Free pardon and forgiveness of all my sins And as For my body to bee buried In Christian buriall att the Discrettion of my Executores heare nomminated. First itt is my will and minde and I doe Give and bequeath unto Martha March, the wife of John March of the City of London and in the County of Middellsex, Ten pounds Lawfull mony of England to bee paid with in six months after my Desese. Item I give and bequeath unto James Hundsdon my Granchild in the Parrish St Andrewes Hertford and County as above said the bedd and beddinge wheare on I now ly Exceptinge the Feather bedd. And in the Roome of thatt bede I doe Give and bequeath unto him the s[ai]d James Hunsdon my Granchild one Feather bedd in the Rubb Roome and I doe give and bequeath more anto the s[ai]d James two paire of Flaxen sheetes and two paire of Pillowes and two pudder Dishes of the beste sortt. Item I give and bequeath untto Mary Nickholls my Gran Child Daughteer, to William Nickholls of St Andrewes Harttford and County as above one Trundell bedd and beddinge that beelonges to itt and the old Green Rugg and the beste hangeinge press and the beste Chiste in the Roome over the Washhouse and two paire of the beste Flaxen sheets and two pare of the pillowes and two pudder dishes And the biggiest Cettell and two Green Cheires. Item I give and bequeath unto Susanna Nickholls my Gran Child Daughter of the said William Nickholls two paire of Flaxen sheetes of the beste sortt and two paire of Pillibers and two Pudder Dishis of the beste sortt. Item I give and bequeath unto the poore of the parrish of St Andrewes Hertford the som of one pound to bee ordered as my Executor thinkes Fitt. And Lastely itt is my Will and minde and I doe make my Gran Child John Hunsdon Eldiste sonn to John Hunsdon senior of the Parrish of St Andrews Hertford and in the County of Hertfoordsheir Farmer my whole and sole Executtor of this my Laste will and Testament And doe Give and bequeath unto him the s[ai]d John Hundsdon my Gran Child all my Goods and Chattels that I dye poss[ess]ed on to him and his heires for ever: And doe putt my whole Truste in hem to see my body decentelly buried In my parrish Church so neare my Husben as can bee with Convenience done: he paying all my deptes and Legisess and Funerall Expensess and Revokinge all other Wills and Testaments. In Wittness heareof I the said Mary Pettett have putt on my hand and seall the day and yeare First above Written Mary Petitt Sealled and Delive[re]d in the presence of Henry Marson, Will[iam] Smart, Henry Willson

WILLS AND INVENTORIES FOR HERTFORD, 1660-1725

Inventory Reference: 104HW51
Date of Appraisal: 14 July 1690

A true Inventory of the goods and Chattells of Mrs Mary Pettit of Hartford in the County of Hartford widd[ow] lately deceased taken the 14th day of July Anno D[omi]ni 1690 vizt

In the Parlor	A table, Carpett, six Joynt Stooles, Six turkey worke Cushions, a livery cubbord, cloath, seven leather Chayres, A wodden Elboe Chayre, a pare of Andirons in the passage, one table	02.02.06
In the Stayre case	a Hanging press, a Chest, a Clock	01.12.06
In the Chamber over the Parlor	a Hanging press, a bedsted, cord straw bedd, one Feather bed, one Flock bed, 2 boulsters, one blankett, one rugg, Curtaines and valance, 2 pilllowes, Hedcloath, testerCloath a round table, carpett, 4 Chayres, one livery cubbord, cloath, one looking glass, A pare of Andirons, one Chest, a window Curtaine, rodd, 2 truncks, a great Bible	08.18.00
In the Chamber over the Kitchin	Bedsted, cord, Flock bed, Feather bedd, bolster, pillow, two blanketts, one old coverlid, Curtaines valance, ruggs, one Chayre, window Curtaine, rodd, a brass Fyer shovell, tongs, a pare of Andirons, a Chest, stoole, a trundle bedd, materials belonging	09.03.06
In the Chamber over the Washhouse	a bedsted, cord, straw bedd, a Fether boulster, a Flock pillow, a Coverlid, Curtaine and valance, rodds, a Chest, a Folding table	02.02.06
In the Chamber over the Milkhouse	a Halfe headed bed, cord, Straw bed, Fether bedd, 3 blanketts, two Chests, a stoole	02.03.06

108

WILLS AND INVENTORIES FOR HERTFORD, 1660-1725

In the Kitchin	Nyne a twenty peeces of pewter,	
	3 kitles, one porrage pott, 4 skillets,	
	A brass Chaffing dish, a warmeing pan,	
	a brass washpan, a brass bake pan,	
	a Jack and weight, two spitts, 2 dripping pans,	
	a brass morter and pesell, a pare of Andirons,	
	1 Fier shovell, tongs, a Fyer forke,	
	a pare of bellowes, a gridiron,	
	2 pare of potthankers, 7 Chayres, a table,	
	3 Joynt stooles, a setle bench, earthen parts,	
	a glass case, some other small things,	
	a spice boxe	06.16.00
In the Sellar	two drinke stalls, two small vessells,	
	some botles	00.04.06
In the Wash house and milk house	a Copper, Irons, sixe tubbs, 3 plank formes,	
	a beare stall, 3 other formes,	
	some other Lumber	02.15.10
	The Lynnen	
	12 paire of sheets, 6 pare of pilloberes,	
	A doz[en] and Halfe of napkins,	
	3 table cloaths, some towells,	
	some other things	07.01.00
In the yard	10 Load of wood	07.00.00
	debts sperat and desperat	15.00.00
	Wearing Cloaths, money, plate	10.00.00
In the garrett	some old Lumber	00.03.00
	A cubbord	00.05.00
[Total]		**75.07.10**

These goods were valued and prised by us the day and date First written Will[iam] Guyse, John Hill Praysors

WILLS AND INVENTORIES FOR HERTFORD, 1660-1725

61 Mary Pomfrett   Will Ref: 104HW23
Widow

In the name of God Amen. I Mary Pomfrett of the parish of All S[ain]ts in Hertford in the County of Hertford widow being sick of body but of sound and perfect memory, praise be to God for the same, doe make this my last Will and Testament in manner and forme following, that is to say: First I give and bequeath unto William Catlyn, Son of John Catlyn of Broxbourne in the said county husbandman [and] John Pitkin of the parish of St Johns in Hertford aforesaid husbandman, All those my two Messuages or Tenem[en]ts w[i]th the appurtenances now in the tenure or occupacon of Thomas Fulke and William Read or their assignes situate in the parish of St Johns aforesaid To hold to them their heires and assignes for ever. Item I give and bequeath unto my two kinswomen Alice and Elizabeth Catlyn, daughters of my brother William Catlyn, the summe of tenn poundes apeice to be paid to them w[i]thin five years next after my decease and if in case either of them shall decease before the expiracon of the said five yeares after my decease then my will is the surrvivor of them shall receive both legacies. Item I give and bequeath unto Elizabeth, Alice, Judeth and Mary Brewer fower Daughters of Thomas Brewer of Hoddesdon in the said County Grocer the sume of fiftie shillings a peice to be paid to them w[i]thin five yeares next after my decease. And if in case any of them decease before the expiracon of the said five yeares my will is that the porcon or porcons of the deceasing p[er]son and p[er]sons shall be devided amongst the survivor or survivors of them. Item I give unto my said Brother John Catlyn and to his daughter Mary Catlyn the sume of fourty shillings a peice to be paid to them w[i]thin one yeare next after my decease. Item I give and bequeath unto Phillipp Bridgeman, son of Phillipp Bridgeman of St Johns aforesaid, husbandman, and to his daughters Jane, Mary and Elizabeth the sum of fifty shillings a peice to be paid to them w[i]thin fower yeares next after my decease: And if in case any of them shall decease before the end of the said fower yeers then my will and meaneing is that the porcon and porcons of such deceaseing p[er]son or p[er]sons shall bee devided amongst the survivor or survivors of them. Item I give and bequeath unto my sister Grace Holding, wife of John Holding of the Rye, neear Stanstedd the sume of tenne poundes to be paid to her w[i]thin fower yeares next after my decease. Item I doe will and require my Executor hereafter named to pay the severall legacies hereinafore bequeathed as hereinafore is ? and appointed. Item all my goods, Chattells, household stuffe and implements of household stuffe, moveable and imoveable, whatsoever I give and bequeath unto my said Brother William Catlyn whoe I make and ordaine full and whole Executor of this my last Will and Testament. And Lastly I doe hereby renounce revoke and make void all former and other Wills whatsoever by mee heretofore made. In Wittnes whereof I the said Mary Pomfrett have hereunto sett my hand and seale and published this to be my last Will and Testam[en]t this present sixth day of March in the one and thirtieth yeer of the reign of King Charles the second over England etc And in the yeare of our Lord God 1678 he marke of Mary Pomfrett Sealed and delive[re]d and published in the presence of Joseph Saward, Andrew Goodman, W. Hale

Inventory Reference: H22-1315
Date of Appraisal: 30 May 1682

A Inventory of the goods and chatteles of Marey Pumpret widdo of brickendon in the countey of Hartford as folloth this 30 day of may 1682

Debts owing to the testator

Item for moneys owing from Will Hawkings of Hartford	100.00.00
Item for more money owing from John Runinton of hartford	20.00.00
Item for more moneys owing from the wido Runinton of hartford	10.00.00
Item for more moneys owing from goodman browen of hartford	10.00.00
Item for more moneys from John Smith of nassing	10.00.00
Item for more money owing from the wido Landey of eckellford	10.00.00
Item for more money owing from thomas Collings of hartford	06.00.00
Item for more money owing from thomas Hutchin of St Johns Hertford	05.00.00
waring clothes, purse and money	03.05.00
[Total]	**174.05.00**

apraised by us whos hands are under wrighten Joseph Saward, John Pitkin

62 **James Pendred**
    Maltster   **Bond of Administration: 12 January 1712**

Granted at Yardley to Samuell Penderid and Thomas Coulson before Robert Strutt and witnessed by Nicholas Bickerton and Edmund Pendred

Inventory Reference: H23-1889
Date of Appraisal: 13 December 1712

Ann Inventory of the Goods and Chattels of James Pendrid latley deceased in the parrish of Saint Andrew in the Corpurashon Town of Hartford malsster Aprasid by us who names are under ritten this 13 day of December Ann Dom[ini] 1712

his Waring Aparill, reddey money	15.00.00
malt in the maltlast one hundrid and therty quarters	130.00.00

WILLS AND INVENTORIES FOR HERTFORD, 1660-1725

malt working one the flouer and one the Couch stepid in the sestern nintey quarter	16.00.00
Barley in the barleylast one hundrid and twenty quarters	102.00.00
Aparcill malt dust	01.12.06
Wood in the yeard and wodhos	10.00.00
one wier, one kill to drey malt	08.00.00
one skren, one busshill, shovils	01.00.00
one fether bed, one boulster, two blankits, bedstid, Curtins, one Coverlid	05.00.00
oing to James Pendrid of Book depts	90.07.00
2 malt quornes	01.10.00
[Total]	**440.09.06**

[Appraisers]
Thomas Coulson, Thomas Goose

Exhibited: 12 January 1712

**63   John Radford   Grant of Probate: 3 March 1671   Will Ref: 111HW37
       Baker**

In the name of God amen. the first day of March In the Twentie Third yeare of his Maj[es]ties reigne Anno D[o]m[ini] One thousand six hundred and seventy, I John Radford of Hertford in the Countie of Hertford Baker being sicke in body but of sound and perfect minde and memory, praise be given to god for the same, And knowinge the uncertainty of this life one Earth and beinge desirous to setle things order[ly] doe make this my last will and Testament in manner and forme following: That is to say first and principally I comend my soule to Almighty god my Creator assuredly beleevinge That I shall receive full pardon and free remission of all my sins and be saved by the precious death and merites of my blessed Saviour and redeemer Christ Jesus and my body to the earth from whence it was taken to be decently buried in such Christian manner as to my Executrix here afternamed shall be thought meet and convenient. And as touchinge such worldly Estate as the lord in mercy hath lent me, my will and meaninge is the same shall be imployed and bestowed as here after by this my will is expressed. And first I doe revoke, renounce and frustrate and make void all wills by me formerly made And declare and appoint this my last will and testament. Item I give and bequeath unto my loveinge wife Frances Radford All that my three Cottages or tenements with the appurtenances situate standing and being in Ware and p[ro]fitts there of arisinge for and duringe unto the full end and terme of fourteen yeares next after my decease towards the bringing up of my children and at

WILLS AND INVENTORIES FOR HERTFORD, 1660-1725

the end of the said terme of fourteene yeares. Then Item I give and bequeath unto my three sonns hereafter named, that is to say, John radford, Henry Radford and Francis Radford or the survivors of them their heires and assignes All that one of the aforementioned Tenements with the app[ur]tenances scituate standinge and beinge in the Land ? in Ware now in the possession of James Sixton or his Assignes to be equally devided amongst them by the Judgment of two honest men. Item I further give and bequeath unto my fower daughters here after named that is to say Elizabeth Radford, Mary Radford, Margarett Radford and Phebe Radford their heires and Assignes For ever All those my two fore mentioned Cottages or Tenem[en]ts lyinge one the backesid of the afore mentioned Tenem[en]t To enter upon and have the said two Tenements Just at the end of the afore said Terme of fourteene yeares next after my decease to be equally devided amongst them by the Judgment of two honest men. Item it is my minde and will that my fore mentioned daughters or any one of them shall have free ingresse and grosse regresse ways and Passage to fecthe water at the pumpe that now stands in James Sextons yard, Provided all waies never the lesse and upon this condition, that my said daughters their heires and Assignes whatsoever shall beare their full sheare in the repaireinge and mendinge of the said pumpe as often as need shall require. Item I further give and bequeath unto my said Loveinge wife Frances Radford the use and p[ro]fitts thereof arisinge of All my household stuffe goods and Chattelles whatsoever for and duringe the terme of her naturall life towards the bringinge up of my said Children and from and after the decease of my said wife Frances. Then Item I further give and bequeath unto my aforementioned seven sonns and daughters All the aforementioned household stuffe goods and Chattells whatsoever as aforesaid to enter upon presently next after the decease of my said wife Frances to be equally devided amongst them by the Judgment of two honest men. Item I doe make and ordayne Thomas Herrecke of Hertford aforesaid Praysser and my brother John Draper my two Overseeres of this my last will and Testament, And for all theyr paynes and Care they shall take therein. Item I give and bequeath unto them and to each of them the sume of ten shillinges apeece to be paid by my Executrix. Item I doe further make and ordaine my said wife Frances my sole Executrix of this my last will and testament. Item it is further [my] minde and will that if my said wife Frances shall at any tyme after my decease happen to marrye with any manner of man or p[er]son whatsoever, That man before the marriage day shall put in good securtyes and be come bound in a bond of three hundred pounds of lawfull money of England to my said two Overseeres of this my last will and Testament that the aforementioned household stuffe, goods and Chattells whatsoever shall not be wasted nor imbasselled awaye, but shall remaine and be to the use of my seven children aforesaid presently after the decease of my said wife Frances And thus I finish my last will and Testament. In witnes whereof I have hereto sett my hande and seale the day and yeare first above written John Radford, Signed, sealed, published and declared in the presence of Will[iam] Plumer, Ralph Freeman

WILLS AND INVENTORIES FOR HERTFORD, 1660-1725

Inventory Reference: 111HW37
Date of Appraisa: 22 March 1670/1

A true Inventorie of all and singuler of the goods and Chattells of John Radford latly of Hertford in this Countie of Hertford Baker deceased prized this two and twentieth day of March in the Twentie third yeare of his Maj[est]ies reigne A[n]no D[omi]ni 1670

In the Chamber where he died	One beddsteed, vallans and curtaine, one Feather bedd, Feather boulster, flock boulster, one Rugg, one blanckett, all other furniture belonging to the said beddstead, One trundle beddsteed, flocke bedd, Rugg, blancketts, one presse, one Chest of drawers, a box, a glass case, one wicker chaire, three leather chaires, one wooden chaire, one table and frame, one carpett, sixe Joyne stooles, one paire of Anirons	08.01.00
In the flower Parlor	One Table and frame, sixe Joyne stooles, a side cubboard, three chaires, one paire of Anirons	01.02.00
In the hall	one Table Frame, fower Joyne stooles, one setle, one Cubboard, one Jacke, sixe speets, one paire of Anirons, a paire of Tongs, two paire of Potthangers, one paire of fire racks, two fire shovels, seven chaires, one dipinge pann	03.05.00
In the kitchen	pewter, brass	17.00.00
In the shop	one little Table and Frame, one forme, pottshelfe	00.10.00
In the bell parlor	one Feather bedd, boulster, pillowes, one Rugg, Coverlett, blanckett, Curtaines and vallance, one Table and Frame, Sixe Joyne stooles, one little table, two Chaires, one side cubboard, one livery cubboard, one Fire Irons	07.00.00

WILLS AND INVENTORIES FOR HERTFORD, 1660-1725

In the backe house   one boultinge mill, a flower binn,
two kneding troughes,
some other small things   04.02.00

In the great chamber   two standinge beddsteeds, two Feather bedds,
boulsters, pillowes, Ruggs, blanckets,
Curtaines and vallance, two trundle beddsteeds,
one Feather bedd, two flocke bedd, coverletts,
blancketts, one Table and Frame,
eleven Joyne stooles, one forme, one little Table,
a side cubboard, fire shovell, tongs, Anirons,
three chaires, one Chest
some lumber in the next roome   25.00.00

In the Neather Chamber   Three beddsteads, three Feather bedds,
three feather boulsters,
sixe Feather pillowes, two ruggs,
one Coverlett, sixe blancketts,
Curtaine and vallance, two tables,
three Joyne stooles, one cubboard,
Two great Chestes, a cheire in the passage   18.00.00

In the Cocke roome   one little Table and Frame, fower stooles,
a forme, one paire of Anirons   00.14.00

In the halfe Moune Chamber   Three beddsteeds, two Feather bedds,
a flocke bedd, one paire of Curtaines
and vallance, two Coverletts, fower blancketts,
two boulsters, three pillowes, two Tables,
three Joyne stooles, one Chest   08.00.00

In the Seller   fower beerstalls, a poudering tub   00.10.00

In the white heart Chamber   One standinge bedsteed,
Curtaines and vallance, one Feather bedd,
one boulster, two pillowes, one Coverlett,
blanckett, one Trundle bedd,
flocke bedd, boulster, coverlett,
blanckett, a side cubboard and cloath,
two window curtaines, five chaires,
sixe stooles, one Table, one Truncke,
a lukinge glasse   12.00.00

115

WILLS AND INVENTORIES FOR HERTFORD, 1660-1725

In the Merry Bull Chamber	One standinge beddsteed, Curtaines and vallance, one Feather bedd, boulster, two pillowes, one Rugg, One blanckett, one Trundle bedd, flocke bedd, boulster, two pillowes, one coverlett, blanckett, one little Table and Frame, Carpett, two Joyne stooles, two other littles stooles, one side cubboard, one great Truncke, three paire of Anirons, two paire of Tonges, one fire shovell, one paire of bells, one Joyne Chaire	14.00.00
In the hall Chamber	one standinge beddsteeds, three under beddsteeds, one Feather bedd, three flocke bedds, boulsters, pillowes, Coverletts, blancketts	06.00.00
	ready money in the house	05.00.00
	Linnen in the house his wereinge apprell	05.00.00
	Woode in the yard, hay	08.00.00
	two Mayres, fower hoges	08.00.00
	five load of Meale	05.00.00
[Total]		**186.04.00**

Prized upon the day and yeare above written by us whose names are here under written John Cherl?, W[illia]m Turnere, Tho[mas] Herrick

Exhibited: 30 March 1671

64 John Rogers   Grant of Probate: 16 April 1687   Will Ref: 111HW67
     Cordwainer

The Second day of June 1685, I John Rogers of Hertford in the County of Hertford Cordwayner being aged but of p[er]fect mynd and memory, praised be God, Do ordayne and make this my Testament and last Will in manner and forme followinge. Impr[imi]s I give and bequeath unto Joane Rogers my wife my House in Hertford

WILLS AND INVENTORIES FOR HERTFORD, 1660-1725

aforesaid and the use of all and singuler my goods, Bonds and monyes whatsoever for and duringe the terms of her naturall life. And after her decease I give and bequeath the said Goods, Bonds, and moneyes which she leaves and the House aforesaid to my Daughter Elizabeth Rogers and to her Heires for ever. But notwithstandinge it is my mynd and will that my Son Thomas Rogers shall enjoy that end of my said House, w[hi]ch was formerly John Webb's shopp and the Buttery and the Chamber that is over them And that he shall also enjoy that part of my Woodhouse called the Stable w[i]th free egress and regress at all seasonable tymes and through the Butry into the said Chamber, yard, shopp and stable, and for his owne use of the said yard in comon, w[i]th my said Daughter and those which may live with her or belong unto her; and w[i]th those to whome she may lett the part of the said House unto; soe which last mentioned I give unto my said Son for and during the terme of his naturall life, and that he shall enter upon them, after my said wife's decease, but not before, ? after the decease of my said Son Thomas Rogers I give the said Shopp and Chamber Buttery and Stable, and his right of comon in the said yard ? to my said Daughter and to her Heires for ever. Item I also ordayne and make my said Daughter Elizabeth Rogers sole and only Executrix of this my said last will and Testament, desireing her to p[er]forme it carefully, unto whome I give all the rest that is myne w[hi]ch is not herein before bequeathed, Lastly I caused this my will to be written and read unto me and I heare sett my Hande and Seale to the same and declared and published it to be my very and only last will and Testament, revoakeing all other wills, formerly by me made, the day and yeare first herein and above mentioned John Rogers Signed, sealed, declared and published to be the very and only last will and testament of the said John Rogers in the presence of us John Trott, William Hurrell, John Hunsdon

Inventory Reference: 111HW67

An Invatary of the Goods that are in the house of John Rogers latley Deceased

It[em] in the	2 pewter Dishes, four basons,	
Lower Rome	chamber pot, a Candellbox, A kitell,	
	2 poridg pots, dripin pan, blankit,	
	Coverlid, Cubard, tabell, 4 stoulls,	
	2 Chaiers, 2 stoulls, form, fiershovell,	
	tongs, a pare of Andeyrons,	
	a pare of belles, spit, grideyron,	
	3 smothing eyrons, Looking glas,	
	A Litell Tabell, A worming pan	02.00.00

WILLS AND INVENTORIES FOR HERTFORD, 1660-1725

In the stairhed Rome	an oulld bedstid, beding, an oulld pres, trunck, A form, stoull 4 Litell boxis, 4 pare of shets, 4 pare of pillobears, 2 touiles, 4 napkins, Tabell Cloath	00.02.10
In the Midell Chamber	bed, Beding, A Joynt stoull, 2 Chaiers, A Litell Tabell, a Litell stoull, Trundell bed, beding, a box, another box, a Livery Cubord and Cloath, A pare of Andoyrons, fireshovell, tongs, A Long Chist, 4 pare of sheets, 5 pillobears, 4 Touells, 2 small pillobears, 9 napkins, 3 tabell cloaths	03.00.00
In the butrey	sum small od things, a Tub, a flaskit, fagits in the barn	00.05.00
	his waring Cloaths, money in purs	05.00.00
[Total]		**12.15.00**

65   Edward Reason
Bond of Administration: 13 December 1673

Granted to wife of the deceased, Jane Reason and Edward Bache at Hertford before Thomas Juice and Ralph Battell

Inventory Reference: H23-2003
Date of Appraisal: 27 November 1673

A True and perfect Inventory of all the Goods and Chattells of Edweard Reason of the p[ar]ishe of All Saints Hartford in the County of Hartford late deceased taken by us whose names are hereunder written this 27th November 1673.

Imprimis in the Kitchin	pewter, brasse, Jacke, 3 spitts, other Implements	08.00.00
In the Great Chamber over the Kitchin	ii bed steads, feather beds, Curtaines vallence etc, furniture thereunto belonging	16.00.00
	a long table, i forme, 4 Joynt Stooles	02.10.00

WILLS AND INVENTORIES FOR HERTFORD, 1660-1725

	6 leatherne Chayres, 3 other Chayres	01.10.06
	A side bourd, table, carpett,	
	6 Cussions, a chest	01.00.00
	a fire shovell, toungues,	
	a payre of small andirons	00.06.00
In the Chamber over the Halle	a bedstead, feather bed, boulster, pillows, blanketts, Curtaynes and vallens, Counterpayne, 6 Chayres, Stooles thereunto belonging	16.00.00
	A Lyvery Cubbord w[i]th Cover Cloth, a Table, Carpett	02.10.00
	A payre of andirons, Creepers, fire shovell, toungues, bellowes	01.00.00
	a silver boule, 6 silver spoones	03.10.00
In the Garrett over the Great Chamber	a bedstead, trundle bed, two flocke beds, furniture belonging	05.00.00
	6 chests, boxes in the same roome	01.00.00
Lynning	8 payre of flaxen sheets, 12 payre of towen sheets, nine payre pillowbeers, 6 dussen and halfe napkins, 8 table Clothes, a new fetherbed Ticke	36.00.00
In two other Lyttle Garretts	one bedstead, feather bed, Curtaynes and vallens w[i]th there furniture	06.00.00
	Also a halfeheadedbed, flocke bed w[i]th furniture	01.10.00
	Hay in the Barne, wood in the yarde	14.00.00
	his wearing Apparell, Money in purse	14.00.00
[Total]		**131.16.00**

Wittnessed by us Ed[ward] Bache, James Goodman, Jane Reason

Exhibited: 13 December 1673

WILLS AND INVENTORIES FOR HERTFORD, 1660-1725

66   James Runnington   Inventory Ref:H22-970

An Inventry of the goos and chattles of James Runnington Late of Hertford deceased

Imp[rimis]	1 Bedstead, curtains and valons	00.12.00
In the Best	1 Feather Boule, Bolster, 2 Rugs	02.10.00
Chamber	A chest of Drawers	00.14.00
	Chairs, Stooles	00.10.00
	1 table, carpitt	00.05.00
	1 trundell Bedstead, Beading	00.10.00
	A Pair of Andirons	00.04.00
[Subtotal]		**05.05.00**
In the Staire	1 Bedstead, curtains	00.10.00
Head Chamber	1 Feather Bead, Coverlead, Matt	01.17.06
	1 pallat Bead	00.10.00
	a settle Benche, chest	00.03.06
[Subtotal]		**03.01.00**
In the Backe Chambers	2 Bedsteads, Beading	02.10.00
In the Lower	1 Flocke Bead, Bowlsters	01.10.00
Lodging Room	Blanketts, Rugg	00.09.00
	1 Chest, 2 Chairs	00.04.00
[Subtotal]		**02.03.00**
In the palour	1 table, Stooles	01.00.00
	a pair of Andiorns	00.05.00
	4 Chairs	00.04.00
[Subtotal]		**01.09.00**
In the Cellar	Drinking vesells	01.05.00
In the Hall	1 table, 3 stooles	00.12.00
	6 small chaires	00.05.00
	1 pair of Racks	00.10.00

WILLS AND INVENTORIES FOR HERTFORD, 1660-1725

	1 Jacke, Spitts	00.13.00
	some other things, pott Hoocks	00.15.00
[Subtotal]		**04.00.00**
In the Buttery	1 smal copper	01.00.00
	pewter, Brase	03.00.00
[Subtotal]		**04.00.00**
In the Brewhouse	1 Copper	03.00.00
	Brewing veseals	01.00.00
[Subtotal]		**04.00.00**
In the Shop	a Bolting Mill	00.15.00
	Steales, waites, jackes	01.00.00
[Subtotal]		**01.15.00**
In the yard	2 Hoggs	02.00.00
	Wood, Coales, Hay	04.00.00
[Subtotal]		**06.00.00**
	Linnen	04.10.00
	Wairing apparell, purse and money	05.10.00
[Subtotal]		**10.00.00**
[Total]		**44.03.00**

Appraised this 3rd of March 1678-9 by us William Bennett, Thomas Webb

Exhibited: 7 April 1679

WILLS AND INVENTORIES FOR HERTFORD, 1660-1725

67   Joan Treyherne   Grant of Probate: 3 March 1687/8   Will Ref: 132HW13
    Widow

In the name of God Amen. I Joane Treyherne of the parish of All S[ain]ts in Hertford in the County of Hertford, widow, being sick and infirme of body but of sound and perfect memory and understanding, thankes be therefore given to Almighty God for thesame, doe make and ordayne this to be my last will and testament in Manner and Forme Following. Imprimis I give and bequeath into the hands of Almighty God the soule w[hi]ch he gave me and my body I resigne to the earth from whence it came, assuredly trusting through the meritts and Intercession of my blessed Saviour that they shall be againe reunited and shall appear togeather at a Joyfull Resurreccon. And for the settling and asuring of that worldley estate where w[i]th it hath pleased God to blesse me, I give and dispose thereof as followeth. Item to my loving Brother Mr John Humberston now residing at Aston in the aforesaid County of Hertford I give tenn shillings to buy him a ring to wear in remembrance of me. Item to my loving sister Anne Humberston, Spinster, who now liveth togeather w[i]th me, I give all the Moneys w[hi]ch are due to me by any specialtye or specialties from any p[er]son or p[er]sons whatsoever. Item to my said Sister Anne Humberston I give and bequeath all the rest and residue of my money and debts Goods and Chattels and all other my personall estate whatsoever well knowing my said Sisters great want and need thereof. Item my will is that my body be decently interred in the Church or Church yard of the parish of All S[ain]ts Hertford aforesaid at the discretion of my executrix. And I doe hereby constitute and appoint my said loving Sister my Sole Executrix of this my last will and testament hereby revoking and adnulling all former wills by me made. In witness whereof I have hereunto sett my hand and seale this one and twentieth day of March in the Nyneteenth yeer of the reign of King Charles the second over England etc, the m[ar]ke of Jone Treyherne, Signed, sealed, published and declared to be the last will and testament of the said Joane Treyherne in the presence of Tho[mas] Burges,   Edward Humberston

Inventory Reference: 132HW13
Date of Appraisal: 20 August 1667

An Inventory of the goods and chattells of Joane Trayherne widdow deceased of Hertford in the County of Hertford made and appraized the twentieth day of August 1667 by us Joseph Browne and Edward Humberston as followeth vizt

In her Chamber	a Fether bedd, two fether boulsters, two fether pillowes, a flocke bedd, a matt, a rugg, two blanketts, curtaines and vallance, curtaine roods,

WILLS AND INVENTORIES FOR HERTFORD, 1660-1725

bedsted	06.10.00
two ioyned chests, two trunkes, a chaire, two cushions, other smale things	01.10.00
a silver spoone, her waring apparrell	10.00.00
good debts	115.00.00
ready money	00.05.00

[Total] 133.15.0

the m[ar]ke of S Humberstone
Joseph Browne, Edward Humberstone

Exhibited: 3 January 1668

68 William Turner   Inventory Ref: 32HW39
     Gentleman   Date of Appraisal: 21 August 1683

A true Inventory of the goods and Chattells of William Turner of Hartford in the County of Hertford gent lately deceased taken the one and twentyeth day of August Anno Dom[ini] 1683 vizt

In the great Parlor one drawing table, seven Chayres,
three Joynt stooles, one litle table,
two Carpetts, sixe turky worke Cushions,
one Cubbord, spice boxe,
one pare of Andirons, one pare of doggs,
Fier shovell, tongs,
a screene to sett before the Fyer,
Curtaine rod about the Fyer, one Jack,
Chayre, two Leaden weights,
one smothing Iron, one sconce or Candlestick,
three window Curtaines,
one long Wooden candlestick,
one warmeing pan, two spitts,
one dripping pan, sixe pewter dishes,
sixe plates, two brass skilletts,
two brass kitles, two brass potts,
a litle brass Fryeing pan,
a brass Morter and pestell, a litle brass ladle,
a brass Candlestick, one Andiron,

WILLS AND INVENTORIES FOR HERTFORD, 1660-1725

	two Iron barrs, one Cloath beater,	
	two old Cushions, pare of Bellows,	
	a pewter pye plate, Cleaver, a pewter bason,	
	a gridiron, 3 pott hookes, a pynt copper pott,	
	a parcell of Earthen ware, a litle siff,	
	some other odd things, a whyte table,	
	two brushes, a pare of sceales, seven weights,	
	a p[ar]cell of tinn ware, a brass sawcell,	
	a brass Chaffing dish	05.00.06
	[ink blot smudged the middle figure]	
In the Garrett	one Flock bolster, one boxe, one pye peele,	
	one wooden Flaskett, eighteene stone botles,	
	one salt boxe, a bedd pan, a Close stoole and pan,	
	a Iron peele, a stone morter pestell,	
	one bole and tray, Five Curtaine rodds,	
	a ? hole Frame, a Iron For the Fyer,	
	an old Cushion, a trevett, 2 tables,	
	a folding Board	01.01.00
In his Chamber	one Chest, one booke stan,	
and Clossett	one case of drawers, a litle forme,	
	one litle Cubbord, one livery Cubbord	
	and Cloath, one Chest of drawers,	
	seven Chayres, one great trunck,	
	one pare of brass Andirons,	
	one pare small Andirons, one other Chest,	
	another Chayre, a Hanging press,	
	Foure window curtaines, one Ironing Cloath,	
	a deske, two boxes, a Clock,	
	a lookeing glass, a Fyer shovell, tongs	02.09.00
In the wood house	3 stack of wood, Halfe a load of Faggotts	02.09.00
Att Mrs Fardons House	two drinkestalls, a botle rack, Henn pann,	
	one bedsted, cord, Matt, a tester Cloath,	
	one great Chest, one old trunck Hooped with Iron,	
	one other old Chest, one old Forme,	
	a wooden rake in the garden,	
	A livery Cubbord [value illegible]	
	his weareing Clothes	15.00.0?

The will of prominent Hertford yeoman and malster Nathaniel Hale, made 30th June 1671. It includes bequests of money to his five sons and three daughters (see page 125).

[Hertfordshire Archives & Local Studies]

The former St Andrew's church, Hertford, c.1820, from a watercolour by George Shepherd. The church was rebuilt in 1869. (from original in the Knowsley extra-illustrated edition of Clutterbuck's History of Hertfordshire, vol V, p 170A).

[Hertfordshire Archives & Local Studies]

	Ready money	11.15.00
[Subtotal]		29.12.06

	six pare of sheets, two dussun of Napkins, four Bordcloths, one pare of pillowbears, four Towels	04.15.01
	six silver spoones, a little cup	02.03.04
[Subtotal]		06.02.06
[Total]		35.15.00

These goods was valued and prized by us the day and date First written John Barfoot, Andrew Bray Praysors

69   Nathaniel Hale   Grant of Probate: 2 March 1671/2   Will Ref: 56HW97
Yeoman; Maltster

In the name of God amen. The 30 of June 1671. I Nathanael Hale doe revoke al former wils and I doe make this my last will and testament in maner and forme folowing: imprimis I doe give and bequeath unto my son Thomas Hale the som of twentipounds of laful monis of Engeland to be p[ai]d him within a yeere after my deces. Item I doe give and bequeath to my sone Nathanael Hale and to my son John Hale five pound apees to bee p[ai]d them within a yeer after my deces. Item I doe give and bequeath to my son Josiah Hale the som of five pound to bee p[ai]d him within a yeere after my deces. Item I doe give and bequeath to my son Samewel Hale the som of fiftipounds to bee p[ai]d within a yeer after my deces. Item I doe give and bequeath unto my two dafters Mare Smart and Sarah Sawerd ten pound apees to bee p[ai]d them within a yeer after my deces. Item I doe give and bequeath unto my dafter Elizabeth Hale the som of a hundered pounds to bee p[ai]d her after my deces and in case ani of those doe die afor the time of ther legases is due there legases shall bee at the Exseqetrix disposal. I doe make and ordaine my loving wif Margaret Hale to bee hole and soale Exseqetrix to see this my last wil and testament performed and ifit hapen soe as mi wif shale depart this life afore mee I doe then make and ordaine mi son Samewel Hale to bee my hole and soale Exseqetrix to see this my last wil and testament performed and fulfilled and therunto have set my hand and sele the daye and yeere above written Nathanael Hale [the will was written in his own hand], witnese thereunto John Parkin, Joshua Morris

WILLS AND INVENTORIES FOR HERTFORD, 1660-1725

Inventory Reference: 56HW97
Date of Appraisal: 10 November 1671

And Inventory of the goods and chattells of Nathaniell Halle in the County of Hertford in the liberty of Brickendon yeomen latly deceased praised by us whose names are heare underwritten this tenth of November 1671

Imprimis in the Hall	on tabell, a presse Cobord, a Clock and other lumber	05.00.00
Item in the parler	a longe tabell, six stooles, two carpets, a short tabell, twelve lether chaires, tenn other chaires, stooles, two paire of Andirons, fiershovell, tonges, a glasse case, Livery cobord, cloath	05.00.00
It[em] In the dary house	a Cheese presse, Milke vessells	02.00.00
It[em] In the brewhouse	a copper, Marsh fatt, other small vessells	02.10.00
It[em] In the chamber over the parler	a bedsted, Fether bed, boulster, pillowes, a tabell, three stooles, chaires, stooles, Fiershovell, tonges	15.00.00
It[em] In the Citchinge	brasse, pewter, a jacke, spitts, Racke and other thinges	15.10.00
It[em] In the chamber over the milkhouse	Bedsted, Fether bed and the furnitur	06.00.00
It[em] In another chamber	a bedsted, fether bed, a hanginge presse, and other things	08.00.00
	twenty seven paire of sheets	15.00.00
	Five duzen of Napkins, three longe tabellcloaths, 15 short ons	07.10.00
	a silver bowle, two silver spoones	03.10.00

WILLS AND INVENTORIES FOR HERTFORD, 1660-1725

It[em] **In the chamber over the Citchinge**	three beds	06.00.00
It[em] **In another chamber**	two Fether beds	04.00.00
It[em] **In the Seller**	5 hogsheads	01.00.00
	Five horse with theire harnest	17.10.00
	Five Mares, two geldings	08.10.00
	two colts	02.00.00
	three Longe carts	03.00.00
	three donge carts	05.00.00
	A wagon	04.10.00
	Six cows, a bull	16.10.00
	Eight Hoggs, Five piggs	10.00.00
	Two Reekes of oats and pease	90.00.00
	A coke of Hay	10.00.00
	Five Bay of barley	55.00.00
	a bay of wheate	17.10.00
	Thirtey Five sheepe	10.00.00
	Waringe Apparell, money in purse	10.00.00
[Total]		**355.10.00**

Praysed by James Goodman, Jon Heath, Nicholas Tuffnell

Exhibited: 2 March 1671/2

70   John Helder   Grant of Probate: 31 March 1688   Will Ref: 59HW1
       Carpenter

In the name of God Amen. The thirteenth day of January 1687. I John Helder of the Towne of Hertford in the County of Hertford Carpenter being weake and sick in body but of sound knowledge mind and memory and being willing to settle that Estate as it hath pleased God to give me before I dye doe therefore make this my last Will and testam[en]t in manner following. First and principlely I comend my soule into the hands of my blessed Saviour and Redeemer and my body I desire may be buryed according to the discrecon of my Exec[utor]s herein after named. And as concerning

WILLS AND INVENTORIES FOR HERTFORD, 1660-1725

my temporall Estate I dispose of it as followeth First I give and bequeath unto Marrable my wife for her life my howses or tenem[en]ts w[i]th their app[ur]tenances in Mill Lane and Kibes Lane in Ware my howses w[i]th their app[ur]tenances at Amwell w[i]th the ground lately bought of Sollomell Fiennes and the messuage or tenem[en]t at Butchery greene whereon I live w[i]th the app[ur]tenances for soe many yeares as shee shall live the same being Leasehold upon condicon notw[i]thstanding that shee keepe them in tenantable repaire as after that shee bring up and maynteyne my son John Helder out of the rents and profitts of the s[ai]d premises as well as maynteyne herselfe out of the same. And after her decease I give the s[ai]d tenem[en]ts in Ware to my son John and to his heires forever alsoe I give to my s[ai]d son John after his ? decease the s[ai]d tenem[en]t at Butchery greene for the Terme of yeares for to come, but my will is that if my son John shall happen to dye before he come to age and w[i]thout Issue, that then I give the moyety of the s[ai]d tenem[en]t at Ware to my son Joseph and his heires forever and the other moyety thereof I give to my brothers Samuell Hemmings of Aston and John Hemmings of Parish Munden and to their heires forever in trust nevertheless for the sole benefitt of my daughter Mary, the wife of Joseph Ansell of Highcrosse, and not of her husband hereof of the s[ai]d Mary forever. And likewise if my son John shall dye as afores[ai]d I give the s[ai]d tenem[en]t at Butchery greene the one moyety thereof to my son Joseph and the other moyety to the s[ai]d Samuell Hemmings and John Hemmings in trust for the sole benefitt of the said Mary my daughter and not of her husband and of such children as shee shall leave behind her. My will is further that if my wife shall happen to marry againe then shee shall only have the s[ai]d messuage at Butchery greene for soe many yeares as she shall live and the tenem[en]ts at Ware in Mill Lane and Kibes Lane shall imediately upon such marriage goe to my son John and his heires as if shee were as truly dead and in case of his death ? as afores[ai]d; and the Tenem[en]ts and ground at Amwell after my wifes decease or in case shee marry againe then upon such marriage I give these to my Son Joseph Helder and to his heires forever. Item I give to my wife Marrable my little tenem[en]t at Butchery greene with the app[ur]tenances in the possession of John Dighton being alsoe Leasehold for all my Tenure. Item I give to the s[ai]d Samuell Hemings and John Hemings and to their heires forever my tenem[en]ts w[i]th their app[ur]tenances in dead Lane in Ware afores[ai]d in trust nevertheles that they pay the rents and profitts thereof as they shall receive the same to my s[ai]d daughter Mary Ansell for her p[ar]ticular mayntenance and benefitt and not that for her husband, but if it shall please God that shee shall overlive her husband then the s[ai]d tenem[en]t in dead Lane to bee to the only use of the s[ai]d Mary and her heires forever, but if the s[ai]d Joseph Ansell her husband shall happen to overlive her then my will is that then my s[ai]d trustees shall bestow the rents and profitts of my s[ai]d last mensoned tenem[en]t after her decease towards the mayntenance and bringing up of the Children which my s[ai]d daughter Mary shall leave behind her and after they shall bee brought up to shift for themselves or live of themselves then to bee to the use of the right heires of my said daughter Mary forever. And as concerning my howsehold goods and furniture in my howse I give them to my said wife. But as concerning my Park of wood and timber debts due to mee and all other my personall estate whatsoever after my just debts that I shall owe at my death and funerall charges shall bee discharged out of the same, my will is that what shall remayne thereof shall bee equally devided into foure parts and I give to my said wife one fowrth part thereof, an other fowrth p[ar]t I give to my Son Joseph, an other fowrth part I give to my Son John and I desire my s[ai]d wife to take care of his share for him and the last part I doe give to the s[ai]d Samuell Hemings and John Hemings to be sold by them at the best price they can and the moneys thereof arising to be payd or layd out for the best benefitt they can of my s[ai]d daughter Mary only and not of husband. And whereas I have one howse more not yet disposed of wherein my s[ai]d daughter Mary and her husband live being at Highcrosse in the p[ar]ish of Standon but I never yet could gett any rent of her husband for it, my will is and I give the said tenem[en]t or Cottage at Highcrosse afores[ai]d w[i]th the appertenances unto the said Samuell Hemings and John Hemings and their heires forever in trust neverthelesse to bee to and for the only benefitt of my s[ai]d daughter Mary only and not of her husband and of his heires forever. Item I give to my s[ai]d Son Joseph all my working tooles whatsoever belonging to my trade of a Carpenter or otherwise howsoever. Lastly I make and ordaine the said Marrable my s[ai]d wife and the said Samuell Hemings and John Hemings Exec[uto]rs of this my will desiring them to see the same faithfully p[er]formed according to the contents and true meaning thereof, thus revoaking all former wills by mee made I make ordaine and publish this to bee my last will and testam[en]t. In Wittnesse whereof I have hereunto sett my hand the day and yeare afores[ai]d. Item I give to my son Joseph and to his heires the tenem[en]t I bought of him in the High Street at Hertford, John Helder Signed, published and declared to bee the last will and testam[en]t of the s[ai]d John Helder in the presence of us Jo Chauncy, Daniell Smyth, Tho[mas] Buncher

Inventory Reference: 59HW1
Date of Appraisal: 28 February 1687/8

Inventory of the Howsehold goods of John Helder Lately Deceased taken And Aprasied by us whowse hands are heerunder subscribed the 28 day of Febry 1687-8

In the Parlor	1 bedsted, Cord, matt, Roods, 1 fether bed, bolster, 1 p[ai]r blankits, Quilts, 1 p[ai]r blew Curtins and vall, 6 Turkey worke Chayres, table, Carpitt, 1 glass, 1 glass shelf, window Curtins, Roods, 2 bas bottom Chayres, one Joynt stoole, Cushin, some pecis of erthen ware	09.00.00

WILLS AND INVENTORIES FOR HERTFORD, 1660-1725

In the Kitching	9 puter dishes, 6 puter porringers, parcell erthen ware, 1 poot shelf 1 table, 6 chayres, 1 table, one Joynt stoole, 1 Candle box, parcell tin ware, 1 spitt, 1 Jack and waight, 2 p[ai]r Andirons, fiershovle, tongs, Gridiron, 1 p[ai]r bellowes, 1 Looking glass, 1 Warming pan, 2 Copper poots, 2 Smothing Iorns, 1 putter bason, pessill and mortor, 1 pothooks, some other od things,	02.10.00
In the Chamber	1 bedsted, cord, matt, 1 flock bed, 2 blankets, 2 Rugg, 1 p[ai]r Curtins and vallans, 1 Cowrt Cobert, 1 table, 2 Chayres, 2 stooles, 4 boxes, 1 forme, 1 old press, window Curtins	02.10.00
In the Best Chamber	Bedsted, Cord, straw bed, Roods, 1 p[ai]r searge Curtins and vallans, 1 fether bed, 2 blankits, 1 wosted Rugge, 1 p[ai]r Chest drawers, 1 press, 5 Chayres, 1 p[ai]r andiorns, fiershovle, Tongs, bellowes, table, box, frame, 1 Large Chest, window Curtin, rood	10.00.00
	The Linin 1 doz napkins, 4 p[ai]r pillobers, 12 Large towels, 6 table Cloaths	02.05.00
In the Seller and Brewhowse	4 Kilderkins, 1 Copper, Brewing vessels, 2 Cittles, 1 brass poot, 3 killits, 2 skimers, 1 brass friingpan, passell bottles, scales, brass sasepann, passell erthen ware, with some od things	
	Waring Aparrill, Mony In pockits	10.00.00
[Total]		**42.05.00**

John Barfoot, Adlord Bowde Aprasors

WILLS AND INVENTORIES FOR HERTFORD, 1660-1725

71 John Hill   Grant of Probate: 8 March 1705   Will Ref: 59HW98
    Shopkeeper

In the name of God Amen. I John Hill of the Burrough of Hartford in the County of Hartford, Shopkeeper, beeing aged and in yeares but of good and perfect memory, thankes be to God, and considering with my selfe the uncertainty of this present mortall life, with my owne handwriteing doe make and declare this my last will and testament (in maner and forme following (that is to say): First I bequeath my soule unto Almighty God my Creator and to Jesus Christ my Saviour and redeemer thorough whose merritts after this mortall life is ended I hope and doe beleeve to have everlasting Joy and happyness in the world to come. And as for such worldly goods that God of his mercy hath lent mee I doe give and dispose of vizt. Imp[rimis] I doe give and bequeath unto Margery my loving wife All that my Mansion house that I lately bought of John Gurrey the elder wherein I now dwell scituate next the Tolebridge in Hartford with all thapp[ur]tenances thereunto belonging (Excepting the two chambers that I built over John Wolmers beare buttery) For and during her naturall life and after her decease then to goe to John Gurrey the younger and the heires of his body lawfully begotten for ever. But for want of such heires then to goe to his Brothers Christopher, Charles and Richard Gurrey or any other brother that shall bee by his Father John Gurrey lawfully begotten hereafter equally betweene them or to be Assigned over by any one of them to each other for ever. I doe give and bequeath unto Margery my loving wife All that my house I bought of Jonathan Francis of Bigleswade in the County of Bedds gent lately deceased with all the Appertancnes thereunto belonging and the two Chambers over John Wolmers beare buttery For and during her naturall life. And after her decease unto John Wolmer and Elizabeth his wife for and during their naturall lifes and after their decease unto their two sonns John and Joseph Wolmer and to the heires of their bodyes lawfully begotten for ever. But for want of such heires or any other Child lawfully begotten of the body of the s[ai]d Elizabeth Wolmer to goe unto the daughter of the s[ai]d John Gurrey the elder equally devided amongst them for ever. Item I doe give and bequeath to Margery my loveing wife the Benefitt of Thomas Hadden lease payeing to the Earle of Salsburry his rent. Item I doe give and bequeath unto John Wolmer and Elizabeth his wife the sume of Five shillings a peece and one shilling a peece to their Children to bee paid to them within three months next after my decease by my Executrix heerafter named And to John Gurrey and Martha his wife three shilling a peece and their Children one shilling a peece to bee paid in like maner. Item I doe give and bequeath unto Joseph Hynd of Stapleford two shillings and six pence to buy him a pare of gloves, And I doe give and bequeath unto Thomas Hill of Cheshunt and Sarah Hill his sister three shilling a peece to buy them a pair of gloves to bee p[ai]d to them within six months next after my decease. Item I doe give and bequeath unto William Peeters of Hartford, Coamer, and Sarah his now wife three shilling a peece and one shilling a peece to his Children to bee paid to them within three months next after my decease And I doe forgive him the debt that hee oweth mee in the shopp. Lastly All the rest of my goods and Chattells bills bonds debts and dues wtsoever to mee belonging I give and bequeath unto Margery my Loving wife whome I doe make and ordayne full and sole Executrix of this my last will and testament desireing her and John Wolmer and Elizabeth his wife to see my body decently burried in St Andrew Hartford Church yard on the left hand the path that leads up to the great dores of the Church a litle above the grave of one Daniell Tuffnell A Cooper. In Witness whereof I have heerunto sett my hand and seale sixth day of September Anno Dom[ini] 1703 John Hill, Signed, sealed, published and declared to bee the last will and testament of the s[ai]d John Hill, William Smyth, The mark of John Tipton, The mark of Sarah Thurgood.

Memorandum before the sealing and publishing of this codicill I doe give grant and bequeath unto Margery my loving wife all that right title and interest in the Queens Armes att Southton in the County of Hartford that I now have and full power and Authority to sell give or grant the same to Mr Hardisty of the Temple of London gent or to any other p[er]sons that will buy the same, paying to the s[ai]d Mr Hardisty his Executor or Assignes the Mortgage money beeing 46 li upon the same. And upon the sale and receipt of the overplus I doe desire her to give Will Peeters of Hartford, Coamer, or his wife or Children Fourty shillings next after sale and receipt of the same. In witness whereof I have heerunto sett my hand and seale the Sixth day of September Ann Dom[ini] 1704 By way of Codicill or schedule to the s[ai]d will confirmeing the s[ai]d will on the other side and this to bee parte thereof John Hill, signed, sealed, published and declared on both sides to bee the true and onely will of the s[ai]d John Hill in the presence of Thomas Smith, Stephen Haynes, Samuell Randall

Inventory Reference: 59HW98

(date of appraisal omitted)

An Inventory of the Goods and Chattells of the late Deceased Mr John Hill, Grocer, in Heartford, Taken and Appraised us whose Names are hear Under written etc

Goods in the Garrate	00.09.00
Goods in the Further backe Chamber	03.09.00
Goods in the Maids Chamber	01.04.00
Goods in the Chamber over the Shope	06.18.00
Lining	03.14.00

WILLS AND INVENTORIES FOR HERTFORD, 1660-1725

Goods in the Chamber over the Kicthing	06.19.06
Goods in the Further back Chamber next the yard	04.19.00
[Subtotal]	**27.12.06**
Goods in the Parlor Chamber	01.00.00
Goods in Johns Chamber	01.15.00
Goods in the Parlor	00.12.00
Goods in the Kicthing	03.04.00
Goods in the Buttrey	02.17.00
Goods in the Shope	75.17.06
Goods in the Brewhouse	03.15.00
In the Yarde 1 horse, 1 Cow, hay, Wood	05.10.00
[Subtotal]	**94.10.06**
[Subtotal]	**27.12.06**
[Total]	**122.03.00**

Wittness Whereof we have heare unto sett our hands the day and date abovewritten
John Barfoot, Andr[ew] Goodman

Exhibited: 8 March 1705

72   Mary Humberston   **Will Ref: 57HW66**
      Spinster

In the name of God Amen. I Mary Humberston of the Towne of Hertford in the County of Hertford Spinster being sick in body but of sounde and p[er]fect mind and memory praised bee God doe make and ordaine this my last will and testament in manner and forme following that is to say: first and principally I comend my soul into the hands of Almighty God hoping through the merits of my blessed Saviour Jesus Christ to have full pardon and forgivenesse of all my sins and to inheritt everlasting life. And my body I comitt to the earth to bee decently buryed at the discression of my Executrix hereafter named. And as touching such temporall estate as it hath pleased God to bestow upon me, I dispose thereof as followeth: First after my debts and funerall charges are defrayed, I give and bequeth unto my very loveing Sister, Anne Humberstone, all my right title, estate, share and intrest of in and to the howse wherein I now live w[hi]ch I hold by Lease together w[i]th the said Lease. And also I give and bequeath unto my said loveing Sister all my Goods and moveables whatsoever w[i]th in my said howse and elsewhere. And of this my last Will and Testament I make my said Sister Anne Humberston sole Executrix. In Wittnesse Whereof I have hereunto sett my hand this fifth day of March in the 36th yeare of the reigne of our Sovereigne Lord Charles by the Grace of God of England Scotland France and Ireland King defender of the faith etc Anno D[omi]ni 1683 her marke Mary Humberston. Wittnessed by us Elizabeth Wren, John Greenings, Charles Fox

Inventory Reference: 57HW66
Date of Appraisal: 21 March 1683/4

An Inventory of the goods and Chattells of Mary Hummerston of the parrish of All Saints in Hartford Spinster lately Deceased Taken by us whose names are under written this 21th day of March in the year of our Lord 1683-4

In the Hall	1 old Chaire, 1 old Court Cubbord, 1 old forme	00.02.06
In the Kitchen	1 old table, 1 old Cubbard, 4 Chairs, 3 Joyne Stoles, 1 Jack, Spitt	00.10.00
In the Buttery	4 Little pewter Dishes, 1 Skillett, A pewter tankerd	00.08.00
In the Parlor	1 Table, pare of Anirons, Dogs	00.05.00
In the Stare Case	1 old Trunck, 1 press, 2 Trundle beds, 1 Bedsted, 1 old Feather Bed, 2 old pillows, 1 old Bolster, 1 old wicker Chair	01.05.00
In the Chamber over the parlor	1 Chest, 4 pare of Shetts, 1 Bedsted, vallens and Curtaines, 1 Flock bed, 1 Blankett, 1 Rugg, 1 Chest of Drawers, 1 pare of Andirons, Fireshovell, Tongs, 2 old Joyne stoles, 1 Table, 6 Napkens, 6 Towells	01.10.00

WILLS AND INVENTORIES FOR HERTFORD, 1660-1725

In the washhouse	1 Little Copper	00.06.00
In the yard	1 Load of wood	00.06.00
	Waring Apperell	01.00.00
	In Dibts Sperat and Desperate	20.00.00
	Total of Goods excluding debts	05.12.06

[Appraisers]
Ro[bert] Warner, William Norris

73   John Turner
   Barber;Weaver   Bond of Administration: 29 August 1699

Granted to Michaell Turner of Pirton, barber, his brother before Thomas Woodward

Inventory Reference: H23-2391
Date of Appraisal: 23 August 1699

An Inventory of the Goods and Chattell of the Late Deceased John Turner Barber and Weaver in the Towne of Hertford; Taken and Appraised by us Whose Names are hear under Written; etc.

the goods in the Garrat	05.12.10
the goods in the Chamber	03.02.06
the Lining	01.00.00
the goods in the Rome bellowe	04.06.00
the goods in the shope	10.12.00
wood, **other things in the yarde**	01.12.06
Wearing Apparrell, Debts Sperat	30.00.00
[Total]	**56.05.10**

John Barfoot, John Barfoot junior Appraisers

Exhibited: 29 August 1699

WILLS AND INVENTORIES FOR HERTFORD, 1660-1725

74   Thomas Wheatly   Inventory Ref: H23-2518
                              Bond of Administration: 18 January 1663

Granted to Elizabeth Wheatly, wife of the deceased
An Inventory of the goods and chattells of Thomas Wheatly deceased

In the Hall	one drawing table, three high joyned stooles	00.08.00
	six old chaires	00.02.00
	one Jack, three spitts	00.06.00
	one payre of Andirons, two payre of tongues, fire shovell	00.02.06
In the Kitchin	Copper, five brasse kettles, foure skillets, one brasse pott, one iron pott, one warming pan	02.00.00
In the Buttery	xi pewter dishes, ten pottingers, two pewter candelsticks, two flaggons, 2 pintpotts, one quart pot, five sawcers, one pewter bason	02.00.00
In the Barne	one Roan horse, one bay mare, one cart with furniture	05.00.00
Chamber over the Hall	Two bedsteds, Curtains and valens, one feather bed, one feather bolster, foure feather pillows, one flock bed, thre flock bolsters, 2 blanketts, tow Coverleds	02.00.00
Chamber over the Kitchin	one Bedsted, Curtaines and valence, two feather beds, two feather bolsters, thre pillows, 9 blankets, 2 Coverleds, one rugg, 2 table Carpetts	03.10.00
	A payre of Andirons, fire shovell	00.04.00
	six payre of shetts, two table cloths, three dozen of Napkins, six towels, six pillowbers	01.15.00
	A debt of eighteen pounds from Thomas Fulkes father in law to the	

WILLS AND INVENTORIES FOR HERTFORD, 1660-1725

	deceased Thomas Wheatly	18.00.00
	His wearing apparell	01.10.00
[Total]		**36.17.06**

[Appraisers]
Tho[mas] Herrick, Will[iam] Carter

Exhibited: 18 January 1663

75   John Woollard
            Bond of Administration: 5 July 1687

Granted to Ann Woollard, wife of the deceased before Samuel Fox and witnessed by Henry Bole, John Smart, John Wackett

Inventory Reference: H23-2557
Date of Appraisal: 26 May 1687

An inventarey of the goodes of John Wollor Latley desesed as falloes

It[em] in the furdist Chamber	one chest of drawers, 1 truncke, 3 bords, 3 chayeres, 1 halfeheaded bedsted, 1 grene Rug, 1 bolster, cord, blanckitt, flock bed, Bolster	02.04.00
In the other Chamber	one Bedsted, cord, mat, to fethetser bedes, one Bolster, one trundell Bedsteed, Sad colored curtaines and valens, 3 blankittes, 1 Rug, to chayeres, a pare of andirones, fier shovell, tonges, Litell table, 1 warming pan	07.04.00
	Linen	01.10.00
In the Hall	to pare of Iron andirones, tonges, fiershovell, clever, pothangeres, gridiron, 1 Jack, 1 spitt, 1 Copord, 4 chayeres, 3 Joynd stowles, 1 Table, a parcill of erthenware	01.05.00

WILLS AND INVENTORIES FOR HERTFORD, 1660-1725

In the Butterey	Puter	01.00.00
	Brase	02.00.00
	Bere, other odd things	00.10.00
[Subtotal]		**15.13.00**
It[em]in the woodhouse	Brewing vesells, wood all in the woodhouse	01.10.00
[Subtotal]		**15.13.00**
[Subtotal]		**01.10.00**
[Subtotal]		**17.03.00**
	his waren Close, Money in his purse	01.10.00
[Total]		**18.13.00**

apraysed By Us John Smart and Will[iam] Guyse

76 John Woolmer **Will Ref: 142HW53**
   Tailor   **Grant of Probate: 30 January 1705/6**

In the name of God Amen. The therd day of december Anno Dom[ini] 1705, I John Wollmore of the p[ar]ish of St Andrews with the Burrough of Hertford in the County of Hertford, Taylor, being very sick and weake in body but of p[er]fect mind and memory, thanks be given to God therefore, calling into mind the uncertainty of this life do make and ordain this my last will and Testament. That is to say, principally and First of all I recomend my soul into the hands of God w[hi]ch gave it hoping that through the merits of my Saviour Jesus Christ to have free pardon of all my sins and to enjoy everlasting life and as touching such worldly estate wherewith it hath pleased God to bestow upon me, I give devise and Bequeath as in manner and forme as Following: Imprimis I committ my Body to the Earth to be decently buried and my debts and Funerall charges to be paid and discharged by my Executrix and Executor hereafter named. Item I give and bequeath unto my well beloved son John Woolmore all that my Freehold estate and tenements and pmises situated att Chapmanes end in the p[ar]ish of Bengeo in the above said County of Hertford now in the ocupation of Francis Harvey unto him and his Heries [sic] for ever. But provided nevertheless that If my said son John Woolmore should depart this life before he attains unto the age of one and twenty years (of age) and without lawfull Issue, then this said Freehold estate,

WILLS AND INVENTORIES FOR HERTFORD, 1660-1725

Lands and p[re]mises shall goe unto my second son Joseph Woolmore to him and his heires forever. Item I further give and bequeath unto my said son Jon Woolmore All that my tennement called little Rickners with the Orchard containing be estimacon one Acre and a half be the same more or less unto him and his heires for ever. Provided nevertheless that if my s[ai]d son John Woolmer should depart this life before he attaines unto one and twenty years of age, and with out lawfull Isue that then this said tenement of Rickners with the said Orchard and p[re]mises shall goe unto my second son Joseph Woolmore to him and his Heires For Ever. Item I give and bequeath unto my dear and loving son Joseph Woolmore one Acre and a half of land in Ansley Feild, one Acre in Hackett Feild one Acre in Berycroft, One Acre and a halfe in Hole Orchard, One Acre and a half in Benjao Field one piece of ground cald Fountains containing two Acres and one half Acre in Broadoake mead, All lying in the p[ar]ish of Benjao Copi hold in the Mannor of Temple Chelsin as appears by one surrender of those pmises bearing date the First day of this Instant december unto him and his Heires for Ever. Item I furthermore give and bequeath unto my said son Joseph Woolmore one p[ar]cell of land called Little Hole Orchards containing by estimation three Acres be the same more or less And one Acre more in Crouch Feild And one Rood in Oldenfield And two Acres more in Ansley Field and berycroft all Copyhold and of the said Mannor of Temple Chelsin in the p[ar]ish of Benjow afores[ai]d As appears by a surrender unto this will wherein is menconed the payment of Fifty pounds unto one Ralph Reed of Hatfeild in the County of Hertford w[hi]ch said fifty pounds my said son Joseph Woolmore is to pay, And then the s[ai]d severalls pieces or p[ar]cells of Land I give unto him and his Heires For ever. Item my will and pleasure is and I do hereby declare that in consideration of the good service and care that my Brother Benjamin Woolmore will have in looking after the said p[re]mises of my said sons John and Joseph, I do order and strickly charge My said sons John and Joseph to pay between in equall proportion when they shall attain unto one and twenty years of Age the sume of five pounds of lawfull money of England within the month after they come unto the said Age of tweentone years. Item I give and bequeath unto my Brother in law John Gurrey the sume of ten shillings to be paid by my Executrix and Executor within six months after my decease. Item I give and bequeath unto my Cosin Mary Ray the sume of ten shillings by my executrix and Executor to be paid within six moths after my decease. Item I give unto John Hall ten shillings provided he helps to laye me out as he useth to do to others to be paid by my Executrix and Executor within six months after my decease. All the Rest of my Estate goods and Chattles whatsoever I give and bequeath unto my dear and loving Wife Elizabeth Woolmore And my son Joseph Woolmore whom I make my Full and sole Executix and Executor coequall of this my last Will and Testament. Furthermore I desire of Mr Joseph Duke to be my trustee and by this my last will do impower he the said Joseph Duke to enter upon any of the said p[re]mises to see what repaires are necessary and that no wrong may be done unto my said sons John and Joseph in their Lands and tenements and further power to examine and look into the goods and Chattles left in my house so as my dear and loving wife may not any wayes be injured. And for this his trouble all Charges w[hi]ch he shall reasonably demand shall be paid by the respective person or person with which he may or shall be concern'd and for non payment of his said Charges I do by these p[re]mises impower him to sue Arrest or detach any of the said p[re]mises to reimburse his said Charges together with all Charges of suit this being the true intent and meaning of this my last Will and Testament Lastly I do hereby utterly disallow, revoak and disanull all and every other former Wills or Testaments, legacies, request and Executors by me in any wayes before this time named Willed and bequeathed Ratifying and Confirming this and no other to be my last Will and Testament. In Witness whereof I have hereunto set my hand and seal the day and year before writen John Wollmer. Signed, published and declar'd by the said John Woolmore as his last will and testament in the present of us John Gurrey, The mark of W[illia]m North, Ben[jamin] Manning

Inventory Reference: 142HW53
Date of Appraisal: 11 January 1705

A true Inventory of the goods and Chattells and Houshold stuffe of John Wolmer of Hartford in the County of Hartford Tayler Lately deceased taken the Elevnth day of January Anno Dom[ini] 1705 vizt

In the Hall	severall goods	01.00.00
In the litle Buttery	severall goods	00.18.00
In the Shopp	severall goods	00.06.00
In the Kitchin	severall goods	08.00.00
In the best Chamber	severall goods	07.10.00
In the Chamber over the Kitchin	severall goods	01.15.00
In the Chamber over the Shopp	severall goods	02.05.00
In the garrett over the gate house	severall goods	00.10.00
In the garrett over the shopp	severall goods	01.00.00
In the garretts over the great Chamber	severall goods	01.10.00

WILLS AND INVENTORIES FOR HERTFORD, 1660-1725

	The Lynen	07.09.00
In the yard	with the wearing Cloaths	18.10.00
	Plate	04.00.00
[Total]		**54.13.00**

These goods and Chatells and Householdstuff was Appraysed by us and sett downe upon a double stamp sheete of paper the day and date first above written by us John Hill, Will[iam] Smitheman Praysors

Exhibited: 30 January 1705

77   **Henry Yates**   **Will Ref: 151HW18**
        Collarmaker

In the Name of God Amen. The four and twentith day of July in the yeare of our Lord God One thousand six hundred eighty two. I Henry Yates of Hertford in the County of Hertford, Collermaker, being sick and weake in Body but of sound and perfect mind and memory I praise God therefore And considering the uncertaine estate of this transitory life doe make this my last Will and Testament in manner following (that is to say): First and principally I Resigne my Soul into the hands of Allmighty God my Creator stedfastly believeing to receve pardon and forgiveness of my Sins through the alone meritts and mediacon of my Blessed Saviour and Redeemer Jesus Christ. And my Body I comitt to the Earth from whence it was formed to be decently buryed according to the discretion of my Executrix herein after named. And to such worldly estate as the Lord in mercy hath bestowed upon me, I dispose of the same as followeth: Imprimis I give and bequeath to my Loveing Wife Elizabeth Yates the sume of Forty pounds of lawfull money of England to be paid unto her within three months next after my decease. And moreover I give and bequeath to my said Wife the Goods and Chattells following now being in my dwelling house in Hertford aforesaid (that is to say): The Bedstead Bedd and bedding with thapp[ur]tenances whereon shee usually lies And also sixe pewter dishes, One brasse pott, One Greate brasse Kettle, One smale Brasse Kettle, two Skilletts, four pair of Sheetes, four pillowbeares, the Cupboard in the Parlor, the table by my Bedside, two Chests, One box, three flaxen Tablecloths, One dozen of Flaxen napkins, three Chaires, two litle joint Stooles with other such smale things for her necessary use as my executrix shall thinke fitt. Item I give and bequeath to my Sonn Henry Yates two shillings and six pence If he demands the same within twelve months next after my decease. Item I give and bequeath to my daughter Mary Tingey, the wife of Job Tingey of Ware, two shillings and six pence to be paid her within three months next after my decease If shee lawfully demands the same. Item All the rest residue and Remainder of my household stuffe, Money, debts owing to the Wares, Comodites,

WILLS AND INVENTORIES FOR HERTFORD, 1660-1725

Goods and Chattells whatsoever (my debts and funerall Charges being paid) I doe give devise and bequeath to my Loveing Daughter Elizabeth Yates whome I make appoint and Ordaine Sole Executrixe of this my Last Will and Testament. And I doe revoke and hereby make void all other Wills and Testaments heretofore by me made in or by word or writing and publish and declare this to be my only Last Will and Testament. In Wittnesse whereof I have hereunto sett my hand and seale the day and yeare first abovewritten Henry Yates Signed, Sealed, published and declared in the presence of John Jones, John Catlin, Jo. Richards

Inventory Reference: 151HW18
Date of Appraisal: 16 March 1682/3

An Invytary of the goods of Henry Yates Hertford Lately deceased March the 16th 1683/2

In the Hall	pewter	00.12.00
	Brass	02.00.00
	one Jack, spitts, Irons, fier shovell, tonges, Irons belongin to the fier	00.11.00
	an old Table, stoole	00.05.00
	three old Cupboards	00.06.00
	old Chaire	00.03.00
In the Chamber	three Beds with all belongin to them	04.00.00
	on Chest	00.05.00
	3 old Hutches	00.06.00
	one smale hangine press, 4 boxes	00.07.00
	two little Tables, two stools	00.04.00
	one old Chaire	00.01.00
	Lynine	02.10.00
	wearing Cloaths Hatt Stockins and shoos	02.00.00
	Earthen ware, trenchers	00.01.06
	two Little drinke Vessells, 2 wooden platters	00.03.00
In the Yard	Wood, two washin Tubbs	02.02.00
Goods In the Shop		05.00.00
	Cushins, two Window Kirtins	0.03.00
	Bellows, Candlbox, a desk	00.01.00
[Total]		**21.00.06**

valued by us Robert Nichollsone, John Greeninge

Glossary

Probate documents include a number of words which may appear unfamiliar, either because they are no longer in use, or because of unstandardised spelling: many of the writers wrote phonetically. For this reason, many letters are used interchangeably: s and c, y and i, u and v. This glossary has drawn very heavily on those definitions which appear in the following works by Lionel Munby and I am therefore indebted to his scholarship. Additional definitions have been taken from the Shorter Oxford English Dictionary (SOED).

Munby L.M. (ed), *Life and Death in Kings Langley. Wills and Inventories 1498-1659* (Kings Langley Local History and Museum Society 1981)

Munby L.M., *All My Worldly Goods* (Bricket Wood Society 1991)

ANDIRONS: large fire dogs designed to support a spit for cooking in an open hearth

APPURTENANCE: a minor property, right or privilege, subsidiary or incidental to a more important one (SOED)

BAIZE: a coarse, usually green, woollen stuff with a long nap (SOED)

BLOCK: log of wood, possibly used as a chopping block

BOLE: bowl

BOULTING HUTCH: a trough used for sifting meal

BRASEN: made from brass or resembling brass in colour

BUTTERY: (1) a place for storing liquor; (2) a place for storing provisions

CARPET: a thick fabric, generally made of wool, and in the seventeenth century generally used to cover tables, beds and cupboards

CELLAR: any store room, sometimes used as a brewery, but not necessarily underground

CESTERN: cistern or large vessel used for storing liquids

GLOSSARY

CHAFER, CHAFING DISH: small brasier containing coals for heating food and drink

CHARGER: large flat dish

CLOSE: (1) a yard for cattle; (2) an enclosed field

CLOSE STOOL: a commode

COBIRONS: irons on which a roasting spit turns

COLT: young male horse less than five years old but having left its mother

COPYHOLD: land held by copy of a manor

CORDS: the tight cords woven across a bed frame to support a mattress

COUNTER: a desk or writing table where accounts could be compiled

COUNTERPANE, COUNTERPAIN: a bedspread

COURT CUPBOARD: a two-tiered sideboard, either with or without doors

COVERLID, CUVERLETT: a bed cover

CREEPER: small fire-dog

CUSTOMARY: established or based on custom, rather than common law or statute (SOED)

DAMASK: a heavy fabric, generally of silk, with an interwoven design

DESPERATE (DEBTS): debts of which there was little hope of recovery; a bad debt, as opposed to a 'sperate' debt

DIAPER: a twilled linen cloth woven with a diamond pattern and used for napkins, towels and tablecloths

DICKER: a quantity of hides, generally ten in number (SOED)

DOUBLET: a close-fitting body-garment worn by men

GLOSSARY

DRAPE: woollen cloth

DRIPPING PAN: pan placed beneath spit to catch meat juices

DRUGGET: a coarse woven fabric generally used for floor and table coverings (SOED)

ELL: a measure of cloth: in England this was 45 inches

EWER: a jug with a wide mouth, often used in bedrooms (SOED)

FAGGOTS: small bundles of sticks

FAN, FANNE: a broad, shallow wicker basket

FATTE: vat or tub containing more than half a barrel of water and used in brewing and cheese making

FIRKIN: a small cask containing half a kilderkin or a quarter of a barrel. The measure varied according to the commodity: eg. 8 gallons of ale; 9 gallons of beer; 56lbs. of butter

FLASKETT: a shallow washing tub or clothes basket

FLOCK: wool refuse used for stuffing mattresses and pillows

FRAME: a wooden structure, generally used for supporting a table-top

FRIEZE: a coarse woollen cloth with a nap

FUSTIAN: a coarse cloth made of flax and cotton; 'cotton' in the sixteenth and seventeenth centuries was made of wool

GALLEY POT: a small earthen glazed pot

GARRETT: attic

GLASS CASE: a case or cupboard with an upper part made of glass for display

GRIDIRON: an iron grate with short feet and a long handle for cooking meat over a fire

GLOSSARY

HALF HEADED BED: a bed with short corner posts and without a tester canopy

HOG, HOGGE: (1) a pig reared for slaughter; (2) a young sheep before its first shearing

HOGSHEAD: a large cask for storing liquids, generally containing a little over 50 imperial gallons

HOLLAND: a linen fabric of both fine and coarse texture

HOSE: breeches, worn with a doublet

HUTCH: a chest of less sturdy construction than a normal chest

IMPRIMIS: firstly

JACK: a mechanical device activated by weights and gears to make a spit turn automatically

JOINED, JOINT, JOYNT: furniture made by a joiner using mortice and tenon joints secured by wooden pegs, and of superior craftsmanship to simple carpentry

KEELER: vessel for cooling liquids

KERCHER, KERCHIEF: a cloth for covering the head

KETTLE: an open cooking pot suspended over a fire

KILDERKIN: a cask for liquids equivalent in measure to half a barrel

KIMMEL, KIMNEL: a household tub with a variety of uses, but often used for brewing, kneading and salting meat

KNEADING TROUGH: a wooden trough for kneading dough

LADDERS: wooden framework fixed to the side of a wain to take a load of hay and corn

LAVER: a washing vessel

LENT CORN: any spring crop

GLOSSARY

LIVERY CUPBOARD: a shelved cupboard with perforated doors or bars for storing livery, a small meal taken at about 8 or 9pm, or any provisions taken into the night chamber

MALTMILL: mill for grinding malt before brewing

MARK: two-thirds of a £1 = 13 shillings and 4 pence

MASHING FAT: vat containing the malt mash when brewing beer

MESSUAGE: formerly, the portion of land intended to be or actually occupied as a site for a dwelling-house and its appurtenances (SOED).

MOIETE, MOIETY: a half share

MONETH: month

MONTEITH: a large ornamental punch-bowl, often silver with a scalloped rim

MOULDING BOARD: pastry board

NEATHER, NETHER: lower

OVERSEER: a person appointed to supervise the carrying out of the terms of a will to assist an executor

PARCELL: a part or portion of land

PECK: a measure for dry goods, equivalent to a quarter of a bushel or two gallons; also the vessel used to measure a peck

PEELE: a shovel or shovel-shaped implement, often used by a baker in oven baking

PILLOWBEER: a pillowcase

PIPKIN: small earthenware pot or pan

PORRINGER, POTTINGER: a bowl for pottage, broth or soup

POSNETT: an iron cooking pot with a long handle and three feet

GLOSSARY

POT HANGER, POT HOOK: hook and chain attached to a bar in the chimney and holding a cooking pot

POUDERING, POWDERING TROUGH: a salting tub used for preservation

PRESS: a large cupboard or wardrobe

PUTTER: pewter

QUARN, QUERN: stone handmill used for grinding corn, generally consisting of two circular stones

RACK: iron bar or bars used to hold a spit

RUGG: a rug or piece of rough woollen material

SAUCER, SAWCER, SAUSER: (1) until the mid-eighteenth century a dish or deep plate for solding salt and sauces; (2) a circular dish or plate

SETTLE: a long bench, usually with arms and a high back and a locker or box under the seat (SOED)

SKILLETT: a metal pan with a long handle and three feet for setting in an open fire

SKIMMER: a flat perforated metal ladle or plate, used in dairying for skimming cream from milk and in cooking for removing surface scum from a boiling liquid

SMOOTHING IRON: a flat-iron used for laundry purposes

STANDING BED: a high bedstead underneath which a truckle bed could be rolled

STEELYARD (or Roman Balance): a balance consisting of a lever with unequal arms which moves on a fulcrum, the article to be weighed being suspended from the shorter arm and a counterpoise slid along the longer arm until the lever balances (SOED)

STUFFE: a woollen cloth without nap or pile

TAN, TANN: crushed tree bark used as a source of tannin for converting hides into leather (SOED)

GLOSSARY

TENEMENT: holding or dwelling

TERRACY: made of marble (SOED)

TESTER: a flat wooden or cloth canopy over a bed

TILTE, TILTH: being under cultivation or tillage (SOED)

TOWEN: a coarse cloth made of tow, the shorter fibres of flax or hemp

TRIVET: a three-footed stand for a pot, placed over an open fire

TRENCHER: a flat piece of wood used for cutting and serving meat

TRUCKLE BED, TRUNDLE BED: a low bed running on truckles or wheels and pushed beneath a high or standing bedstead when not in use

TURKEY WORK: Turkish tapestry work or embroidery in this style (SOED)

VALLANCE, VALLENS: a border of cloth hanging from the bed canopy or from the mattress to the floor

WAINSCOT: a high quality foreign oak used in furniture and wall panelling

WORSTED: a smooth woollen textile made from twisted yarn

Index of Names

The Arabic numerals given throughout the index are the number references given to each will or inventory not the page number. Those in bold type refer to a testator of that name. Roman numerals refer to the introduction or references.

Surnames are listed under that most commonly used, with alternative spellings shown in parentheses afterwards. Christian names are abbreviated wherever possible using the key below. No attempt has been made to indicate the number of times an individual name appears in each will or inventory.

Abbreviations used:

Abi	Abigail	Jas	James
Abr	Abraham	Jon	Jonathan
And	Andrew	Jos	Joshua
Arch	Archibald	Judi	Judith
Art	Arthur	Kath	Katherine
Aud	Audrey	Lau	Laurence
Bart	Bartholomew	Law	Lawrence
Ben	Benjamin	Leo	Leonard
Cath	Catherine	Margt	Margaret
Chas	Charles	Mat	Matthew
Chris	Christopher	Mic	Michael
Dan	Daniel	Nat	Nathaniel
Deb	Deborah	Nich	Nicholas
Dor	Dorothy	Phil	Philip
Edm	Edmund	Reb	Rebecca
Edw	Edward	Ric	Richard
Eliz	Elizabeth	Robt	Robert
Fran	Francis	Sam	Samuel
Geo	George	Ste	Stephen
Han	Hannah	Thos	Thomas
Har	Harry/Harrold	Tim	Timothy
Hen	Henry	Wm	William
Hump	Humphrey	Zach	Zachariah
Is	Isabell(a)		

INDEX OF NAMES

Adams (Addams), Ann, 26; Josiah, **26**; Wm, 18
Allen, Sarah, 58
Ambrose, Edw, 6
Ansell, Jos, 70; Mary, 70
Arnold, John, 3; Mary, 3; Thos, 3, 14
Axtell, John, **45**; Mary, 45

Babb, John, xxx, **25**
Bach(e), Anne, 17; Edw, 7, 65; John, xiii, xx, xxi, xxxi, **17**
Baker, Eliz, 54; Joan(e), xviii, xxv, **12**; Thos, 54
Barber (Barbor), Mary, **27**
Barnes, Geo, 46
Battell, Ral, xiii, 6, 14, 65
Bayford, John, **46**; Susan, 46
Beecher, Jas, 22
Bennett, Wm, **28**, 66
Berry, Jas, 20
Best, Jo, 5, 10
Bevis, Thos, 1, 3
Bickerton, Aud, 47; Edm, **47**; Edw, 47; Nich, 62
Bigg(e), Wm, 44
Birdsey, Nich, 52
Bole, Hen, 75
Bond, Frances, 59
Bowd(e), Adlord, xiii, xxxi, xxxii, 5, 15, 17, 39,42, 47, 49, 54, 70; Ann, 25; Dan, 25; John, 25; Lidia, 25; Sarah, 25; Susannah, 25
Boyce, Geo, **29**
Brace, Eliz, 12; John, 9; Mark(e), 12
Bradley, Sara(h), 50
Bradney, Ben, xxi, 30; Emery (Amery), **48**; Jos, 48
Bran, Mark(e), 12
Bratt, John, 4; Thos, xxvi, 4
Bray, And, 34, 68; Mary, 57; Nat, 57; Sarah, 57
Brewer, Ali, 61; Eliz, 61; Judi, 61; Mary, 61; Thos, 61
Briden, John, **52**
Bridgeman, Eliz, 61; Jane, 61; Mary, 61; Phil, 23, 38, 61; Wm, **31**
Brit(t)ain(e) (Britan), Eliz, 19; Hump, 19
Brown(e), Edw, 3; Goodman, 61; Jane, 3; Jas, 24; John, 32; Jos, 6, 67; Margt, 3; Wm, 3, 15, 20, 22
Bucket, Wm, 24
Budd, David, 41
Bull, Robt, 54
Buncher, Thos, 70
Burges(s), Thos, 67
Burton, John, xxxi, 56

Carter, Ric, 10; Wm, 3, 8, 10, 27, 30, 35, 48, 74

Casely, Mary, 58
Cater, Geo, 26
Catlin (Catlyn), Ali, 22, 61; Eliz, 61; John, **53**, 61, 77; Mary, 22, 53, 61; Susannah, 53; Wm, xviii, xxv, **22**, 31, 61
Chamberl(a)in (Chamberlane), Jas, senior, 33, **55**; Jas, junior, 55; John, 33; Mary, 55
Chauncy, Jos, 70
Cherl, John, 63
Child, John, 18. 19
Churchman, Eliz, senior, 54; Eliz, junior, 54; Ric, xxxi, **49**, 54; Susannah, 49
Clapham, Jas, 23
Clark(e) (Clerke), Ann, 11; Dan, 51; Edw, 11; Fran, **11**; Hump, 49, 54; John, 8; Mary, xxvi, 12; Robt, 11, 12; Thos, 49; Wm, 54
Clisby, Is, 51; Luke, **51**
Clowes, John, 59
Collins, Wm, 23
Cooke, Ann, 56; Jas, 56; Margt, 56; Mary, **56**; Thos, 56
Cornell, Mary, xxv, **50**
Cotton, Edw, 9
Coulson, Thos, 62
Craven, Wm, 53
Croft, John, 8
Crook(e), Peter, 19
Crouch, John, 51
Curlis, John, junior, 18

Damport, Wm, 3
Dancer, Roger, 16
Dawes, Eliz, 23
Day, Judi, **57**
Dearmer, Thos, 52
Defoe, Daniel (writer), xiv, xviii
Dellawood, Susan, 6
Dighton, John, 70; Ric, 1, 3
Down(e)s, John, 2, 6, 7, 8; Jos, 24, 59
Draper, John, 63; Liddy (Lidia), 19
Dryden, John (writer & poet), viii, xxxiv
Dyer, Ali, **35**

East India Company, xxxv(n 9)
Edmonds, Wm, xiii, xxxviii, 11, **32**
Ewanns, Edw, 9

Fair(e)man, Robt, 5; Wm, 8
Fardon, Mrs, 68
Field (Feilde), Dan, 10; Eliz, 10; Fran, 25; Zach, 16
Fiennes, Sollomell, 70

152

INDEX OF NAMES

Finch, Eliz, 3, 58; Thos, 58
Fordham, Sam, 1
Fox, Chas, 72; Sam, 75
Francis, Jon, 71
Freeman, Ralph, 63
Fulke (Fulkes), Thos, 61, 74

Gable, a nurse, 6
Gardiner (Gardner), Wm, 30, 48
Gaze, John, 3; Margt, 3
Gifford, John, 3; Thos, 3
Goodman, And, 61, 71; Jas, 5, 41, 44, 48, 65, 69; John, xxiv, xl, **36**, 57; Ric, xxii, **5**; Sarah, 5; Sibbell, 5
Goose, Thos, 62
Gore, Ralph, 51
Gray, Edw, 1; John, 1; Jos, 1; Mat, 1; Thos, xxix, **1**
Green(e), R-, 59; Thos, xxxvii
Greeninge (Greenings), John, 72
Greeve, Kath, 9; Wm, 11
Grimes, Chris, 6
Gurney, John, 29, 45
Gurrey, Chas, 71; Chris, 71; John, senior, **40**, 71; John, junior, 71, 76; Ric, 71
Guyse, Wm, xxvii, xxxi, xxxii, 14, 17, 28, 54, 57, 59, 60, 75

Hadden, Thos, 71
Hale, Eliz, 69; John, 69; Josiah, 21, 69; Margt, **69**; Nath, senior, xix, 69; Nath, junior, 69; Sam, 69; Thos, 69; Wm, 61
Half(e)head (Halfhide), Edw, 13; John, 13; Mary, 13; Thos, 13; Wm, **13**
Hall, John, 13, 76
Harbor, Susan, 58
Harbutt, Hen, junior, 23
Hardisty, Mr, 71
Harvey, Fran, 3, 76; Frances, 3; Jane, 3; Mary, 3; Wm, 3
Hawkin(g)s, Eliz, 22; Mary, 22; Wm, xviii, 22, 61
Haynes, Joan(e), 3; Ste, 71; Thos, 3
Heath, Edw, 24; Geo, 11; Isaac, 27; Jo(h)n/Jonathan, 69; Thos, 10
Helder, John, senior, xxvi, xxix, xxxi, **70**; John, junior, 70; Jos, 70; Marrable, 70
Hemmings, John, 70; Sam, 70
Herrick(e), Hen, 7; Thos, 41, 47, 63, 74
Heyward, Margt, 3
Hill, John, xxx, xli (n 93), 11, 16, 29, 34, 43. 46, 58, 60, **71**, 76; Margery, 71
Hillock, Eliz, 24; Jos, 24

Hodgson, Geo, 20
Holding, Grace, 61; John, 61
Holt(e), Susan(n)a, 25
Holyoak(e), Mary, 13; Robt, 13
Humberston(e), Anne, 67, 72; Edw, 67; John, 26, 67; Mary, xix, **72**; S-, 67
Hunsdon, Jas, 60; John, 60, 64
Hurrell, Wm, 17, 34, 42, 57, 64
Hutchin, Thos, xviii, 61
Hynd, Jos, 71

Ince, Thos, 46

Jenkins, Wm, 18, 19
Johnson, John, **41**; Susannah, 41
Jones, John, 77
Juice (?Joyce), Thos, 65

Kemson, Thos, 19
Kene, Wm, 18
Kent, Han, 57; Mary, 57
Keynton, Israel(l), 17
King, John, 35
Kingitt, Mary, 17
Kirby(e) (Kirbey, Kerby(e)), Anna, 42; John, xxxi; Ric, 42; Thos, 5, 44

Lane, Thos, 58
Larken, Thos, 1
Lathbury, Edm, 54
Lawrence, Edw, 6
Lawson, Ric, 23; Robt, 6
Lea, Judah, **58**; Robt, 3; Thos, 3
Lloyd (Loyd), Eliz, 3

Man(n), Jas, 25
Manning, Ben, 76
March, John, 60; Martha, 60
Mar(r)iott, Geo, 16; Ric, 16; Robt, **16**
Marshall, Jos, 21
Mars(t)on, Hen, xxvii, 1, 17, 19, 34, 36, 60
Martin, John, 37; Ric, 40, 42, 52
Miles (Myles). Jane, 10; John, 10; Sarah, **43**; Tim, **43**
Mills, Wm, 6, 49
Moores, John, xxviii, **18**
Morris, Joshua, 69
Mountford, John, 9
Mynors, Wm, xiii

Nash, Dan, 23; Eliz, 5; Geo, 23; Sam, 5; Wm, 13

153

INDEX OF NAMES

Nicholls (Nickolls, Nicolls), Chris, 7; John, 7; Margt, 7; Mary, 60; Robt, 56; Susan(na), 7, 60; Wm, senior, 7; Wm, junior, 7, 60
Nichol(l)son(e), Ann, 59; Mat, 59; Robt, **59**
Noble, Thos, xxviii, **6**
Norris, Wm, 72
North, Wm, 76
Nutting (Nutten), John, 18

Oddall (Odell), of Wadesmill, 1
Offley, Harmer, 15; Mary, 15
Omans, Esias, 59

Page, Fran, 12; Margt, 12
Palmer, Arch, xxxi, 55; John, 21, 23
Parkin, John, 69
Paswater, Jas, 1
Pavett, Mary, 22; Thos, 22
Pegg(e), John, 2, 5, 10
Pendred (Penderid), Edm, 19, 62; Eliz, 19; Jas, xviii, xxv, xxviii, 19, 62; John, 19; Jos, 19; Mary, 19; Robt, 19; Sam, 19, 62; Wm, 19
Penington, Maria, xxxiii
Pen(n)yfather, Ric, 1
Per(r)in, John, 14
Perkins, Art, 25; Edw, 52
Peters (Peeters), Sarah, 71; Wm, 71
Pettit, Mary, xxvii, **60**
Pile, Robt, 9
Pitkin, John, 61
Plum(m)er, Wm, 63
Pomfrett, Mary, xviii, **61**
Pondman, Sam, 36
Poole, Ali, 22; Ann, 22; John, 22; Mary, 22; ...,Ric, 22; Susan, 22; Wm, 22; ..., author, 25
Pool(e)y, Ric, 32
Porter, Eliz, 8; Mary, 8
Potter, Eliz, 11; Goodman, 11
Potts, Anne, 17
Pratt (Prat, Pratts), Fran, 13; Hosiah, 31; John, 33; Thos, 6
Prentis, Jos, 57
Prichard, -, 53
Pryor (Pryer), Wm, senior, 1, 38
Purcell, Susanna, 13; Thos, 13
Pusey, Thos, 13

Radford, Eliz, 63; Frances, xxvi, 63; Fran, 63; Hen, 63; John, senior, xxi, xxvi, 63; John, junior, 63; Margt, 63; Mary, 63; Ph(o)ebe, 63
Randall, Ann, **20**; John, 20; Sam, 20, 71; Thos, 20

Randolph, Art, **37**
Ray, Mary, 76
Rayner, Wm, 15
Read, Dorothy, 3; John, 3; Wm, 61
Reason, Edw, 2, **65**; Jane, 65
Reed, Ralph, 76
Reeve, John, 56
Richards, Jos, 77
Richardson, John, xxi, **21**; Mary, 21; Thos, 21
Rogers (Rodgers), Eliz, 64; Joan, **64**; John, 64; Thos, 64
Rooding, John, 12; Mary, xxvi, 12
Run(n)ington (Runenton), Eliz, 14; Hen, 14, 22; Jas, 22, **66**; John, 14, 61; Mary, 14, 22; Melitabell, 22; Sarah, **14**, 22, ëwidowí, 61
Russell, John, 8

Saban, Jas, 57
Sake, Mat, 57
Salisbury, Earl of, 71
Sanders, Jos, 50; Mary, 10; Ric, 10
Saward (Sawerd), Ann, 23; Jos, senior, xix, **23**, 61; Jos, junior, 23; Sarah, 23, 69; Wm, 23
Scant, Dor, 9
Scigges (Skeggs), Jas, 21
Seale, Mat, 57
Sexton (Sixton), Jas, 63
Sibley, Sarah, 19
Silverside, Eliz, 11
Skingle, Dan, 3
Smart(e), Ann, 18; Ben, 18; Dan, 15; Eliz, 15; Grace, xxxi, **15**; John, 75; Jon, 15, 17; Jos, 18; Mary, 15, 18, 69; Ralph, 15; Sarah, 18; Ste, 15; Susannah, 18; Thos, 18; Wm, 3, 15, 18, 60
Smith (Smyth), Ann(e), **24**; Cadwallader (Cadwallinder), 7; Dan, xxvi, xxx, 24, 70; Eliz, 2; Geo, 2, 8; Jane, 2; John, **2**, 7, 8, 10, 61; John, junior, 2; Jon, 20; Martha, senior, 24; Martha, junior, 24; Mary, 2, **8**; Robt, 26; Sarah, 24; Thos, 24, 71; Wm, 2, 8, 71
Smitheman, Wm, 28, 53, 76
Smyth *see* Smith
Spencer, Thos, 23
Sprat(t), Grace, **38**
Squire, Jon, 4
Stave, John, 54
Stoakes, Ann, 20; Eliz, 20; Joan, 20; Mary, 20; Wm, 3
Stothard, Robt, xviii, xxi, xxxi, 35, **39**
Stout, John, 19, 25
Strong(e), John, 1; Mary, 1

154

INDEX OF NAMES

Strutt, Robt, 62
Sweeting, Hen, 19

Thomas, Art, 18; Ric, 19, 55
Thorowgood (Thurgood, Thurrowgood), David, 14; Hen, 14; John, 14; Jonas, 23; Robt, 14; Sarah, 23, 71
Thurston, John, 57; Margt, 57
Tingay, Job, 77; Mary, 77
Tipton, John, 71
Toller, Bostock, 17, 22, 24
Tre(y)herne, Joan, xviii, **67**
Trott, John, 64
Tuffnell (Tuffnaile, Tuffnall), Ann, 9; Conor, xxvi, xxviii, 9; Dan, 71; Edw, xx, xxvi, xxviii, 6, 8, **9**; Nich, 56, 69; Thos, xxviii, 9
Turner(s), Ben, xxx, 24; John, 73; Mic, **73**; Wm, 3, 36, 40, 63, **68**

Wackett, John, 75
Wade, Mary, 55
Wall, Ben, 17
Warner, Robt, 54, 72
Waterman, Ann, 6; Eliz, 6
Webb, John, 64; Margt, xxv, **3**; Thos, 18, 66
Wheatl(e)y, Eliz, 74; Thos, **74**
Whis(s)ton, Is, **10**
White, Thos, xxv
Whittaker, Eliz, 23
Widdowes, Martha, 10
Wilding *see* Wylding
Willis, John, 50
Wil(l)son, Hen, 13, 60
Wilshire, Ric, 6
Wood, Ann, 9; John, 9
Woodward, Thos, 73
Woollard (Wollard), Ann, 75; John, **75**
Woollmer (Woolmer, Wolmer), Ben, 76; Eliz, 71, **76**; John, senior, 43, 71, 76; John, junior, 76; Jos, 71, 76
Wren, Eliz, 72
Wylding, Ric, 6

Yardley, John, 45, 55
Yates, Eliz, 77; Hen, senior, **77**; Hen, junior, 77

Index of Places

Places cited are in Hertfordshire unless otherwise indicated. Modern spellings are used for main towns; field names are generally spelt as in the original document; alternative spellings are shown in parentheses where appropriate.

Amwell, Great, 3, 70
Ardeley (Yardley), 62
Aston, 6, 67, 70

Barnet, 19
Bedfordshire, county of, xi
Bengeo, xxi, 1, 9, 76
  Ansley Feild, 76
  Bengeofeild, 76
  Berycroft, 76
  Broadoake Mead, 76
  Chapmans End, 76
  Chaymer, 1
  Cromers, 1
  Crouch Feild, 76
  Fountains Orchard, 76
  Hackett Feild, 76
  Hole Orchard, 76
  Little Hole Orchards, 76
  Oldenfield, 76
  Temple Chelsin, 76
  Tonwell (Tunell), 9
Benington (Bennington), 6
  Three Crosses, 6
Berkhamsted, xxxvii
Biggleswade (Beds), 71
Bramfield (Bromfeild), 58
Brickendonbury, Manor or Liberty of, 2, 5, 21, 69
  Castle Street, 2, 5
  Gilliaports, 5
  Loc-meads, 2
Broxbourne, 61

Cheshunt, 71

Datchworth, 19
Digswell, 1, 18

Essendon (Easingdon), 11

Hadham (Haddon), 1, 6
Hatfield, xx, 10, 19, 76

Newgate Street, 10
  Swan Inn, 9
Hertford (Hartford), x, xv, xvii, xxi, xxii, xxvii, 1
  Deanery of, xiii
  Inns: see subject index
  Parishes: All Saints, x, xii, xiii, xxviii, 2, 5, 6, 7, 10, 11, 14, 23, 24, 35, 41, 47, 48, 51, 55, 56, 61, 67, 72
  St Andrew, xi, xii, 3, 6, 18, 36, 37, 57, 58, 60, 71, 76
  St John, 12, 19, 20, 22, 43, 52, 61

  Places:
  Allings, 23
  Back Street, 56
  Blackfeild, Great and Little, 23
  Butchery Green, 70
  Castle Street, 2, 5
  Corner House, 2
  Cowbridge, 24
  Ducketts, 22
  Edwards Lands, 23
  Floodgates, 1
  Floodgaty Parke, 1
  Gilliaports, 5
  Grove, The, 23
  High Street, 70
  Market Place, 2
  New Close, 52
  Peas Croft or Peasfeilds, 23
  Port Hill, 24
  Quaker Burial Ground, 24
  Sprats Feild, 23
  Tollbridge, 71
  Underwood, 23
  West Street, 14
  Wilkins Feild, 23

Hertingfordbury (Hartingfordbury), 1, 12, 13, 17
  High Cross, 70
Hoddesdon, 6, 61
  Rye, 61

INDEX OF PLACES

Ickleford (Eckellford), 61

Langley, Kings, xlii (n 104)
Lea (Lee), River, x, xi, xxxviii
London, xi, 1, 3, 60
   Temple, 71
London Colney, 11

Munden, Great or Much, 1, 3, 70
Munden, Little or Parva, 5, 70

Nazeing (Essex), xviii, 22, 61
New England (USA), 10
Newgate Street see Hatfield

Pirton, 72
Pulloxhill (Beds), 20

Rye see Hoddesdon

St Albans, x
Sacombe, 1, 19
   Burralls Green, 19
   Chaymer, 1
   Cromers, 1
Standon (Stondon), 3, 70
Stapleford, 71
Stevenage, 10, 13, 15

Tewin, 1
Thundridge see High Cross
Towcester (Northants), 16

Wadesmill (Wardsmill), 1
Walkern, 6
Ware, x, 63, 70, 77
   Kibes Lane, 70
   Mill Lane, 70
   Sexton's Yard, 63
Watton at Stone (Wotton), 6, 16, 19
Welwyn (Wellwyn), 18

Index of Subjects

The Arabic numerals given throughout the index are the number references given to each will or inventory not the page number. Numbers in roman type refer to the pages in the introduction. Numbers in bold type e.g. under occupations, refer to the testator.

No attempt has been made to indicate the number of times specific items such as tables, beds etc appear in each inventory. Common items such as andirons, pots and fire shovels have been entered under **kitchen utensils** even though they may have been listed in other rooms according to the inventory. Rooms referred to in an inventory as 'the Hall' may contain cooking utensils and equipment even though a separate kitchen is included eg Number 46 (p 84).

Names of rooms and outbuildings within a property are mostly indexed from the names printed in bold type at the left hand side of each inventory. Sometimes, however, outbuildings such as barns appear only at the end of an inventory as eg 'Hay in the barne' and occasionally in the will only (for example see number 24).

animals: bull/bullock, 21, 69
    cows/calves, xix, 14, 21, 23, 31, 36, 38, 45, 46, 54, 57, 69, 71
    hogs, xix, 23, 28, 30, 32, 36, 39, 44, 47, 48, 54, 63, 66, 69
    horse, xix, 11, 13, 20, 21, 23, 25, 28, 31, 32, 36, 38, 39, 41, 45, 46, 47, 56, 57, 63, 69, 71, 74
    colt, 47, 69
    harness, 6, 20, 21, 31, 32, 38, 46, 57, 69
    pigs (swine/sows), 6, 13, 17, 21, 31, 32, 38, 39, 43, 46, 69 *see also* hogs
    poultry, 31
    sheep/lambs, 8, 31, 38, 57, 59, 69
    skins/hides, 28, 36, 57
Archdeaconry, of Huntingdon, xiii; of St Albans, xiii arms, xix, 23
    pistols, xx, 17

barrels, 48, 52
bee hives, 18
bees, 18
bell, 17, 63, 64
beneficiaries *see* wills
bishopric, of Lincoln, xiii; of London, xiii
books, xix, xxi, xxiii, 10, 23, 25, 30
    bookstand, 68
    Bible, 25, 46, 57, 60
    Book of Common Prayer, xiii

    Perkins, Arthur *Works*, 25
    Poole's *Annotations*, 25
brewing equipment & utensils: 7, 23, 30, 39
    basket, 17
    bottle rack, 68
    cider cask, 14
    cistern, 62
    cooler, 14, 17, 40, 45, 48, 49
    copper, 7, 14, 17, 30, 39, 40, 45, 48, 49, 54, 57, 66, 69, 70
    fatt, *see* vat
    irons, 4, 17
    jett, 17
    kilderkin, 28, 70
    kiln (drying), 62
    kimnel (kimmel), 17, 18, 38
    pipe(s), 14
    pump, 17
    quern (quorn), malt, 62
    screen (skrene), 62
    shute, 17
    stalls/racks, 17, 18
    still, 30, 48
    trough (troues), 14
    tubs, 14, 17, 45, 57
    tun, 14
    vat (fatt), 36, 69
    vessels (unspecified), 48, 49, 54, 66, 69, 70, 75

INDEX OF SUBJECTS

wire (weir), 62
see also drink
building materials & equipment: bricking tub, 28
bricks, 23
floorboards, 55
burial, 13, 24, 60, 67; in chancel, 6; in churchyard, 2, 67, 71

cart, 21, 23, 32, 38, 46, 69, 74
  cart wheels, 32
  see also waggon
census, Compton (1676), x, xi, xii, xxxvii (n 23)
charitable bequests *see* wills
Church of England *see* Religion
churches, bequests to, xxviii
clothes beater, 68
clothing: xxiii, 1, 2, 3, 5, 6, 7, 10-15, 17, 18, 21, 23, 24, 26-31, 33-49, 52-54, 57, 59-62, 64-70, 72, 74-76
  apron, 58
  breeches, 1
  coat, 1, 42
  doublet, 1
  hat, 1, 42, 77
  petticoat(e), 58
  shirt, 25
  shoes *see* footwear
  stockings, 77
  wa(i)stcoat, 58
coal (coales), 17, 30, 41, 47, 48, 49, 66
shovel, 14, 49
communications, x, xi
consumerism, ix, xxi, xxii, xxxiii, xxxv (n 7)
countryside, ix
courts, archdeaconry, xiii
Prerogative of Canterbury, xiii; of York, xiii

crops: barley, 19, 21, 23, 31, 32, 38, 62, 69
  bran, 20
  chaff, 23
  corn/grain, xix, 17, 25, 38, 57
  grass, 57
  hay, 7, 11, 17, 20, 21, 23, 28, 32, 39, 41, 44, 45, 46, 47, 49, 59, 65, 66, 69, 71
  hops, 30
  malt, xxii, 24, 62
  oats, xxii, 17, 21, 23, 24, 31, 39, 69
  peas, 21, 23, 31, 32, 69
  rye, 30, 32
  straw, 23, 28

tares (tearss), 21
wheat, 7, 21, 23, 30, 31, 32, 38, 69

debts, xviii, xxii, 19, 23, 28-30, 34, 36, 37, 39, 41, 42-44, 46-49, 52, 53, 57, 60-62, 72,74
drink: ale, 17, 48
  beer (bere), xx, 7, 11, 17, 30, 39, 49, 54, 75
  cider, xx, 14, 17
  hogsheads (unspecified), 14, 17, 30, 39, 48, 54
  malt, 51, 57, 69
  wine, xx
  port, xx, 17
  sack, xx, 17
  drinking trough, 41; drinking vessels, 17, 30, 36, 51, 57, 60, 66, 72, 77 *see also* household goods
dung, 13, 17, 23
dung cart, 69

economic factors: consumption, household, xiv
  debt, *see separate heading*
  economic growth, viii, xxxiii
  influence of London, x-xi, xxxiii
  'key goods', xvii, xx, xxi, xxii, xl(n)
  moneylending, xviii
  personal income, xiv, xvii
  prices, xviii
  spending, consumer, xxii, xxxiii
  taxes, *see separate heading*
  wealth, xviii
engine (unspecified), 37
executors *see* wills

farm machinery & equipment: xix, 21
  see also, cart; waggon
  crib, 21
  dragrakes, 23
  fork, 21
  grindstone, 21
  harrow, 21, 23, 31, 32, 38, 46
  plough, 21, 23, 31, 38, 46
  shovel, 21, 36
  trough, 21
  farms, 17
  firearms see arms
foodstuff: butter, 30
  cheese, 30, 38
  spices, 30
  see also crops
footwear, 42, 77
furniture *see* household goods

159

INDEX OF SUBJECTS

gentleman *see* status
gentry *see* status
grain *see* crops
guardian (of children), 58

harness *see* animals: horse
hen/chicken house *see* house:outbuildings
hides/skins *see* animals
horn, 57
house: rooms, xxiv-xxv
  bar, 17
  bottle room, 17
  bedroom, 7, 49
  buttery, 8, 11, 12, 13, 17, 18, 21, 28, 30, 33, 36, 38, 40, 43, 44, 46, 54, 55, 64, 66, 71, 72, 74-76
  cellar (selere, seller), xx, 7, 14, 17, 21, 23, 34, 39, 48, 49, 51, 53, 54, 56, 57, 59, 60, 63, 66, 69, 70
  chamber, best; great; over, 2, 7, 8, 11, 13-15, 17, 18, 21, 25, 28-31, 33-49, 51, 53-57, 59, 60, 63-66, 68-77
  closet, 23, 25, 30, 47, 68
  garret, 8, 11, 14, 17, 21, 25, 29, 30, 37, 39, 44, 47-49, 54, 60, 65, 68, 71, 73, 76
  hall, xix, xxiv, 1, 2, 7, 8, 10, 12-15, 17, 18, 23, 28-31, 33-36, 38, 39, 41-49, 53-57, 63, 65, 66, 69, 72, 74-77
  kitchen, 1, 2, 7, 8, 14, 17, 20, 21, 23, 25, 31, 34, 35, 38-40, 44, 47, 49, 51, 53-55, 59, 60, 63, 65, 69-72, 74, 76
  lodging, 66
  loft, 55
  maid's chamber, 28, 71
  pantry, 21
  parlour, xix, xx, xxiv, 2, 7-10, 13, 14, 17, 23, 33, 34, 36, 38-41, 44, 49, 53-57, 59, 60, 63, 66, 68-70, 72
  pastry, 7
  scullery, 17
  staircase (stairhead), 57, 60, 64, 66, 72
  store, 17, 40
house: outbuildings, outhouses and yards, 12, 17, 21, 23, 24, 45
  bakehouse, 7, 30, 48, 63
  barn, 8, 16, 17, 23, 24, 30, 31, 33, 38, 57, 64, 65, 74
  bin house (bin houss), 21
  boiling house (bowling house), 1
  brewhouse, 7, 14, 17, 21, 23, 30, 39, 40, 44, 48, 49, 54, 66, 69-71

  cheese press house, 21
  corn house (quarn houss), 21
  cowhouse, 16
  dairy (milk house), 21 23, 31, 38, 46, 60, 69
    cheese press, 23, 38, 69
    cheese tubs, 31
    churns, 23
    milk churns, 23, 31
    pails, 46
    vessels, 69
  gatehouse, 39, 49, 54
  hen house (hen pen), 17, 41, 68
  'kill house' [?slaughter house], 16, 57
  manger (mainger), 11
  milk house *see* dairy
  shed, 43, 57
  stable, 11, 16, 17, 24, 31, 38, 59, 64
    horsepen, 28
  tannery, 57
  wash house (workehouse), 28, 45, 60, 72
    copper, 60, 72
    tubs, 77
  wood house, 59, 64, 68, 75
  yard, 7, 11, 14, 16, 17, 23, 24, 33, 34, 36, 39, 40, 43-46, 48, 55, 60, 62, 63, 66, 71-73, 76, 77
household accounts, xiv
  see also housekeeping
household goods & chattels: xviii-xxii, xxiii (table)
  ash bin (ash pan), 17
  barrel, 14, 23, 57
  basin (bason), 8, 11, 17, 28, 30, 42, 47, 50, 64, 68, 70, 74
  basket, 11, 41
    flaskett, 68
    hop basket, 17
  bed pan, 17, 68
  bellows, 8, 10, 17, 28, 39, 41, 46, 49, 54, 55, 60, 65, 68, 70, 77
  bottles, 2, 17, 28, 38, 41, 50, 57, 70; of stone, 68
  box, 10, 14, 46, 50, 55, 57, 58, 63, 64, 65, 68, 77
  candle, 17, 28, 64, 77
    ēdrudginí, 17
    pepper, 17
    salt, 68
    spice, 60, 68
    wainscott, 25
  'candle mole', 45
    snuffer, 57
  candlesticks, 11, 14, 17, 28, 38, 39, 42, 47, 49, 54, 55, 57, 68, 74

INDEX OF SUBJECTS

sconce, 17, 68
chamber pot, 2, 8, 11, 17, 39, 42, 46, 47, 49, 54, 55, 64
china, xxiv
    coffee pots, xxiv
    tea pots, xxiv
    see also basin; crockery
clock, xix, xxi, xxii, xxiii, 23, 25, 28, 57, 60, 68, 69
coal shovel, 14, 49; *see also* kitchen utensils, fire shovel
crockery, xx, xxiii
    cups, 30, 46, 57, 68
    dishes, 18, 46
    plates, xxii, 14, 17, 25
    saucers, 18, 39, 74
    see also basin; china
curtains *see* soft furnishings
cutlery, xxi
    forks (meat, table etc), xxi, 14, 17, 39
    knives (shredding, table etc), xxi, 17, 39
        chopping, 57
    spoons, 13-15, 17, 25, 30, 38, 47, 57, 67-69
        alchymie, 55
dog(g)s *see* fire dogs
drying horse, wooden, 39
earthenware, xxiii, 28, 33, 38, 40, 46, 50, 55, 57, 58, 60, 68, 70, 75, 77
ewer, 8
fender, 14, 49, 55, 57; *see also* grate
firedogs (dog(g)s), 28, 42, 49, 68, 72
floor covering: carpet, 8, 17, 30, 35, 47, 60, 63, 65, 66, 68, 69, 70, 74
    mat, 8, 14, 28, 35, 39, 42, 50, 54, 59, 66-68, 70
    tapestry, 41
flour bin, 63
flower pots, 14
grate, fire, 14, 17, 30, 49, 55, 58
    'bread grate', 14
kimnel (kimmel) *see* brewing equipment
household: furniture, xxiv
    beds/bedsteads, xxi-xxii, 1, 2, 5, 7-9, 11, 13, 14, 17, 18, 23, 25, 26, 31, 33, 35, 37, 39-41, 45, 46, 48, 49, 51, 54, 55, 58-60, 62-68, 70, 72, 77
    feather, xxii, xxiii, 2, 5, 7-9, 14, 17, 25, 27, 30, 35, 36, 38, 39, 41, 42, 46, 47, 49-51, 54, 55, 57, 59, 60, 62-67, 69, 70, 72, 74, 75
    flock, xxii, 10, 13-15, 17, 25, 26, 28, 30, 36, 38, 39, 46-48, 55, 57-60, 63, 64, 66, 67, 70, 74, 75
    halfhead, xxi, 7, 10, 36, 38, 39, 44, 46, 54, 60, 65, 75
    'joynt', 38
    pallet (pallat), 66
    settle, 30
    straw, 35, 38, 39, 41, 57, 60
    trundle, xxi, 1, 7, 8, 11, 14, 17, 28, 30, 35, 36, 39, 41, 44, 50, 54, 58-60, 63-66, 75
bench/form, 1, 2, 10, 11, 14, 17, 30, 38, 39, 41, 44, 46, 49, 54, 57-59, 63-65, 68, 70, 72
chairs, xix, xx, xxiv, 7, 8, 11, 14, 17, 18, 23, 26, 28, 30, 33, 35, 38-42, 45-49, 51, 54, 55, 57, 60, 63-70, 72, 74, 75, 77
    elbow, 57, 60
    'joyne', 63
    leather, 8, 17, 48, 54, 57, 60, 63, 65
    rush, 13, 17
    serge, 57
    turkey work, 14, 54, 57, 70
    wicker, 10, 11, 63, 72
chest, 1, 5, 7-10, 14, 15, 17. 18, 23, 25-27, 30, 31, 33, 36, 46, 47, 50, 54, 55, 57, 60, 66, 68, 72, 73
    linen, 48, 49
chest (or case) of drawers, 14, 17, 25, 30, 33, 35, 39, 40, 45, 47, 50, 55, 57, 65, 66, 68, 70, 72, 75
coat rack, 17, 45
couch, 17, 41, 45
cupboard (cobert), 1, 5, 9-11, 17, 18, 28, 30, 33, 35, 38, 39, 47, 54, 55, 57, 58, 64, 68, 72, 75, 77
    court (cowrt), xxi, 7, 8, 39, 44, 58, 70, 72
    livery, xxi, 2, 14, 41, 54, 59, 60, 63-65, 68, 69
    press, 2, 8, 30, 39, 41, 46, 48, 59, 63, 69, 70
    hanging, 17, 48, 57, 60, 68, 69, 77
    side, 17, 63
    tobacco, 30
desk, 41, 50, 68, 77
dresser, 17, 28, 45
    kitchen, 14, 17, 49
form *see* bench
looking glass, xix, xx, xxii, xxiii, 6, 17, 23, 47, 54, 55, 57, 60, 63, 64, 68, 70
press *see* cupboard
settle, xix, 8, 17, 35, 36, 41, 57, 60, 63, 66
sideboard, 7, 14, 65
stand, 17
stool (also joyned/joynt stool(e)), xix, 2, 7-11, 13, 14, 17, 18, 23, 28, 30, 31, 35, 36, 38-40,

161

INDEX OF SUBJECTS

42, 44, 46, 47, 49, 54, 55, 57-60, 63-66, 68-70, 72, 74, 75, 77
close stool (and pan), 17, 35, 68
tables (and frame), xx, xxii, xxiii, 1, 2, 7-11, 13, 14, 17, 18, 23, 26, 28, 30, 31, 33, 35, 36, 38-42, 44-49, 51, 54, 55, 57-60, 63-66, 68-70, 75, 77
   drawing, 2, 8, 41, 68, 74
   folding, 60
   side, 42
   spanish, xx, 17
trunk, xxi, 6-9, 11, 14, 17, 27, 30, 59, 60, 63, 64, 67, 68, 72, 75

household: kitchen utensils and equipment
and irons, 2, 7, 8, 10, 11, 13, 14, 17, 28, 30, 35, 38, 38, 41, 42, 46, 47, 49, 51, 54, 55, 57, 59, 60, 63-66, 68-70, 72, 74, 75
apple roaster, 57
bin, 41
bowl, 10, 17, 30, 55, 68, 69
'bread grate', 14
brushes, 17, 68
chaffing dish/chafer *see* dishes
chopping block, 17
cleaver, 14, 17, 39, 68, 75
colander (culinder), 17, 28, 39
copper, 14, 17, 30, 74; *see also* brewing equipment
creepers *see* fireirons
cruet, 17, 35
dishes: chaffing (chafer), 11, 14, 17, 28, 38, 39, 54, 57, 60, 68
   earthenware, 38, 46
   pewter (putter), xx, 11, 14, 17, 25, 31, 38, 39, 42, 46, 47, 50, 51, 54, 55, 59, 64, 68, 70, 72, 74
   sawcer (sawcell), 68
   serving (servers), 28
'drudgin box', 17
firedogs see household goods
fire 'creepers', 8, 9, 14, 39, 41, 47, 65
   fork, 55, 60
   irons, 8, 14, 36, 37, 39, 57, 63, 68, 77
   rack, 63
   screen, 14, 68
   shovel, 7, 8, 11, 13, 14, 17, 25, 28, 30, 35, 38, 39, 41, 42, 46, 49, 51, 54, 55, 60, 63-65, 68-70, 72, 74, 75, 77
   see also tongs
flagon, 2, 11, 14, 38, 39, 42, 46, 47, 49, 54, 74
glasses, drinking etc, 17, 30, 36, 51, 54, 57

graters, 17
gridiron, 8, 10, 11, 13, 17, 25, 28, 30, 42, 54, 55, 60, 64, 70, 75
iron, box, 28
   smooth (smothering), 17, 35, 55, 57, 58, 64, 68, 70
ironing cloth, 68
jack, 7, 11, 13, 14, 17, 23, 25, 28, 30, 39, 41, 46, 47, 49, 54, 55, 57, 59, 60, 63, 65, 66, 68-70, 72, 74, 75, 77; *see also* weights
kettle (kitle, cittle), 8, 11, 18, 25, 28, 30, 31, 38, 39, 42, 46, 47, 49, 50, 54, 55, 57-60, 64, 68, 70, 74
ladle, 17, 28, 39, 55, 68
lampblack (lamblack), 28
mortar (and pestle) *see* pestle
pail, 8, 17, 25, 38
   milk, 46
pans, 10, 35, 38, 39, 54
   bake, 60
   cake, 57
   dripping, 2, 11, 14, 17, 25, 28, 30, 35, 38, 39, 42, 46, 47, 54, 55, 57, 63, 64, 68
   frying, 10, 11, 14, 17, 25, 28, 46, 54, 55, 57, 68, 70
   patty, 17
   pudding, 28, 39, 46, 57
   stewing, 17
   wash, 60
peele, iron, 68
   pie, 68
pepper box *see* household goods
pestle & mortar, 17, 28, 38, 54 (mortar only), 57, 58, 60, 68, 70
pipkin, 17
plates, 42, 45, 47, 50, 54, 55, 68
   pie, 68
   tin, 34
platters, 2, 17, 77
pot hanger/pot hooks, 8, 10, 11, 17, 28, 38, 39, 54, 55, 57, 58, 60, 63, 66, 68, 70, 75
pots, xx, xxiii, 11, 17, 28, 31, 38, 47, 49, 50, 54, 68, 70, 74
   butter, 17
   chamber *see* household goods
   drinking, 11, 17
   galley, 17
   iron, 8, 10, 57, 58, 74
   milk, 17
   porridge (porrage), 9, 11, 17, 25, 28, 51, 54, 64

INDEX OF SUBJECTS

porringer (pottinger), 38, 39, 46, 50, 55, 70, 74
posnett (posurt), 8, 11
pottage, 55, 57
racks, 14, 17, 42, 54, 66, 69
salt(s), bin, box, cellar, pot, 11, 14, 17, 39, 47, 50, 55
saucepans (sasepann), xx, xxi, xxii, xxiii, 17, 28, 47, 70
scales, 17, 20, 25, 30, 68, 70
sieve (siff), 17, 68
skewers, 28
skillet, xx, 2, 9, 14, 17, 18, 25, 28, 38, 39, 42, 46, 47, 49, 51, 54, 55, 57, 60, 68, 70, 72, 74
skimmer (scummer), 17, 25, 28, 39, 42, 55, 57, 70
slice (slise), 14, 17
spit, 2, 7, 11, 13, 14, 17, 23, 25, 28, 30, 35, 38, 41, 42, 46, 49, 54, 55, 57, 59, 60, 63-66, 68-70, 72, 74, 75, 77
toasting fork, 39
tongs, fire, 7, 9, 13, 14, 17, 25, 28, 30, 35, 38, 39, 41, 42, 49, 51, 54, 55, 57, 60, 63-65, 68-70, 72, 74, 75, 77
tray, 17, 38
trenchers (trenikers, trenches), 17, 28, 38, 46, 77
trivet (trevett), 68
troughs *see* household goods
tubs, 17, 30, 36, 46, 52
   meal, 55
   powdering (poundering), 23, 24, 38, 63
weights, 14, 17, 25, 30, 39, 46, 49, 54, 57, 60, 66, 68, 70
   and measures, 25
   see also jack
household:linen (linin, lining, linnen), xxv, xxxi, 6, 7, 10-12, 15, 17, 18, 23, 27, 30, 31, 34, 38, 40, 43-45, 47-49, 51, 53, 54, 56, 66, 71, 73, 75
   bed/bedding, xxi, xxiv, 1, 11, 19, 33, 44, 64
    blanket, 1, 5, 8-10, 13-15, 17, 25, 27, 28, 30, 35, 36, 38, 39, 41, 46-50, 54, 55, 57, 59, 60, 62-65, 67, 70, 74, 75
    bolster (bowlster), xxi, 5, 8-10, 13, 14, 17, 27, 28, 30, 35, 36, 38, 39, 41, 46, 47, 49-51, 54, 55, 58, 60, 62, 63, 65-70, 72, 74, 75
    coverlet (coverlid), xxi, 8, 10, 13, 14, 27, 28, 30, 35, 36, 38, 38, 41, 47, 48, 50, 54, 55, 57, 60, 62-64, 66, 74
    counterpa(i)ne, 17, 65
    mattress, xx, xxii, 8
    pillow, xxi, 8, 13, 14, 17, 27, 28, 30, 36, 38, 39, 41, 46-48, 50, 57, 58, 60, 65, 67, 69, 72, 74
    pillowcases (pillowbeer), xx, xxi, 8, 9, 14, 17, 28, 30, 36, 41, 50, 57, 58, 60, 64, 65, 68, 70, 74
    quilt, 17, 49
    rug(s), xxi, 2, 9, 13-15, 17, 25, 28, 35, 38, 39, 41, 42, 46-49, 51, 54, 55, 59, 60, 63, 66, 67, 70, 72, 74, 75
    sheets, xx, xxi, 2, 9, 14, 15, 17, 28, 30, 35-38, 54, 55, 57, 58, 60, 64, 68, 69, 72, 74
     flaxen, 3, 42, 50, 65
     holland, 3
     towen (towan), 3, 8, 41, 42
    tester, xxi, 39, 42, 54, 60, 68
    vallance (rods and curtains), xxi, 2, 7, 9, 13, 23, 25, 30, 35, 36, 38, 39, 41, 42, 46-49, 54, 55, 57, 59, 60, 63, 64-67, 70, 72, 74, 75
   board cloths, 68
   handkerchief, 1
   napkins, xx, 2, 8, 9, 14, 17, 28, 30, 36, 37, 39, 41, 42, 50, 54, 55, 57, 60, 64, 65, 68, 69, 70, 72, 74
   table cloth, xx, xxiii, 2, 4, 8, 30, 36, 39, 41, 42, 46, 54, 55, 57, 58, 60, 64, 65, 69, 70, 74
   towels, 9, 17, 28, 30, 36, 37, 42, 46, 50, 57, 58, 60, 64, 65, 68, 70, 72, 74
household: soft furnishings, xxiv
   curtains (and rods), xxii, xxiii, 7-10, 13-15, 17, 23, 30, 35, 38, 39, 41, 42, 46, 47, 49, 51, 54, 57, 63, 68, 70, 77; *see also* linen, bed vallance
   cushions, 6, 11, 17, 28, 30, 35, 39, 42, 57, 58, 60, 65, 68, 70, 77
   see also needlework and wallpaper
house keeping, organisation and management, xxii ff
hutches, for animals, 58, 77

illiteracy *see* literacy
inheritance *see* wills
inns, 9, 17, 71
   Hatfield - Swan, xx, 9
   Hertford - Anchor, xx, 17
    Dolphin, xx, 17
    Groom, xx, 17
    Magpie, xx
   Maidenhead (Maydenhead), xxi, 9
   Ship, xxi, 17
intestacy *see* wills
irons *see* household goods
inventories, xiii, xiv, xvii-xxiii
   appraisal, xiv, xviii

INDEX OF SUBJECTS

appraisors, xv, xix, xxiii, xxiv, xxxi, xxxii
   exclusions from, xiv, xv
   problems regarding, xiv, xv, xxiv
   valuations, xxiv, xxxi, xxxii, 41

jewellery, rings, 25

'key goods' *see* economic factors
kitchen utensils *see* household

ladder, 17, 21, 28, 39, 55
lantern (lanthorne), 17, 28
leather, 36, 42; *see also* animals, skins/hides
lifestyle *see* social grouping
literacy, xxvii, xxviii
   illiteracy, xxvii
livestock *see* animals

malt *see* crops
marriage, xxvi, 63, 70
metalwork: brass, xxiv, 7, 10, 23, 33, 35, 36, 37, 40, 41, 45, 48, 63, 64, 65, 75, 77
   copper, xxiv
   iron, xxiv, 10, 36, 47, 68
   pewter, xx, xxii-xxiv, 7-10, 23, 30, 33, 35-37, 40, 41, 45, 48, 57, 60, 63, 65, 75, 77
   silver, xxiii-xxv, 15, 25
   tin (tinware), xxiv, 49, 55, 68, 70
mills, 25
   bolting (boulting), 7, 45, 63, 66
   dressing, 48
   flour, 7, 20
   hand, 36
   quern (quorn), 62
   water, 57
money, personal and loose, 7, 14, 15, 17-19, 21-24, 27, 29, 31, 33-36, 41, 44-53, 57, 59, 61-70, 75
   gold, 24
musical instruments, virginal, xxv, 50

needlework: tapestry, 41
   turkey work, xxii-xxiv, 14, 54, 57, 60, 68, 70

occupations and trades, xiv, xv, xviii
   baker, xxi, 7, **24, 63**
   barber, 73
      barber surgeon, xx
   brazier, 25
   brewer, 8, 10
   bricklayer, xviii, **53**
   brickmaker, 18

butcher, 15
carpenter, xviii, xxvi, xxxi, 10, **55, 70**
chapman, **11**
collarmaker, 77
comber (coamer), 71
cooper, 71
cordwainer, xviii, xxxi, 18, **42, 64**
currier, xviii, **28**
dealers, xvi, xviii
farmer, xvi, xix, 60
glazier, xviii, **29**
grocer, **40**, 61, 71
husbandman, xvi, xxvi, **4**, 16, **46**, 61
innkeeper, xxi, xxxi, **39, 49**
joiner, **16**
labourer, 10, 11
locksmith, xviii, 2
maltster, xviii, xxv, **5, 18**, 19, **62, 69**
mealman, xxv, xxx, **20, 25, 31**
nurse, 6
patternmaker, 22
peruke-maker, xv
plumber, **29**
sawyer, 10
schoolmaster, 5
servant, 6
shopkeeper, **45, 71**
surgeon (chirurgien), **9**
tailor, **52, 76**
tanner, xviii, xxiv, 18, **34, 35**
tobacconist, xv, **37**
turner, **18**
watchmaker, xv
weaver, 73
webster, 15
wig-maker *see* peruke-maker
woolstapler, 24
oil, 28

paintings, 17
pistols *see* arms
plate, 14, 15, 17, 23, 30, 39, 76
poor, xxviii, xxxi, 1-3, 6, 19, 57, 60
population, growth, viii, xxxvi (n 16 & 17), xxxvii (n 23)
   of Hertford, x, xxxvii (n 23 & 26)
   of Hitchin, xxxvii (n 23)
   of London, x, xi
prices *see* economic factors
probate *see* wills
property, copyhold, xx, xxi, 23, 76

164

INDEX OF SUBJECTS

distribution of, xvii-xxix, 18, 23
pump, 14, 17, 57, 63

quern *see* brewing equipment

razor, 13
Reformation, English, xxviii
religion: church, failure to attend, xxvi
   denominations: Church of England, xxvii
     Congregationalist, xxvii
     Dissenters, xxxiv
     Friends, Society of *see* Quakers
     Quakers, xi, xxvii, xxviii, 18, 24
     burial ground, Hertford, 24
     Roman Catholicism, xi, xxvii
   religious beliefs, xxvii, xxviii
     in Hertford, xi, xii
Restoration, the English, viii, ix, xxi
rooms *see* houses

sacks/sacking, 25, 30, 48
saddle and harness *see* animals
scaffold/scaffolding, 14
sconce *see* household goods
screen, 20
   fire, 14, 68
shelf/shelves, 9, 11, 14, 17, 49, 50, 70
   glass, 54, 70
   pot, 63
shop, 3, 25, 28-30, 33, 37, 39, 40, 42, 44, 45, 47, 48, 55, 64, 66, 71-73, 76, 77
shute (shoott), 17, 57
social groupings, xiv, xv
   lifestyle, xiv, xxii, xxiv, xxxi, xxxiv
   see also status
spinning wheel, 17, 41
spinsters *see* status
stall, beer and wine *see* brewing equipment
status, social/economic, xiv-xvi, xviii
   batchelor, xv, **13**
   gentleman, xv, xviii, xxiv, xxv, **6**, **17**, **32**, **68**
   gentry, xvi, xviii, xxxvi (n 16)
   spinster, xv, xvi, **50**, **67**, **72**
   widow, xv, xviii, xxv, xxxix (n 58), **3**, **8**, **10**, **12**, **14**, **15**, 19, **27**, 45, 46, **48**, **54**, **57**, **60**, **61**, **67**
   yeoman, xv, xvi, xviii, xix, xxiv, **1**, **21**, **22**, **23**, **59**, **69**
Statute of Distribution (1670), see wills
steel(s) (steales), 47, 66
steelyard (stillyard), 17
stove, 17

tankard, 13, 14, 17, 55
taxes: Hearth Tax (1663), xiv, xxxi, xxxviii (n 40)
timber *see* wood
tins, biscuit, 17
tobacco, xxi, 30, 37
   pipes, 37
tools: garden, rake, 68
   working, xxv, xxxi, 28, 33, 36, 47, 55, 57, 70
   die, 42
   hammer, 42
   knife, 55
   last, 42
   seals, 42
   shave & block, 57
   shovel, 62
   tan fork, 57
towns, social and cultural development, ix
trade, ix
trough, 14
   drinking, 41
   kneeding (dough), 10, 17, 18, 30, 55, 63
   pig, 14
   poundering (powdering), 23, 24, 38, 41
'tummill', 17
turkey work *see* needlework

valuation, of goods *see* inventories
vats, 36, 39
   tanning, 57

waggon, 21, 23, 46, 69
wallpaper, 17
   drugget (druggett), xx, 17
warming pan, 8, 9, 11, 14, 17, 18, 25, 28, 30, 38, 46, 49, 54, 55, 57, 60, 64, 68, 70, 74, 75
wash block, 17, 39
wealth, xviii-ix, xx
wheelbarrow, 17, 28, 57
widows *see* status
wills: beneficiaries, xxviii-xxxi
   bequests, xxvi, xxviii-xxxi
   charitable, xxviii
   children, xxvi, xxviii
   executors, xxxii
   inheritance, xxvi, xxviii-xxxi
   intestacy, xiii, 41, 42
   inventory *see* separate heading
   nuncupative, xxv, xxvi, 4, 12
   land given in, xxxi
   overseer, xxx, xxxi
   primogeniture, xxviii

INDEX OF SUBJECTS

probate, xiii, xxxi
problems regarding, xiv
property, distribution of, xvii-xxix
scribes, xxv, xxvii, xxviii
siblings, xxx
signing of, xxvii
Statute of Distribution (1670), xxviii
testators, xiii, xxviii, xxix-xxx, xxxii
witnesses, xxv, xxxi
writing of, xix, xxv, xxvi
women, influence of, xxii, xxiii
wills, differences in, xxxi
wood: bark, tanning, 57
   beams, 28, 57
   faggots, 7, 17, 19, 41, 64, 68
   fire wood, 10, 17, 21
   floor boards, 55
   furniture see household goods
   timber, cut/uncut, 7, 8, 11, 18, 23, 25, 28, 30, 32, 33, 35, 39-41, 44, 46-49, 57, 59, 60, 62, 63, 65, 68, 72, 73, 75, 77
   trestle (tressel), 39
wool, 38

yarn, 30
yeoman *see* status

H31 893 456 3

A CHARGE
IS MADE FOR
REMOVED OR
DAMAGED
LABELS.

A	Cowe Bridge
B	Old Croße
C	S. Andrews
D	The mill
E	S. Nicolas
G	S. Maries
H	Hony lane
K	Back ſtret
L	Highe ſtret
M	Alhallowes
N	Caſtle ſtret
P	Weſt ſtret